# ON BOTH BANKS OF THE JORDAN

*To my mentor
the late Uriel Dann
(1922–1991)
Teacher, scholar and
gentleman*

# ON BOTH BANKS
# OF THE JORDAN
## A Political Biography of
## Wasfi al-Tall

## Asher Susser
### *Tel Aviv University*

FRANK CASS

First published in 1994 in Great Britain by
FRANK CASS & CO. LTD.
Newbury House, 900 Eastern Avenue,
Newbury Park, Ilford, Essex IG2 7HH

and in the United States of America by
FRANK CASS
c/o International Specialized Book Services, Inc.
5804 N.E. Hassalo Street
Portland, Oregon 97213-3644

Copyright © 1994 Asher Susser

British Library Cataloguing in Publication Data

Susser, Asher
On Both Banks of the Jordan: Political
Biography of Wasfi al-Tall
I. Title
956.9504092

ISBN 0-7146-4542-7

Library of Congress Cataloging-in-Publication Data

Susser, Asher.
[Ben Yarden le-Falestin. English]
On both banks of the Jordan : a political biography of Wasfi al
-Tall / Asher Susser.
    p.    cm.
Includes bibliographical references and index.
ISBN 0-7146-4542-7
    1. Tall, Wasfi, 1919–1971. 2. Prime ministers—Jordan—Biography.
3. Jordan—Politics and government. 4. Palestinian Arabs—Politics
and government. 5. Munaẓẓamat al-Taḥrīr al-Filasṭīnīyah.
    I. Title.
DS154.52.T34S8713   1994
956.9504'3'092—dc20
    [B]                                                              93-10856
                                                                       CIP

Typeset by Vitaset, Paddock Wood, Kent
Printed in Great Britain by Bookcraft (Bath) Ltd

# Contents

List of Illustrations        vii

Preface        ix

**Introduction: The Jordanian Regime and**
**the Palestinians**        1

**1. Wasfi al-Tall – The Early Years**        9

**2. The Beginning of a Political Career (1945–49)**        14

The 'Arab Offices'        14
The Army of Salvation (*Jaysh al-Inqadh*)        15
Lessons of the 1948 war        19

**3. Jordanian Government Service (1949–61)**        23

Senior civil servant        23
The spokesman for the regime        29
The propaganda war against Eygpt        30
Relations with Iraq        32
Jordan's ambassador in Baghdad        33
Anti-Nasserist plots in Lebanon        34

**4. Prime Minister (1962–63)**        36

The appointment        36
Purging the bureaucracy        39
The Amnesty Law        41
Elections under controlled liberalization        42
Jordan's initiative on Palestine        47
Confrontation with ´Abd al-Nasir        53
Support for the royalist cause in Yemen        57
A new government: increasing domestic opposition        59
The Ba´thi coups in Iraq and Syria –
    Husayn back on the defensive        65

**5. Confrontation with the PLO (1965–67)**        70

Back to the Prime Minister's office        70
The merits of political indoctrination        72
*Shura* but no more        73

The General Amnesty                                              75
The price of the 'summit spirit'                                76
The challenge of the PLO                                        78
Tall and Shuqayri – negotiations between rivals                 82
Peparations to thwart the PLO                                   84
Fruitless attempts at compromise                               87
The March 1966 agreement                                       93
The suppression of the oppositon and
    popular PLO support                                        94
Mounting tension with the PLO                                  96
Crisis and rupture                                             99
Tall's assault on 'Shuqayri's PLO'                            102
The disintegration of the 'summit spirit'                    103
The impact of the Samu´ operation                            109
Opposition within the establishment                          117
Jordan's counter-offensive                                   119

6. **Behind the Scenes (1967–70)**                           **123**

Tall and the Six Day War                                      123
The arch-enemy of the Fida'iyyun                             132
'Black September'                                             137

7. **The Final Eviction of the Fida'iyyun (1970–71)**        **141**

Tall, the Fida'iyyun and the question of
    'law and order'                                          141
Relentless pressure                                          145
The final expulsion                                          150
Political rehabilitation of the Kingdom                      156
Tall and the future of the West Bank                         160
Between Tall and Husayn                                      163
The assassination in Cairo                                   168

**Conclusion: Wasfi al-Tall and the East Bank Political Elite** **172**

**Notes**                                                    **182**

**Bibliography**                                             **196**

**Index**                                                    **204**

# List of Illustrations

*Between pages 90 and 91*

1   Wasfi al-Tall at the High School in Salt.

2   Wasfi al-Tall with his wife Sa´diyya.

3   Wasfi al-Tall as Director of Jordanian
    Radio.

4   Tall sets fire to domestic intelligence
    dossiers.

5   Wasfi al-Tall and King Husayn.

6   Wasfi al-Tall's final return to Cairo.

*Picture credits*
All photographs are taken from *Wasfi al-Tall: An Illustrated Record*
by Isam Arida (1972) and reproduced by courtesy of the Jordan
Press Foundation.

# Preface

More than any other single issue, Jordan's complex and often contentious relations with Palestine and the Palestinians have shaped the historical development of the Hashimite Kingdom. Perhaps more than any other individual, with the exception of King ´Abdallah, the founder of the Kingdom, and his grandson, King Husayn, it was the East Bank politician and statesman, Wasfi al-Tall, who personified Jordan's determination to preserve its political and territorial integrity.

No Jordanian, outside the Hashimite royal family, has ever embodied the Jordanian state and its struggle for survival with greater resolve and power than Wasfi al-Tall. All the fundamental characteristics of the Kingdom became integral components of Tall's political consciousness. During his rather brief political career, cut short by the bullets of assassins, he matured into one of the most representative examples of those East Bankers who compose the Jordanian political elite, the backbone and mainstay of the Hashimite regime.

Wasfi al-Tall was one of King Husayn's closest confidants and one of Jordan's senior statesmen from the early 1960s until the early 1970s. During this period he served three terms as prime minister, all at decisive junctures in the unfolding competition and confrontation between Jordan and the Palestinian national movement. It was in the last of these terms of office, in 1970–71, that he orchestrated the expulsion of the PLO from Jordan. Ironically, Tall's political career, which began in the 1940s, when he devoted himself to the Arab political and military struggle in Palestine, was abruptly terminated when he was gunned down by Palestinians, who condemned him as the architect of their defeat in Jordan.

Writing the political biography of a Jordanian politician while unable to visit Jordan to interview those who worked closely with him has its obvious drawbacks. I have tried to compensate with interviews with the late Anwar Nusayba and two former US ambassadors to Jordan, Findley Burns and William Macomber, to all of whom I remain particularly grateful for their co-operation. My main sources, however, came from the wealth of available written material: Tall's own writings, speeches, interviews and press conferences; Jordanian and other Arab press articles and broadcasts covering Tall's entire career; and secondary sources on Jordan published in Jordan and elsewhere.

Much of this study was originally published in Hebrew (a first edition in 1983 and a second in 1986). This English version has been revised in places, following the publication of some new source material. It differs from the Hebrew edition in two main respects. The first chapter, 'The Early Years', has been partly rewritten in view of the publication in Jordan of a collection of biographies by Sulayman Musa which included new material on Tall's childhood and youth that had hitherto been unavailable to me. I have also written a new concluding chapter on the Jordanian political elite which did not appear in the Hebrew book.

To quote my friend and colleague, Dr Martin Kramer, 'when done with sensitivity, the telling and reading of lives increase our empathy for people of other times, other places, other cultures' (Martin Kramer (ed.), *Middle Eastern Lives: The Practice of Biography and Self-Narrative* (Syracuse University Press, 1991), p. 19). I do sincerely hope that this book meets these criteria.

There are many to whom I owe a debt of gratitude and without whose help this book would never have been completed. I am especially grateful to the late Professor Uriel Dann and to Mr Daniel Dishon who read the manuscript of the English version and made most valuable suggestions. I am similarly most grateful to my parents, Gideon and Minnie, for their painstaking assistance in preparing the initial draft of the English translation. For 20 years my academic home has been the Moshe Dayan Center and Shiloah Institute at Tel Aviv University. It is to that institution and its fellows, and particularly to its former head, Professor Itamar Rabinovich, that I owe an extraordinary debt of gratitude for friendship, inspiration, co-operation and material support. Edna Liftman and Amira Margalith, who turn the wheels of publication and office administration, were as indispensable as always. Lydia Gareh, who typed the manuscript with painstaking precision, has become an institution in her own right in the eyes of all who have ever had the pleasure of working with her. Last, but not least, I want to thank by wife Miriam and my two sons, Boaz and Eyal, who have lent a special sense of purpose to the demands of academia.

Asher Susser
*Tel Aviv, May 1993*

# Introduction: The Jordanian Regime and the Palestinians

For centuries inhabitants of the East and West Banks of the River Jordan have been linked by bonds of kinship and economic inter-action and, at times, by administrative and political ties as well. The British Mandate for Palestine initially included both banks, and the British authorities noted, with considerable historical justification, that for economic reasons as well as in some geo-graphical aspects the two areas were essentially one unit.[1]

In 1921 the Emirate of Trans-Jordan was established to serve both British imperial interests and Hashimite dynastic ambitions. Henceforth, Trans-Jordan developed as a separate political unit. Nevertheless, Trans-Jordan remained part of the British Mandate for Palestine, until it achieved independence, as the Hashimite Kingdom of Jordan, in 1946. Jordan's political fate continued to be intimately connected to that of Palestine. King ´Abdallah, the grandfather of King Husayn and the founder of Hashimite Trans-Jordan, never concealed his political aspirations in respect of Palestine. He regarded the establishment of an independent Arab state in Palestine as a potential threat to his throne and therefore sought to ensure Hashimite supremacy in the settlement of the Palestinian question. Jordan's occupation of the West Bank in 1948 and the formal annexation of the territory in 1950 forestalled the immediate threat to the Kingdom, but did not suffice to overcome the deep-seated hostility which many Palestinians felt for the Hashimite regime. From the outset, the relationship between the regime and the large Palestinian population that was absorbed into the Kingdom was characterized by considerable tension and repeated political confrontations. At times, the regime's very existence was endangered. Yet, despite the challenge, the Jordanian political entity remained stable, consistently defined by the follow-ing characteristics:

- A Kingdom, hereditary in the Hashimite family, successor to the British-mandated Emirate of Trans-Jordan, and heir, as far as possible, to its political, social and psychological values. The

1

King is the linchpin of the political system and the real head of the decision-making process.

- The monarchy is backed by a political elite which is predominantly Trans-Jordanian. This elite is supportive of the status quo and is apprehensive of any change that may deny it access to, and control of, the key positions of state, government and army. Power resides disproportionately with East Bankers. Palestinian influence has never been commensurate with their demographic weight.
- The regime relies heavily on the army and other security forces. These are employed against the opponents of the regime, upon the King's instructions, whenever he perceives it to be in serious danger. It should be noted, however, that King Husayn does not relish the use of force against his subjects, and tends to do so only in extreme situations.
- The regime is fearful of any radical ideology – Nasserist, Ba´thi or Communist on the one hand, or revolutionary Islamic on the other. It treats all who show any sympathy for these ideological trends with suspicion, and it does not hesitate to confront them, at times even resorting to force.
- Jordan has always been connected with the West, first to Britain and later to the United States, from which it has received much of the political, economic and military assistance that has been essential for the Kingdom's survival.[2]

In its attitude to the regime, the political public was traditionally divided into two fairly clearly defined groups: the supporters of the existing political structure, namely, the ruling political elite, composed in the main of Trans-Jordanians, supported by a Palestinian minority; and its opponents, among whom Palestinians have always figured prominently, backed by a minority of Trans-Jordanians.

Palestinians probably constitute just over half of the population of the East Bank of Jordan and some two-thirds of the population in both Banks combined.[3] A large proportion of this Palestinian political public rejected the traditional 'image of Jordan' as defined above and strove for radical change. They objected to the centrality of the monarchy and opposed the supremacy of the Trans-Jordanian elite. They also rejected the regime's traditional alliance with the Western powers, on whose shoulders the Palestinians tended to place much of the responsibility for their national calamity in 1948. Most of the Palestinian political elite identified with, and drew revolutionary inspiration from, precisely those ideological trends that were anathema to the regime.

The role of the Palestinians in the upper echelons of the government and the military has always been marginal. Even so, a not insignificant number of Palestinians threw in their political and personal lot with the regime, and displayed unswerving loyalty to the throne, even in times of crisis between the regime and the Palestinian population.

Some of the Palestinians who supported the regime originated from the Nashashibi camp in Palestinian politics, which formed during the years of the British Mandate. They maintained strong ties with the Amir (later King), 'Abdallah. The Nashashibis and 'Abdallah chose to join forces against their mutual enemy, Hajj Amin al-Husayni, then leader of the Palestinian national movement. Others had economic interests which they wished to safeguard by links with the establishment. Yet another group was composed of those whose support for the monarchy stemmed from their loyalty to government *per se*, and from a realistic appraisal of the balance of forces in Jordan. They did not believe that there was a reasonable chance of change and therefore preferred not to pay the price of sterile opposition. One cannot ignore those who chose to co-operate with the regime for reasons such as the aspiration for status, prestige and authority, or other personal rewards. On the other hand, there were also Palestinians who genuinely identified with the regime's pragmatic and relatively moderate policies on the struggle with Israel, in inter-Arab affairs and the economy.

From among East Bankers who have traditionally filled key positions, southerners of tribal Bedouin origin have often been preferred to urban northerners. Since the earliest days of 'Abdallah's rule, northerners, from the towns of Irbid and Salt, have been at the core of the Trans-Jordanian opposition.

The Bedouin have played a central role in the Jordanian establishment. From the outset, most of their chieftains were closely associated with 'Abdallah, who cultivated a special relationship with the Bedouin, and since their recruitment to the Arab Legion in the 1930s the Bedouin have been the backbone of the crack fighting units of the army, the mainstay of the regime. The number of nomadic or semi-nomadic Bedouin has been steadily declining for many years. In 1960, they accounted for less than ten per cent of the East Bank population,[4] and by 1980 their number had dwindled further, to some five to seven per cent of an East Bank population of well over two million.[5] Today, that figure is even smaller, in a population that exceeds three million.

The proportion of nomadic, semi-nomadic and recently sedentarized Bedouin in the army, particularly in key units, far exceeds their relative weight in the overall population. Their devotion to the Hashimite monarchy rests to a large degree on the unique status of the King. He has become the focus of a supra-tribal loyalty, which, to a certain extent, has replaced the traditional more circumscribed tribal solidarity. This special relationship has engendered a remarkable and almost complete identification of the army with the regime.

The Jordanian army, contrary to a number of other Arab armies, developed as a relatively apolitical and professional military machine that has suffered only marginally from subversion. There have been isolated attempted coups but these never seriously eroded its loyalty. It has been employed on various occasions by the King against his domestic enemies. The army's reputation for unswerving loyalty to the regime has also probably deterred many would-be plotters. The causes for the army's exemplary loyalty are not related solely to the fact that it is based on the Bedouin nucleus, but also to the systematic cultivation of its *esprit de corps*; long-term service under relatively good material conditions; good leadership from the throne downwards; and the fear of the officer class for its position under a regime rejecting the 'image of Jordan'.[6]

In recent decades social change and modernization had had a far-reaching impact on the Bedouin. The process of sedentarization and the influence of education and communications have reduced the level of tribal awareness and identity. Moreover, since the institution of conscription in 1976, the relative weight of the Bedouin in the army has declined.[7] These factors might eventually have a negative effect on army loyalty. At present, however, there are no indications that the army has undergone significant change in this respect.

Many of the conscripts, as opposed to career recruits, are placed in service jobs and most do not remain in the army after their two years of duty are up.[8] The Bedouin, on the other hand, are still largely inclined to seek career fulfilment in the military,[9] and, as a result, the fighting units and the officer corps are still disproportionately Bedouin. Available evidence even suggests that the weakening of tribal solidarity and the diminishing authority of tribal shaykhs has actually tended to reinforce the King's role of 'shaykh of shaykhs'. Modernization and change have thus promoted a more direct identification of the individual with the Jordanian nation-state, which is replacing the traditional identification through the collective tribal association with the regime.[10] The bond between the Bedouin troops and the King, therefore, is still very strong.[11]

The political leadership, with the King at the centre of the decision-making process, is composed of a very small number of senior officials and members of the royal family. It includes only some members of the cabinet, usually the Prime Minister, the Minister of the Interior (responsible for domestic security), and the Minister of Information. As opposed to the situation obtaining in many Western countries, the role of the Foreign Minister is, for the most part, restricted to the execution of policy laid down by the King and to the supervision of the diplomatic corps. The authority of the Minister of Defence is similarly confined and his role is limited, in the main, to administrative matters; the formulation of policy is the exclusive domain of the King and his inner group.

Since the annexation of the West Bank, there have always been Palestinians in Jordanian cabinets. Until Jordan's disengagement from the West Bank in 1988, usually about half of the ministers in any given cabinet were of Palestinian extraction. At times, some were entrusted with the portfolios of Defence and Foreign Affairs. However, it is only in rare instances that they have held those portfolios which entail membership of the restricted decision-making group at the very top.

Generally, the most senior officers in the defence establishment are associated with this inner group, including the most senior army officers and the directors of the domestic security forces – General Intelligence (the internal security service) and General Security (the police). None of these positions has ever been held by a Palestinian.

Outside the functional categories, there is a circle of 'King's friends' who may or may not hold official appointments, but who have the King's ear and who are regularly entrusted with missions of political importance.[12] This circle would normally include various members of the royal family, such as the King's younger brother, Crown Prince Hasan, and, in Husayn's earlier years, the Queen Mother and some of Husayn's uncles; the Chief of the Royal Court; one or two very close personal advisers; and a select few of former senior officials.

Husayn selects the members of his inner council and those who fill important positions according to their personalities and political proclivities in order to facilitate the satisfactory execution of policy, as formulated by him, at any particular juncture. Policy is determined in the palace and not by the cabinet, which is chiefly concerned with its execution and its explanation at home and abroad. But it is the cabinet which is far more exposed to public scrutiny than the palace. Consequently it is the cabinet which invariably attracts criticism for a policy in fact laid down by the King. Changes in government in response to such criticism serve as a mechanism designed to protect the King. They occur frequently, particularly in times of stress, but do not necessarily herald any change in policy. However, they do tend to create the impression of impending change, thus acting as a most important 'shock absorber' in times of crisis.

Any opposition whose objective is to obtain a meaningful share in political power, let alone assume power, in order to change the traditional image of the Kingdom is perceived by the regime as a form of subversion and thus not tolerated. This does not mean that the opposition is completely deprived of any freedom of action. The measure of freedom it is allowed is a function of the King's self-confidence and the risk he is prepared to take at any given time. In recent years Jordan has undergone a process of liberalization. However, the regime has never had the intention of permitting the opposition to have real influence on the decision-making process.

The Jordanian parliament (*Majlis al-Umma*) is bi-cameral. Until Jordan's disengagement from the West Bank, the Senate (*Majlis al-A'yan*) had 30 members appointed by the King from among the notables, former prime ministers, ministers and ambassadors; and an elected Chamber of Deputies (*Majlis al-Nuwwab*) which had 60 members, equally divided between East Bank and West Bank constituencies. Following the disengagement, membership of the Senate was increased by ten and the Chamber of Deputies by 20 members, representing constituencies solely from the East Bank. The constitution requires that they be elected for a period of four years, in regional, secret and direct general elections.

The appointed Senate tends to ensure that a certain skein of conservatism is woven into the fabric of the legislature.[13] Moreover, until quite recently, the regime resorted to a number of other measures to guarantee that parliament was not transformed into a vehicle of the opposition. The existence of political parties in Jordan was forbidden, and elections were therefore held on a personal basis. In spite of the fact that the constitution requires that elections should be free, they were generally 'directed' by the government, with the object of minimizing the representation of the opposition. Candidates considered undesirable by the government were sometimes prevented from running in the elections by various forms of pressure brought to bear upon them by the domestic security apparatus. In order to ensure the success of its favoured candidates, the regime also often adopted a variety of fraudulent procedures in the voting and in the counting of votes.

The antagonism prevalent between a large segment of the Palestinian political public and the Hashimite regime made it a constant facet of Jordanian policy to limit Palestinian attempts to attain key positions; moreover, the government deprived them of the ability to organize any political power-base which would be independent of the central government. One of the essential elements of this policy was the attempt by the Hashimite regime to assimilate the Palestinians into the Jordanian state by systematically de-emphasizing their Palestinian identity, so as to transform them into loyal Jordanian subjects. This, however, was diametrically opposed to autonomous Palestinian efforts to maintain their national identity and to the general Arab consensus on this issue. The predominant trend in the Arab world was to preserve the Palestinian identity and to allow for its organizational expression through the notion of a 'Palestinian entity' (*kiyan Filastini*). It was the coalescence of this Palestinian effort and the Arab consensus that spurred the formation of the Palestine Liberation Organization (PLO) in 1964.

Before the establishment of the PLO, the Palestinian opposition in Jordan expressed itself through the medium of various radical political parties until these were banned in 1957. Indeed, the Palestinians were the backbone of a variety of opposition parties all subscribing to a revolutionary social and political platform. On the left, these were the Ba´th, the Communists, the Arab Nationalist Movement (*Harakat al-Qawmiyyin al-´Arab*), and the less radical National Socialist Party led by Sulayman al-Nabulsi; on the right (a term chosen for convenience rather than accuracy) there were the religious-fundamentalists organized in the Muslim Brotherhood and the Islamic Liberation Party. All these groups rejected the traditional image of Jordan in one way or another. In October 1956, as a result of elections that were freer than usual, opposition candidates won a majority in the Chamber of Deputies. Nabulsi formed a government which soon threatened to overturn the traditional political order. Husayn, aware of the danger, bided his time for a while, but then, in April 1957, cracked down and smashed the opposition. He dismissed the Nabulsi government, imposed martial law and banned all political parties.[14]

The formation of the PLO threatened yet again to provide the Palestinians with a framework for political organization against the government. Like the parties of the 1950s, it presented the regime with a political challenge, only now the threat was even greater. The PLO purported to provide a political framework potentially appealing to the majority of the population in a manner liable to threaten the very existence of the Jordanian state far more directly and more seriously than any of the banned parties had done.

In the annals of the Jordanian–Palestinian confrontation, one could hardly point to a more outstanding Jordanian personality than Wasfi al-Tall. Tall's entire political career was interwoven from beginning to end with the Palestinian saga and the impact it had on Jordan.

8

# 1

# Wasfi al-Tall – The Early Years

Wasfi al-Tall was born in 1919 and grew up in Irbid in northern Jordan. The family has its origins in the Bani Zaydan tribe which migrated from the Najd region in Arabia to Syria in the middle of the eighteenth century. Some members of the tribe settled in the Irbid area while others chose the area of Zabdani in south-western Syria.[1] The Talls became one of the most distinguished families in Trans-Jordan and some of them rose to positions of prominence even during Ottoman times, well before the founding of the Emirate of Trans-Jordan in the early 1920s.[2] The first to achieve real fame, or rather in this case notoriety, was Wasfi al-Tall's cousin ´Abdallah al-Tall. He was a battalion commander in the Jordanian army and military governor of the Old City of Jerusalem in 1948. ´Abdallah al-Tall was sentenced to death *in absentia* for his part in the assassination of King ´Abdallah in 1951. During Wasfi al-Tall's second term as prime minister, at the beginning of 1965, ´Abdallah was pardoned and allowed to return to Jordan from his extended exile in Cairo.

Wasfi al-Tall was the son of Mustafa Wahbi al-Tall, a well-known Jordanian poet who had not always been favourably disposed towards the Hashimite regime. Wasfi's mother was a Kurdish woman whom his father had married during a sojourn in ´Arabkir (Arapkir, in present-day Turkish Kurdistan). Mustafa Wahbi was caught up there on his way to university in Istanbul during the First World War. Wasfi al-Tall was born in ´Arabkir and it was there that he spent his early childhood, until his family resettled in Irbid in 1924.[3] Wasfi was tall and had a dark complexion inherited from his Tall forefathers and from his Kurdish mother. He always looked younger than his years. Even when he reached the age of 50, his thick jet-black hair gave him the appearance of a younger man. His sharp and stern facial features corresponded with his character which was essentially serious, strict and tough.

But people who knew him well maintained that these features belied some of his more humane and gentle traits. He had a fine sense of humour, a deep affection for his friends and a romantic streak, attested to by his love of nature, his profound appreciation for the desert poetry of the Bedouin and for the traditions of village life, which he cherished. As a mature politician, Tall was the image of self-confidence and he was prone to demonstrations of arrogance and disdain towards his opponents. But even when in high office he did not find it unbecoming to work very long hours and to take simple meals of bread and laban, falafil or humus, sitting on the floor like the Bedouin and the villagers.[4]

As a young boy Wasfi al-Tall was obstreperous, aggressive and mischievous and it was already apparent in his early youth that he had a mind of his own. He received his elementary education in Irbid and in 1936 he enrolled at the high school in Salt, which was the only government high school in Trans-Jordan in those days.[5] These were the beginnings not only of his formal education but of his political schooling as well. He and his classmates came under the influence of their history teacher, Sa´id al-Durra, who inspired in them a powerful sense of identification with the Arab nationalist cause. Tall and some of his peers became so emotionally involved with the Arab cause in Palestine that they decided to form a secret society called 'The Black Hand'.[6] These were the years of the Arab Rebellion in Palestine and one of the most prominent groups responsible for the promotion of the armed rebellion was 'The Black Hand', led by the legendary Shaykh ´Izz al-Din al-Qassam. Qassam was killed in a clash with the British in 1935,[7] and one may assume that Wasfi and his friends had Qassam in mind when choosing the name of their society. Theirs was but a youthful and quite innocuous adventure. But they did succeed in getting themselves into serious trouble. One night in order to register their protest against their own government's moderation and restraint on the Palestine question, they packed an old bombshell with explosives and tossed it at the home of the local *Mutasarrif* (district governor). They were immediately arrested, but Wasfi's father intervened on their behalf and bailed them out.[8]

Tall graduated from high school in 1938 and went to Lebanon to pursue his university education at the American University in Beirut (AUB). The AUB was then the most distinguished institution of its kind in the Arab world. It was the intellectual hub for the educated young of the most respectable families from a number of Arab countries and, as such, became the training ground for numerous Arab leaders of the future. The three years he spent at the AUB were an educational and political inspiration to Wasfi al-Tall, as he entered his twenties.

He came into contact with students from all over the Arab world in a highly politicized college atmosphere. The ideas of Arab nationalism were expounded to them by some of the leading Arab intellectuals. The most prominent of these at the AUB was Qustantin Zurayq, a distinguished medieval historian and, as Albert Hourani has put it, a 'consulting don to a whole generation of nationalists'.[9] It was around the likes of Zurayq that the nucleus of what was later to become the Arab Nationalist Movement was formed in the late 1930s and early 1940s, when Zurayq published some of his most important works on Arab national consciousness.

When British forces intervened in Iraq, in early 1941, to put down the pro-Axis Rashid 'Ali movement, many students at the AUB, including Wasfi al-Tall, staged demonstrations in support of Rashid 'Ali. Tall and others, fired with enthusiasm for the Arab nationalist cause, volunteered to fight for Rashid 'Ali and left Beirut for Baghdad. However, they turned back before reaching their destination when they heard the news of Rashid 'Ali's defeat.[10]

Wasfi al-Tall studied physics, chemistry and philosophy, but it was for the last of these that he developed a real passion. The Arab nationalists with whom Tall was associated at the time had initially been influenced by European fascist thought. Tall became an admirer of German philosophy, particularly Nietzsche's theories on power.[11] He was convinced that societies and nations had no life without the acquisition of power and that work and power were the very essence of existence. The idea of power, he contended (in an essay he wrote in his final year at the AUB), was associated with Islam from its very beginning. The object of Islamic teachings, he wrote, was to make the individual strong in his beliefs and in his spirit, and powerful in his relations with others, and thus to ready him for struggle.[12] Tall's acquaintance with Nietzsche's philosophy was to have a lasting impact.

His student days at the AUB turned Tall into an avid reader.

11

Most of his reading was on politics, philosophy and history, particularly military history. His library included Plato's *Republic*, the philosophy of Nietzsche, books on the history of the Roman Empire and numerous works on war, especially the Second World War and the memoirs of the great leaders who fought it. But there were other interests too, like the novels of Lawrence Durrell and books about animals, for which he had an especially soft spot.[13]

Wasfi graduated from the AUB in 1941 and returned to Trans-Jordan. He taught very briefly at a school in the southern town of Karak before being transferred to his *alma mater* in Salt. He taught chemistry, but he was far too much of a political being to confine his classes to the subject at hand. Instead, they often drifted into political sessions on the threat of Zionism to the Arabs and the need for Arab unity.[14]

In the summer of 1942 Wasfi's father was appointed to the position of *Mutasarrif* of Salt. However, he soon fell out with the Prime Minister, Tawfiq Abu al-Huda: after having deliberately and provocatively challenged Abu al-Huda's authority, Mustafa Wahbi al-Tall found himself in prison. Wasfi was outraged. He sought an interview with the Prime Minister, but Abu al-Huda refused to see him. In the corridor outside the Prime Minister's office, Wasfi launched into a tirade of curses and abuse, which could not but have been overheard by the Prime Minister. Having lost his temper, Wasfi now lost his job as well. Abu al-Huda had Wasfi join his father in prison where they spent the next three months together.[15]

Having served a prison sentence, a return to teaching was out of the question. The moment had come for a new departure. He tried to join the Arab Legion, but was turned down by Glubb Pasha – it was said on account of the fact that he was a university graduate.[16] In late 1942, the tides of war in the Middle East began to change in favour of the Allies. The anti-British and pro-German mood that had prevailed in much of the Arab world in the early years of the Second World War (and which had not passed over Wasfi al-Tall himself during his studies in Beirut) was beginning to subside. At the end of 1942, Wasfi al-Tall decided to enlist in the British Army. One cannot dismiss the notion that he enlisted for reasons similar to those which, at least to some extent, had motivated the Jews of Palestine to join the British Army – that is, to obtain military

12

training for the imminent conflict over the fate of Palestine.[17] It was during his service in the British Army that he acquired the habit of pipe-smoking. In later years he was seldom seen without one, though he liked cigarettes as well and generally smoked a lot. In early 1943, Tall completed an officers' course at the British base at Sarafand in central Palestine, where he was commissioned as a second lieutenant. At the end of the war, he was demobilized with the rank of captain.[18] Shortly thereafter, he began his political career, at the heart of which was the struggle for Palestine.

# 2

# The Beginning of a Political Career
# (1945–49)

## THE 'ARAB OFFICES'

Following his release from the British Army Wasfi al-Tall joined the 'Arab Office' in Jerusalem, apparently at the beginning of 1946.[1] This was one of the 'Arab Offices' proposed by Musa al-´Alami, at the preparatory conference of the Arab League, where ´Alami represented the Arabs of Palestine. The preparatory conference, held in Alexandria in September–October 1944, was followed by the inaugural conference of the Arab League in March 1945. The latter adopted ´Alami's proposal and 'Arab Offices' were opened in Jerusalem, London and Washington a short time afterwards. Their purpose was to engage in publicity for the Arab cause, particularly on the issue of Palestine. Musa al-´Alami was the Director of the 'Offices' and recruited his staff in Palestine and in the member states of the Arab League, mainly from the ranks of former government officials and from the young intelligentsia.[2]

In the course of his work at the Arab Offices, Tall divided his time between the offices in Jerusalem and London.[3] He was hard-working, devoted and intelligent and his military experience left a marked imprint on his style and conduct. He took nothing for granted. His competence soon drew the attention of Musa al-´Alami who made him his permanent secretary. In the spring of 1947, ´Alami also made Tall a member of the select committee he appointed to prepare a report for the United Nations Special Committee on Palestine (UNSCOP).[4]

In December 1947 Iraq suspended its financial support to the Arab Offices, and, as a result, the scope of their activities was considerably reduced.[5] This happened to coincide with the decision of the Arab League, taken just after the UN Partition Resolution of the previous month, to establish *Jaysh al-Inqadh* (The Army of Salvation) – to be composed of volunteers from the Arab states – to assist the Palestinian Arabs in their struggle against partition. Tall

14

resigned from the Arab Offices and was among the first to enlist in *Jaysh al-Inqadh*,[6] as it was being formed in Syria.

It is difficult to give a clear and definite appraisal of Wasfi al-Tall's political inclinations at this juncture, but the nature of the activities of the Arab Offices does give some indication. At the time of his appointment as representative of the Palestinian Arabs to the Arab League, Musa al-'Alami was associated with the Husayni camp in Palestine. However, the two soon entered into political confrontation when 'Alami was pressured by the Husayni camp to allow the Palestinian Higher Arab Committee to control the activities of the Arab Offices. This was particularly so after the Higher Arab Committee was re-formed in June 1946 in a manner which gave the Husaynis and their supporters absolute control. Among the Palestinian Arabs there were some who accused the Arab Offices of being pro-British, or of loyalty to Iraq.[7] At the end of 1947, the British Foreign Office considered Musa al-'Alami to be a moderate leader, at the head of the camp of those Palestinian Arabs who opposed Hajj Amin al-Husayni. Shortly after the UN Partition Resolution, while 'Alami was in London as the director of the Arab Office there, he expressed his view, in a conversation with an official of the Foreign Office, that one of the possible solutions to the Palestinian problem was for King 'Abdallah to take control of substantial portions of Palestine, including large areas allocated to the Jewish State in the partition plan.[8] It is therefore, quite clear that the Arab Offices did not serve the enemies of the Trans-Jordanian regime among the Palestinian Arabs, and certainly not the Husayni camp.

That Wasfi al-Tall was genuinely devoted to the Arab cause in Palestine is shown by his volunteering for *Jaysh al-Inqadh* (see below). There was nothing anti-British or anti-Hashimite about that, though one still cannot point to any clear evidence in this period of the unflinching loyalty to the Hashimite regime in Jordan that was to emerge and develop in the later stages of his life.

## THE ARMY OF SALVATION (*JAYSH AL-INQADH*)

Following the secret resolutions of the representatives of the Arab states in Cairo in December 1947, the organization of the first units of *Jaysh al-Inqadh* began in Syria.[9] Its commander in chief was the Iraqi General Isma'il Safwat. He was aided by a number of staff officers, among them Wasfi al-Tall, his assistant for operations. Starting with the rank of captain,[10] Wasfi was soon promoted to major. The capture of Nazareth and the surrounding villages by the Israelis (in July 1948) shattered the morale of *Jaysh al-Inqadh*, and it was swiftly reorganized. Wasfi al-Tall, who had meanwhile become a lieutenant-colonel, was given command of the 4th Yarmuk Battalion, deployed near the villages of Maghar, ´Aylabun and Kafr Manda in Lower Galilee.[11] After the Israelis had taken Galilee, *Jaysh al-Inqadh* was redeployed in southern Lebanon , its command was disbanded and its units, renamed the Yarmuk Forces, were attached to the Syrian Army. When Lebanon signed an armistice agreement with Israel in March 1949, the Yarmuk Forces were moved to the Syrian front. Tall's battalion was stationed near Qunaytra.[12]

Tall and a number of other former senior officers of *Jaysh al-Inqadh*, incensed by the humiliation of defeat, had made up their minds to oppose any ceasefire or armistice agreement. They dispatched representatives to Damascus to inform the Syrian President, Shukri al-Quwatli, of their resolve to continue the struggle, even if they had to take Damascus and depose Quwatli to do so. On the night they had taken this momentous decision, the Syrian Colonel Husni al-Za´im arrived at the headquarters of the Yarmuk Forces at the front and informed the prospective rebels of his own plans to lead a coup against Quwatli. He expressed his support for their stand and carried out his coup at the end of March 1949, with their benevolent approval. Once in power, however Za´im embarked on a totally different policy. When Tall learned of Za´im's own plans to conclude an agreement with Israel,[13] he convinced the officers in his battalion to move, with their men, to Nablus and Tubas in the West Bank to continue the struggle. All the officers agreed and preparations were made to cross into Jordan and from there over the Damiya bridge into the West Bank. Some of the officers, however, informed Syrian intelligence of their plans and Za´im, who obviously did not think highly of Tall's demonstration of independence, summoned him to Damascus. The two men had a stormy encounter after which Za´im had Tall locked up for three months in the notorious al-Mazza prison. After Syria and Israel signed an armistice agreement in July 1949, Tall was released and left the country.[14]

It is said of Wasfi al-Tall that he was a gifted officer who was intelligent and well aware of the realities of the situation at hand. He warned his commander, Safwat, of the military potential of the 'Haganah', and of 'the deplorable state' of his own forces.[15] Safwat, himself had a realistic appraisal of the military potential of the Jews in Palestine. He made a concerted effort to convince the Arab states to make the necessary preparations to commit their regular armies to the conflict. He met with only limited success. His lack of confidence in the Arab effort was reflected by his decision not to let Tall's pessimistic report reach any of the Arab leaders. He advised his young aide that 'if some of the Arab governments read this they will refuse to take the risk of sending their armies to Palestine'.[16]

None of the Arab armies, with the exception of Jordan's Arab Legion, made any significant preparations for war. One substantial act of such preparation was a 15-page plan for the invasion of Palestine drawn up by Tall. Though Tall may well have had some doubts about the Arab capacity to implement the plan, it called for a joint Arab effort to defeat the Israelis in an 11-day campaign. The plan envisaged a thrust from the north by the armies of Lebanon and Syria and by *Jaysh al-Inqadh*. The northern thrust was to be spearheaded by an Iraqi armoured force to capture the port of Haifa, while a narrow thrust from the south by the Egyptian Army would seize Jaffa. Thus the new State of Israel would be deprived of the ports that Tall knew it would need to bring in men and arms after the British departure. At the same time, the Arab Legion and the balance of the Iraqi forces would aim to cut the Jewish settlement in half by thrusting across the coastal plain from the Judean hills to the sea north of Tel Aviv. To implement the plan, Tall had asked that virtually all of the Arab armies be placed under a single supreme commander.[17] Like other Arab intentions in the war of 1948, Tall's plan was never implemented. The Arabs suffered a traumatic defeat, but Tall, according to one of his comrades in arms, had acquitted himself exceptionally well in battle. During the fighting in eastern Galilee, after the fall of Nazareth, Tall, though wounded in the leg, continued to lead his men. His valour was, however, of no avail. The Israeli forces broke through the lines of an 'Alawi battalion of *Jaysh al-Inqadh* west of Safed and began attacking the remaining Arab forces from the rear. Fawzi al-Qawuqji, the field commander of *Jaysh al-Inqadh*, chose not to counter-attack and ordered all his forces to retreat from Galilee to southern Lebanon. At first, Tall refused to comply with the order, but eventually he had no choice but to withdraw. The Arab fight for Galilee was lost.[18]

Arab historians have severely criticized the poor performance of *Jaysh al-Inqadh*.[19] Tall was no different, and he too sharply condemned its dismal record. Things went wrong from the very beginning, he wrote later. Those responsible for recruiting accepted anyone, without question. Thus, many who joined the ranks of *Jaysh al-Inqadh* were fugitives, criminals, reckless adventurers or mercenaries. The weapons supplied to *Jaysh al-Inqadh* were an assortment, and many were defective. Some weapons and munitions were so obsolete and unreliable that they inflicted more casualties on *Jaysh al-Inqadh* than on the Israelis, Tall recalled.[20] The army's showing in the field was most unimpressive. For example, Tall maintained that in the abortive attempt to overrun Kibbutz Tirat Zvi in February 1948 *Jaysh al-Inqadh* was incredibly inept. The battle plans, he explained, were good, but the attacking force was badly organized and its equipment was defective. The Jews had advance knowledge of the planned attack and were well prepared for it. At the time of the attack, the companies lost their way to the objective, and thus less than half of the planned force actually took part in the initial phase of the offensive; about 70 per cent of the weapons did not function properly; the intelligence was inaccurate; the retreat seemed more like flight than an organized withdrawal and the Arab force suffered many casualties; the attacking force was undisciplined and the officers lost control of their men. What made matters worse was that the Arabs did not learn from this experience, and went on to repeat their mistakes for the entire course of the war.[21]

The reports of the inefficiency of *Jaysh al-Inqadh* reaching the Palestinian Arabs, after its failure on the battlefield at Tirat Zvi, and later at the battle of Mishmar Haemek, seriously undermined their faith in this force.[22] Furthermore, the men of *Jaysh al-Inqadh* failed to win the sympathy of the local Arab population, who regarded them as arrogant outsiders who, at times, abused their authority and mistreated the local inhabitants.[23] The testimony of Tall reveals a certain ambivalence towards the Arabs of Palestine. Thus, for example, he showered praise on the Palestinians for their bravery in the fighting at Bab al-Wad near Jerusalem and in parts of the upper Galilee towards the end of the war and he rebuked those Arabs who held the Palestinians entirely responsible for the defeat. Tall also recruited many Palestinians to serve in his own battalion, even though this contradicted the policy of his superiors, who preferred not to do so because of their political differences with Hajj Amin al-Husayni.[24] But his testimony also points to a certain bitterness or even contempt towards the Palestinian Arabs. He castigated the Arabs of Nazareth and the surrounding villages for not even firing a shot against the advancing Israelis, even though they were well armed.[25] Tall similarly tells of an incident in which armed men from the village of Sakhnin denied entry into their village to the forces of *Jaysh al-Inqadh*, arguing that this would provoke a Jewish attack. According to Tall, that same night a delegation from Sakhnin asked the Jews to move into the village, and this was done. The command of *Jaysh al-Inqadh* decided to take revenge on the inhabitants, and on the following day the village was retaken. According to Tall, the soldiers of *Jaysh al-Inqadh* dealt the people of Sakhnin the kind of retribution befitting a captured Jewish settlement.[26]

## LESSONS OF THE 1948 WAR

Wasfi al-Tall summarized the reasons for the military defeat of the Arabs in Palestine with the force, incisive candour and scathing style that were subsequently to become his personal trademarks. A major factor in the Arab defeat was, in his opinion, the lack of a unified command. There was no operational co-ordination and the different Arab commands competed with each other in an atmosphere permeated with mutual distrust. This enabled the Israelis to concentrate their efforts on the various fronts, alternating as they chose. Conversely, the Arab invasion plan was not based on a concentration of the major part of their forces for decisive battles. Furthermore, the Arab armies moved slowly and with exaggerated caution, which allowed the Israeli forces to stop them with relative ease. The Arab armies were worn down in secondary engagements and tended to call for reinforcements well before they had attained any main objective. Consequently the Arabs lost the initiative they had held at the beginning of the invasion. A transfer of the initiative to the Israeli enemy, Tall explained, was the logical result not only of the low level of training and combat-readiness of the Arab forces, but also of the deficient intellectual and professional standards of the Arab command, in comparison with those of the Israelis.

Tall maintained that the Arab appraisal of the Israeli force was unrealistic, an error of judgement compounded by the fact that the Arab leaders who took the decision to invade Palestine did not correctly assess the real strength of their own forces either. Their assessment of the situation was influenced by the mood of the mob, emotion and hyperbole and an excessive reliance upon 'the valour of the Arabs and the cowardice of the Jews', based on 'stories, fanciful tales, and rumours'. According to Tall the assessment of the situation by those in authority was so imaginary as to become an instrument of deception. He was, however, especially harsh in his censure of the enemies of the Hashimites who led the Palestinian Arabs:

(a)  Tall complained that the domestic front of the Arabs of Palestine had disintegrated during the decisive years preceding the war. For this he blamed the local Arab leadership which had occupied itself with internal power struggles instead of preparing for the coming campaign and keeping track of the preparations of the Jews.

(b)  The organizations and political institutions of the Palestinian Arabs were lacking in moral fortitude: they preferred to keep silent instead of explaining the reality of the situation to the population, thus allowing the Arabs of Palestine and the Arab states to continue deluding themselves.

(c)  In retrospect, Wasfi al-Tall argued that the Arabs had failed to focus on the real determinants of war. While the enemy was diligently preparing for a military campaign, the Arabs (including Tall himself, in his work at the Arab Office) busied themselves with propaganda offensives, polemics and declarations to the press about their historical right to Palestine.

(d)  Utter disregard of information: despite the fact that the Arab leadership was informed of their defective combat readiness in comparison with that of the Jews, no action was taken to remedy the situation. It was well known to the Arabs that the Jews had acquired military experience during the period of the

20

British Mandate and that they were firmly resolved to fight, but the Arab leadership in Palestine and elsewhere preferred to ignore this.

Tall accused the Arabs of threatening war at every opportunity, but all these threats, he said, were just empty words. No serious attempt was ever made to learn the lessons of the past 'because the exaggerated stories of valour, glory and heroic death prevented the Arabs from learning from mistakes and failings'. In his typically pugnacious style Tall concluded that, though he had no intention of detracting from the merits of the fallen, 'the object of war is to win and not to sing songs of praise to valour'.[27]

When Tall wrote this account in mid-1955, he was already in pursuit of office in the Hashimite regime. He prudently avoided any specific reference to the controversial Jordanian role in the war and ʿAbdallah's understandings and common interests with the British and the Jews in Palestine.[28] Whether these understandings were ultimately detrimental to the Arab war effort, or enabled the Arabs to hang on to the West Bank, which might have otherwise been occupied by the Israelis, remains a moot question.

Tall drew attention to the fact that he had deliberately abstained from any reference to treachery and conspiracy. This was simply because he was convinced that the Arab military effort, such as it was, 'without treason, conspiracy or imperialist plots, was not enough to achieve victory and prevent the disaster'. There was no point in looking for the reasons for the defeat in the deeds of others, without first meticulously examining the contribution of the Arabs themselves to their own calamity. He argued that blaming imperialism for the disasters of the Arabs would do them no good. Even if it were true that imperialism was the enemy of the Arabs, this was no reason for the Arabs to evade responsibility for their own deeds and misdeeds. On the contrary, if the Arabs would not assume responsibility for their actions, and make amends for their short-comings, they would remain weak and unable to stand up to their enemies and would thus only inflict further disasters upon themselves. He urged the Arabs not to bury their heads in the sand, but to recognize their failings and deal with them honestly. 'The remedy begins with unity, followed by training and preparation, along the same lines and in the same manner adopted by the enemy.'[29]

21

Tall's critical and straightforward analysis is indicative of his down-to-earth attitude towards political issues that was to characterize him later on, when he was at the height of his political career. He had nothing but contempt for the view, widely held in the Arab world, that every change in policy and every political development could always be explained by theories of plots and conspiracies.[30]

The war, it seemed, had a considerable impact on Tall's political perceptions. One can indicate three lessons which were to leave their mark on his future political behaviour: his appreciation of Israel's power; his suspicion and distrust of the other Arab states; and a certain ambivalence towards, or even irreverence for, the Palestinian national movement, though not for its cause.

# 3

# Jordanian Government Service (1949–61)

After leaving Syria, Wasfi al-Tall moved to Jerusalem, where he became involved with young intellectuals then active in various political clubs in the city. At the beginning of 1950, he joined a group of them in the publication of a weekly called *al-Hadaf*, their cause being to extricate the Arab nation from its predicament in the aftermath of the defeat in Palestine. In this endeavour Tall collaborated with such personalities as Anwar al-Khatib, Yahya Hamuda, Hazim Nusayba, 'Abdallah Na'was, 'Arafat Hijazi and Musa al-Husayni, who were all involved in the publication of the weekly or contributed to it.[1]

The publication did not last very long, and the participants went their separate ways. Some were incorporated into the Jordanian establishment, like Tall himself. Anwar al-Khatib, after a brief period in opposition, became the Jordanian Ambassador in Cairo and then the governor of Jerusalem, and after the Six Day War was one of the stalwarts of the pro-Jordanian camp in the West Bank under Israeli control. Hazim Nusayba served for years as Foreign Minister in the governments of Wasfi al-Tall, later became Jordan's representative at the UN and then returned to serve in various ministerial positions. Others took a very different political course. Yahya Hamuda succeeded Ahmad al-Shuqayri as chairman of the PLO, after the Six Day War; 'Abdallah Na'was became one of the founders of the Ba'th Party in Jordan; 'Arafat Hijazi became a journalist with anti-establishment leanings, and as such clashed with the Wasfi al-Tall government in 1971; and Musa al-Husayni was hanged in 1951 for his part in the assassination of King 'Abdallah. Different paths indeed!

It was at this time that Tall renewed his association with Musa al-'Alami, and began to work at the 'Constructive Enterprise', which 'Alami had established near Jericho as an educational and agricultural project.² During this period, a lifelong, intimate relationship was established between Wasfi al-Tall and Musa's wife, Sa´diyya. She and Musa al-´Alami were divorced in 1950, and Sa´diyya married Tall in 1951. It is therefore quite understandable that Musa al-´Alami preferred to tell Geoffrey Furlonge that after 25 years his marriage 'became a casualty of the Palestine débâcle' and in so doing engendered so much bitterness that he did not wish to dwell on it. Sa´diyya was charming, intelligent and educated. She was the daughter of Ihsan Jabri, who was the head of one of the great Arab families of Aleppo, Syria, and a figure of eminence in the Arab world.³ (Sa´diyya was older than Wasfi al-Tall and they had no children.)

In these circumstances, Tall could hardly have stayed on at the Constructive Enterprise. He left for Amman, where he assumed employment in the civil service.

The early 1950s were the formative years of Wasfi al-Tall's political career. While an official in the General Statistics Bureau and later on in the Internal Revenue Department, Tall never withdrew from politics. As a highly politicized and energetic man of action, he must have been bored to distraction in the government bureaucracy. At first, he was closely associated with members of the Arab Nationalist Movement. They believed that the Arabs had to rehabilitate themselves in the aftermath of their defeat by means of radical reform. This was essential in order to bring about the demise of Israel, for whose establishment they blamed the weakness of the Arabs, Western Imperialism and the UN.⁴ Although he was not one of the rank and file members of their organization, articles by Tall were often published in their weekly, *al-Ra'y*, which appeared in Amman between 1953 and 1956. It was actually Tall who had chosen the name for the paper, whose editor-in-chief, ironically enough, was none other than Dr George Habash.⁵ Habash, a Palestinian refugee, was subsequently to become the leader of the violently anti-Hashimite and anti-Western Popular Front for the Liberation of Palestine. He and Tall were, therefore, destined to become mortal enemies and the staunch defenders of two very different political entities – Habash in the radical wing of the PLO, and Tall at the helm of the Jordanian government.

Tall's articles in *al-Ra'y* were not extreme, but he was critical at

24

times of the Jordanian regime, even if only by implication.[6] As opposed to the more committed members of the Arab Nationalist Movement, Tall never developed any anti-Hashimite ideology nor any deeply felt hostility towards the West. Moreover, he was instinctively suspicious and distrustful of the Soviet Union. The real shift became increasingly apparent during the course of 1955, when, in contradistinction to the adherence of the Arab Nationalists to 'Abd al-Nasir, Tall emerged as an ardent opponent of almost everything 'Abd al-Nasir stood for. His service in the British Army in the Second World War, his ties with Musa al-'Alami and his work in the Arab Offices all contributed to his conviction that it would be in the best interests of the Arabs to ally themselves with the Western powers rather than with the Soviet Union. Tall did not keep his ideas to himself and, at the beginning of 1955, he published an article in the Beirut daily *al-Hayat*, in which he explicitly rejected 'Abd al-Nasir's brand of neutralism. He argued that the Arab world did not possess the intrinsic power to sustain a neutralist posture between the two blocs. It was, therefore, incumbent upon the Arabs to choose to rely on the West and to support Western plans to defend the Middle East from Soviet penetration, as exemplified by the Baghdad Pact.[7] This pact, which had come about on the initative of the Western powers, was signed at the beginning of 1955 and joined Britain, Iraq and Turkey in a defence agreement which was anathema to 'Abd al-Nasir. The Jordanian body politic was deeply divided over the Baghdad Pact issue. King Husayn's attitude was decidedly favourable, but in the eyes of much of the public, swayed by the magnetic appeal of 'Abd al-Nasir, the pact meant surrender, treason and utter humiliation.[8] By publicly expressing his support for the pact, Wasfi al-Tall caught the eye of the Jordanian government. On 11 December 1955, at the height of the confrontation with Egypt over Jordan's possible accession to the Baghdad Pact, Tall received his first political appointment in the Jordanian establishment, as Director of the Department of Publications.[9] This department, together with Jordan's broadcasting service, constituted the 'General Directorate for Guidance and Information', which was under the direct supervision of the Prime Minister's office.[10]

The Prime Minister at the time of Tall's appointment was Sa'id al-Mufti, but more important was the fact that the Minister of the

Interior was Tall's old high school chum, Hazza´ al-Majali. Majali was reputedly the most determined of the Baghdad Pact supporters and one may safely assume that he was the prime mover behind Tall's elevation to a position of political significance at this particular juncture.[11] Personal ties and political persuasion drew the two men together. Both were to pay with their lives for their politics.

During the month of December 1955 Jordan was rocked by unprecedented political turmoil. On 6 December the British chief of the Imperial General Staff, General Templer, arrived in Amman to clinch the deal on Jordan's accession to the Baghdad Pact. Tension in the country neared explosion point. Sa´id al-Mufti resigned the premiership and was replaced by Hazza´ al-Majali on 15 December. Majali's reputation as a supporter of the pact gave rise to a ferocious public reaction. Within a day, Amman and every town in the West Bank erupted in riots the likes of which had never been seen in Jordan. They were certainly fanned from Cairo and, in no small measure, managed by Egyptian personnel in Jordan.[12] But even without Egyptian encouragement, to many in Jordan, particularly the Palestinians, an association with the Western powers (which they felt had failed them in Palestine) directed against the Soviet Union (which they did not perceive as an enemy) was simply intolerable. After only six days in office Majali's cabinet resigned. The next government, led by Ibrahim Hashim, did not last very much longer. In early January 1956 the tough and experienced former Prime Minister, Samir al-Rifa´i, was recalled to office and order was restored. The Baghdad Pact, however, was out. Husayn succumbed to the Nasserist onslaught once he came to the conclusion that the 'game was no longer worth the candle'.[13]

In his job at the Department of Publications, Tall was responsible for the inspection and censorship of all the publications brought into Jordan from foreign countries, certainly a key position at a time when Jordan was on the receiving end of an incessant barrage of propaganda from Egypt. But Tall, due to his characteristic zest, political convictions and his friendship with Hazza´ al-Majali, committed himself above and beyond the call of duty. He had the courage of his convictions and was not the kind of person who was afraid to air his views, however unpopular they may have been. Despite the propaganda war waged by Egypt's

*Sawt al-'Arab* radio station and the belligerent mood in Jordan at the time of the crisis, Wasfi al-Tall offered to give a lecture at the Arab Club in Amman, to explain the advantages of the Baghdad Pact to Jordan.

The Arab Club was the leading forum for political debate in Amman at the time. Frequented by the young intelligentsia, the prevalent mood in the club was one of extreme opposition to the pact, and was, therefore, a political lion's den for people like Wasfi al-Tall. Nevertheless, here as elsewhere he spoke his mind undeterred. The essence of his argument was that Western influence in the Arab world was a fact of life, which the Arabs were incapable of eradicating. As long as this was so, it would be preferable to co-exist with it and seek to harness Western influence to check the 'Zionist onslaught'. His lectures were not well received, and he was sharply criticized.[14] He failed to make much of an impact, but he stuck to his guns to the very end. It was during the Baghdad Pact crisis that Tall developed his deep-seated suspicion, distrust and, indeed, loathing of 'Abd al-Nasir and his drive for hegemony in the Arab world, a predisposition that was to come to rather extreme fruition later on in his political career. Tall was convinced that Jordan knew best where its real interests lay and he found submission to 'Abd al-Nasir humiliating.[15]

Shortly after assuming the premiership, Samir al-Rifa'i announced that his government had no intention of joining the Baghdad Pact. Husayn, now bent on riding the Nasserist wave through conciliation rather than confrontation, also abruptly dismissed Glubb Pasha, the British Chief of Staff of the Jordanian Army, in March 1956. In these circumstances the regime had no immediate political use for a devout anti-Nasserist like Wasfi al-Tall. On 23 February he was transferred to the post of Assistant Director of the Internal Revenue Department, and a short while thereafter, in May 1956, he was shifted yet again, this time to the Foreign Ministry.

Tall had aspired for a long time to work in Jordan's foreign service. He had applied for a transfer to the Foreign Ministry in September 1953. Then, since he was still associated with the Arab Nationalist Movement, his application was not even answered.[16] Now, however, almost three years later, things were very different, and Tall's loyalty was unquestionable. From 1956 to 1957 Tall served as a counsellor at the Jordanian Embassy in Bonn. On his return from Bonn he was appointed Chief of Protocol at the Royal Palace (also a Foreign Ministry post), a position that must certainly have afforded the opportunity to cultivate a personal rapport with King Husayn. After a few months in the palace he was transferred to the Jordanian embassy in Tehran as the chargé d'affaires. An indication of the King's appreciation of Tall is that at the beginning of 1958 he awarded him the Medal of Independence, Second Class.

Having become part and parcel of the establishment, Tall supported Jordan's positions and political credo not only because of an agreement in principle but also out of personal interest. He had finally and irrevocably tied his political fate to that of Hashimite Jordan. While serving in the Jordanian embassy in Bonn, in early 1957, when the opposition government of Sulayman al-Nabulsi was in power in Jordan, he wrote a letter to his friend, ´Abd al-Halim al-Nimr, who was deputy Prime Minister and Minister of the Interior in the Nabulsi government, in which he warned the government against breaking with Britain and gravitating towards the Soviet Union and the clutches of 'communist imperialism'. He urged the government to base the stability of the Kingdom on close defensive and economic ties with Hashimite Iraq, and not on an association with Syria, which might threaten the very existence of Jordan as an independent state and provoke Israeli expansion at the expense of the Arabs.[17] In April 1957 Husayn dismissed the Nabulsi government. However, Tall's fears of Soviet penetration were aroused again in 1958, while he was serving at the Jordanian embassy in Iran, this time in regard to North Africa. He suggested to the Foreign Minister of the then existing Jordanian–Iraqi Federation, that it should form an expeditionary force to be sent to fight the French in Algeria. His purpose was to reduce the reliance of the Algerian Revolution on Soviet aid. Tall even suggested that he would join this unit himself if it were established.[18] Just as he felt that federation between Jordan and Iraq was in harmony with his political concepts, so was he shaken to the core by the revolution in Iraq, and the liquidation of the Hashimite regime there, in July 1958. His wife, Sa´diyya recalled that when he heard of the revolution he was so devastated that he ate nothing but laban for ten days.[19]

His identification with the Jordanian regime was complete. On

17 May 1959, having returned to Jordan from Iran, he took up the important post of director of the state-controlled broadcasting system.

## THE SPOKESMAN FOR THE REGIME

On 25 August 1959, the government of Hazza´ al-Majali, which had come into office some two weeks before, also appointed Tall acting director of the General Directorate for Guidance and Information, and thus gave him authority over the entire Jordanian information and publicity system. These were trying times for the Jordanian regime in the inter-Arab arena, particularly because of the ingrained hostility of ´Abd al-Nasir and the United Arab Republic (UAR) and the revival of the question of the Palestinian entity as a central issue in Arab affairs. The appointment of Tall to so senior and sensitive a post was, therefore, not only a significant advance in his political career but also an indication of the extent to which his dedication and loyalty had been recognized. Hazza´ al-Majali, who must have remembered Tall's good service to the government and to Majali himself during the Baghdad Pact crisis, wanted Tall at his side as he assumed the premiership. Jordan and the UAR were locked in a propaganda war conducted over the air. The Director of Broadcasting was clearly a position of importance. As information was supervised directly by the Prime Minister, Tall's new office was in the Prime Minister's offices, just across the corridor from Majali.[20]

In the late 1950s and early 1960s, before the advent of television in Jordan, the radio still functioned as the most important medium of communication with the masses. As was the case in other Middle Eastern countries, its importance derived from the fact that political and other messages transmitted by radio reached the length and breadth of the country, even to those who did not have radio sets themselves, thanks to the loudspeakers installed in shops and cafés in the cities and villages. The relatively high rate of illiteracy and the not very wide circulation of a small number of newspapers and other printed media transformed the radio into the principal instrument for moulding public opinion. Moreover, especially in the context of the flowery rhetoric and extreme statements that were such an integral part of the inter-Arab political discourse, the spoken word had a more direct emotional appeal.[21]

These facts were known only too well to Jordan's leaders. In the years of intensive confrontation, particularly between Jordan and the Egyptian–Syrian Union (the UAR), they attached great weight to the continuous propaganda exchanges. This would explain the rapid development of Jordan's broadcasting capacity at that time. In March 1959, shortly before the appointment of Wasfi al-Tall as the Director of Broadcasting, a new broadcasting station was opened in Amman; in August 1959, new broadcasting studios were inaugurated in Jerusalem; and in August 1960 a powerful transmitter was installed in Amman, to increase the broadcasting range of the station. King Husayn repeatedly emphasized the importance of the radio as an instrument in the struggle against the pseudo-Marxist and Nasserist 'imported ideologies' and for 'national guidance' generally.[22] The importance of broadcasting was appreciated not only by the regime but also by its enemies. In August 1960, when Prime Minister Hazza´ al-Majali was assassinated by agents of the UAR, their objectives were not only to murder Majali but also to destroy the broadcasting station. In this latter mission, however, they failed.

### THE PROPAGANDA WAR AGAINST EGYPT

As already mentioned, at the time of Tall's new appointment, relations between Jordan and the UAR were particularly poor as the two engaged in a rather vicious propaganda war. At the end of July 1959, mediation by the Secretary General of the Arab League, ´Abd al-Khaliq Hassuna, succeeded in improving relations and brought the propaganda war between the two countries almost to a complete standstill. But at the beginning of 1960, the hostile exchanges were resumed with even greater intensity.

At the deliberations of the Arab League Council in September 1959 and February 1960, Jordan's representative had opposed the proposals of the UAR in regard to the revival of the Palestinian entity. As a result, in March 1960, the UAR mounted a venomous propaganda attack against Jordan, accusing it of sabotaging the efforts of the UAR to create a Palestinian entity and to form a Palestinian army.[23] UAR propaganda constantly incited the Jordanians to assassinate King Husayn and to overthrow the regime. The Egyptians did not restrict themselves to a war of words, and their propaganda was coupled with sustained subversive activity in Jordan. The Jordanians for their part accused ʿAbd al-Nasir of splitting the Arab ranks and of oppressing the people of Syria, who were called upon to rise in revolt against him. Jordan also reviled ʿAbd al-Nasir for his inability to confront Israel. As evidence of his impotence the Jordanians regularly cited Egypt's acquiescence in the presence of UN forces on Egyptian sovereign territory and in the free passage of Israeli shipping through the Straits of Tiran.[24]

In August 1960, the Arab Foreign Ministers' Conference met at Shtura in Lebanon. Coinciding with the conference and as a gesture of goodwill, Husayn ordered the cessation of the propaganda broadcasts against the UAR, but this changed nothing. The UAR did not stop its own propaganda broadcasts against Jordan, and at the conference Jordan continued to oppose the recommendations of the UAR and Iraq, which called for the revival of the Palestinian entity and the political organization of the Palestinian Arabs. The Jordanian delegation, of which Wasfi al-Tall was a member, together with the Jordanian Foreign Minister, Musa Nasir, argued that these recommendations would bring about the destruction of the 'Jordanian entity', the majority of whose inhabitants were Palestinians. Tall's impressive appearance and aggressive demeanour earned him the title of 'strong man' of the Jordanian delegation, given to him by one of the Egyptian reporters. It was he who made it quite clear that Jordan would adhere to its position, come what may. If this should result in the failure of the conference that was just too bad. At the end of the deliberations, on the recommendations of the UAR and Iraq, no resolution was adopted.[25]

On 29 August 1960, the day after the conclusion of the Shtura conference, the Prime Minister of Jordan, Hazzaʿ al-Majali was killed by an explosion in his office in Amman. Jordan blamed the UAR for the assassination[26] and Wasfi al-Tall returned from the Shtura conference to orchestrate Jordan's propaganda offensive against the UAR, which was, perhaps, without precedent in its ferocity. For Tall, the death of Majali was the loss not only of his political mentor but of his close friend. He returned from the funeral directly to Broadcasting House where he told the staff that,

31

despite the loss of Hazza´, Jordan was still Jordan, and it could not afford to show any sign of weakness. The best response to the perpetrators was for Jordan to persevere undaunted on its own course.[27]

Sawt al-'Arab, in its broadcasts from Cairo, denied Jordan's accusations. Instead it accused 'the adolescent tyrant' for having brought about the murder of Majali by his policy of 'treachery' and it appealed to the Palestinians in Jordan to rise against the regime.[28] Tall was not intimidated. Jordan's broadcasts dubbed ´Abd al-Nasir a 'murderer and a criminal' and called upon the Syrians to join the Jordanians in 'the battle of Arabism against Nasserism' and against the 'criminal gang' of ´Abd al-Nasir.[29]

Though responsible for information, Tall obviously did not determine the fundamentals of policy towards the UAR. He was, however, responsible for the propaganda aspect of this policy and it was he who gave Jordanian propaganda its pugnacious character. For about a year and a half, Tall exploited the radio in the acrimonious confrontation with the UAR, and to defend Jordan's position against the trend to revive the Palestinian entity. All this was in accordance with the policy of the regime with which Tall identified wholeheartedly.

## RELATIONS WITH IRAQ

During this period, at the end of the 1950s, despite the tension between Jordan and Iraq since the revolution in 1958 which had put an end to the Hashimite regime in Baghdad, the propaganda war between the two countries was less intensive than the one waged between Jordan and the UAR. Furthermore, there was no evidence of subversive activity from either side.[30] In their propaganda broadcasts against Iraq, the Jordanians, as a matter of course, emphasized that Iraq could only have been harmed by Qasim's revolution. Qasim was depicted as the 'new Hulagu' who had taken over Iraq which had lost 'its great Faysal'. (Hulago was the idol-worshipping Mongolian ruler, who had put an end to the ´Abbasid Caliphate, when he devastated Baghdad in 1258. This was therefore a notorious figure of ill-repute in Muslim historiography, and a most derogatory epithet. Faysal was the Hashimite King of Iraq, a cousin of King Husayn of Jordan.)[31]

Between December 1959 and March 1960, the main issue in the propaganda which Tall directed against Iraq was Qasim's call to establish a Palestinian republic in the West Bank and the Gaza Strip.[32] The Jordanian broadcasts castigated Qasim for having become a cat's-paw of 'international Communism' and 'world Zionism' while, at the same time, they warned Jordan's own citizens not to be taken in by the notion of a Palestinian republic.[33]

However, because of the tense relationship both had with the UAR, relations between Jordan and Iraq began to improve gradually from the middle of 1960. The propaganda war between them came to an end in June 1960; Jordan officially recognized the Iraqi republican regime on 1 October; and on 1 December King Husayn appointed Wasfi al-Tall as Jordan's ambassador to Iraq.[34] A principal motive for Jordan's renewal of its relations with Iraq was to extricate itself from the inter-Arab isolation from which it had suffered since the establishment of the UAR and the overthrow of the Hashimite regime in Iraq. Husayn presumably hoped to exploit the *rapprochement* with Iraq as a weapon against the UAR. It is highly likely that such considerations led the King to choose Wasfi al-Tall, whose credentials as an anti-Nasserite made him particularly suitable for the position of ambassador to Iraq at this juncture.

## JORDAN'S AMBASSADOR IN BAGHDAD

On 19 December 1960 Wasfi al-Tall presented his credentials as Jordanian ambassador to the President of Iraq.[35] In the first months of 1961 there were numerous press reports on the further improvement in relations between the two countries. The ambassadors in Baghdad and Amman met with the prime ministers and other ministers, joint committees met, an Iraqi Trade Mission was opened in Amman, and arrangements were made for the shipment of goods to Iraq through the port of Aqaba. Both sides repeatedly issued statements to the effect that relations between them were good, and in July it was reported in the press that about 100 Jordanian students had been accepted at Iraqi universities.

The first Kuwaiti crisis erupted in June 1961 when Iraq demanded sovereignty over Kuwait, which had just obtained complete independence. King Husayn made it clear to Iraq that Jordan did not support its claims. Nevertheless the Jordanians tried to maintain their friendly relations with Iraq. Their participation in the inter-Arab force which was eventually sent to Kuwait to defend its independence was intended not only to restrain the Iraqis but also to prevent Egypt from controlling the force. In any event, Jordan's participation did not prejudice continuation of good relations with Iraq, and, in August, Tall even declared that Jordan's relations with Iraq were better than ever.[36]

However, in January 1962, Jordan's relations with Iraq deteriorated seriously when Jordan received an ambassador from Kuwait. The Iraqi Foreign Minister, Hashim Jawad, had already declared on 26 December 1961, that Iraq would consider the exchange of diplomatic representatives with 'the so-called state of Kuwait' as an 'unfriendly act and [a] violation of Iraq's rights'.[37] Following talks with the Iraqi Foreign Minister, Tall returned to Amman for consultations on 17 January 1962. The following day the Iraqi Foreign Ministry recalled their ambassador to Amman, Brigadier ´Abd al-Karim Shakir, and Jordanian–Iraqi relations became strained for the first time since their renewal at the end of 1960. Tall did not return to his post as ambassador to Baghdad. A few days after his return to Jordan, he was appointed Prime Minister by King Husayn.

## ANTI-NASSERIST PLOTS IN LEBANON

While serving in Baghdad, apart from his activity in promoting bilateral Jordanian–Iraqi relations, Tall had also been involved in contact with anti-Nasserist elements in Lebanon with a view to curbing Egyptian influence there. At the end of December 1961 the National Socialist Party (al-Hizb al-Qawmi al-Ijtima´i, formerly the Syrian National Party (al-Hizb al-Qawmi al-Suri) or more commonly known as the Parti Populaire Syrienne (PPS)) had attempted a coup in Lebanon meant to promote the idea of 'Greater Syria' or 'Unity of the Fertile Crescent'. It was a dismal failure. The charge sheet against the conspirators accused them of having received 20,000 dinars of financial support from official sources in Jordan, although Jordan was not accused by the Lebanese prosecution of having had prior knowledge of the coup.[38]

From the initial stages of the interrogation of the conspirators by the Lebanese authorities, reports and innuendoes in the press linked a number of persons in the leadership of the party with the Jordanian ambassador to Baghdad, Wasfi al-Tall. On 9 January 1962, the Jordanian Foreign Minister, Rafiq al-Husayni, flatly denied the reports published in the Lebanese press to the effect that In´am Ra´d, the party's secretary for information, had been in contact with Wasfi al-Tall in Baghdad during the year preceding the abortive coup.[39] Despite the denials, however, Jordan admitted that there had been some contact with the party. It is therefore reasonable to assume that Tall had, in fact, been in touch with party members during his service in Baghdad. But it appears that neither Tall nor the Jordanian government were involved in the coup itself, and, as we have seen, this was not alleged in the charge sheet either.

At a news conference which Tall held on 21 May 1962, when he was already Prime Minister, he did not deny that Jordan had given material assistance to 'certain circles' in Lebanon, including those involved in the coup. But he denied any direct connection with the abortive coup itself.[40] A short while later, in an interview with the Lebanese newspaper *al-Jarida*, he explained that as far back as 1957 decisions had been made in Jordan to take action against Nasserism in Lebanon. Ties with various groups in Lebanon were initiated for the purpose of combating Nasserist influence there. Jordan had assisted these groups financially because it was convinced, according to Tall, that Lebanon had become a 'center of the Nasserist trend', a fact which constituted a danger to Jordan.[41]

Because of the links between Jordan and the National Socialist Party in Lebanon, there were those who suggested that Husayn and Tall supported the idea of Fertile Crescent unity, which was the basic ideological tenet of the party.[42] However, the generally anti-Nasserist thrust of Jordan's inter-Arab policy, and the views of Tall himself, would suggest that it was the fierce opposition of the National Socialist Party to ´Abd al-Nasir and the brand of Arab nationalism which he represented[43] that served as the common ground with Jordan. The idea of Fertile Crescent unity was unrealistic and not even in Jordan's interest, at that time.

# 4

# Prime Minister (1962–63)

## THE APPOINTMENT

On 27 January 1962, after the resignation of the Bahjat al-Talhuni cabinet, Husayn called on Wasfi al-Tall to form a new government. This was a period of relative tranquility for Jordan in the inter-Arab arena, especially since the dissolution of the UAR in September 1961. Known as the period of secession (*infisal*), it symbolized the receding tide of Nasserism and was characterized, *inter alia*, by the cessation of Syrian subversion in Jordan. Husayn could now enjoy renewed self-confidence and entertain hopes for prolonged stability, after years of pressure and relative isolation in the inter-Arab arena.

Husayn sought to accord the new government an innovative image. He wanted to portray Jordan as standing on the threshold of a new era – a period of concentration on domestic affairs, political liberalization and economic development. Jordan, the King said in his letter of appointment to Tall, was to become a 'model homeland'.[1]

Husayn's choice of Tall to head a government which was meant to lead Jordan into this new era was motivated by a number of factors, the most important of which was Tall's unshakeable loyalty to Hashimite Jordan. Moreover, Tall was a man who exuded self-assurance, he had drive and initiative, he was tough and aggressive and was also relatively young (42), well educated and even acceptable to many Palestinians because of his role in the struggle for Palestine.[2] All these factors combined made him the ideal candidate for the implementation of Husayn's new vision. Furthermore, by this time, the two men had become close friends. Before the appointment, when Tall was still acting as his country's ambassador to Baghdad, it was already quite well known that he was one of the King's closest advisers. Their familiarity was such that neither the King nor Tall thought it out of place for Tall to

36

interfere and give advice even on Husayn's private life. Tall was one of those who tried to dissuade Husayn from marrying Toni Gardiner, subsequently to become the Princess Muna, because of her British origin. Characteristically, he spoke his mind to Husayn in the strongest terms. Indeed, Tall was one of the few, the very few, who would go a long way to impress his views on Husayn, at the risk of displeasing him. But Husayn also liked and appreciated Tall's sincerity.[3] The King found in him a true partner with whom he could share the onus of government and also maintain a correct working relationship, based on mutual esteem and trust.

In the above appointment, Husayn sketched the general guidelines of Jordan's policy objectives. The King laid down that Jordan's mission was to ensure 'genuine freedom, comprehensive unity, and a better life' for its people. Though just a slogan, it nevertheless reflected, to a large degree, the fundamental political proclivities of Husayn and the stalwarts of the Jordanian political elite. It differed not only semantically but also substantively from the Nasserist and Ba´thi slogan of 'unity, freedom and socialism'. Husayn believed in the possibility of transforming Jordan into a sort of success story, and so did Tall. This was to be achieved by means of economic development, efficient administration and the enhancement of the regime's legitimacy – not by the cultivation of an ideology, but by ensuring 'a better life'; not socialism, but pragmatism, and the implementation of a policy the prime objective of which was to establish a socio-economically contented community of citizens, not unduly harassed or oppressed by government. They strove to create a government that would project a liberal image, without actually sharing political power or undermining the basically authoritarian nature of the political order. All this was to be accomplished without infringing upon the unity of the Kingdom on both the East and West Banks. Husayn found it necessary, in view of the attempts to revive the Palestinian entity, to reiterate Jordan's objection to this idea, which, he said, was designed 'to wrest (*intiza´*) the Palestinian brother from the bosom of his Jordanian family'.[4]

Husayn instructed Tall to form a cabinet of young, dynamic and educated people – a harbinger of the change it was to bring about. It was intended to win the support of the young and educated, from whom the opposition – the Ba´th, the Communists or the Arab

Nationalist Movement – recruited many of their adherents. When formed, the new cabinet was exceptional in that not one of its members had ever served in any previous government. Tall himself was the first prime minister in Husayn's reign who had not previously served as a minister.[5] The new ministers, however, had abundant administrative experience in various spheres of government, and, unofficially, formed a kind of 'government of experts'. The Foreign Minister in the Tall government was Dr Hazim Nusayba, a graduate of the American University in Beirut, who had a doctorate from a university in the United States and was the author of *The Ideas of Arab Nationalism*, a widely known book. Before his appointment to the cabinet, Nusayba had served in a variety of senior positions, such as Director-General of the Ministry of Economic Affairs and as Secretary-General and Vice Chairman of the Development Council, the body, established in 1952, responsible for economic planning in the Kingdom and chaired by the Prime Minister. (With him on the council, besides a Deputy and a Secretary-General, were the Directors-General of the Ministries of Economic Affairs, Finance, Public Works and Agriculture, as well as the Governor of the Central Bank and the Director-General of the Institute for Agricultural Finance and three additional members, not associated with government, who were appointed by the cabinet.)

The Minister for Communications, Da'ud Abu Ghazala, who had studied law in Britain, was, before his appointment, Governor of Jerusalem and Chairman of the Aqaba Port Authority. ´Izz al-Din al-Mufti, the Minister of Finance, ´Abd al-Wahhab al-Majali, the Minister for Economic Affairs, and Hanna Khalaf, the Minister of Justice, had all acted as Directors-General of the Ministries to which they were now assigned. Dr Qasim al-Rimawi was the only member of parliament in the new government. He was a graduate of the American University in Cairo, with a doctorate from Columbia University, and had previously served as Deputy Director of the Department of General Statistics.[6]

Particularly noteworthy was the fact that the Minister of the Interior in the Tall government, Kamal Dajani, was a Palestinian. This was exceptionally rare in Jordan, where the Ministry of the Interior is responsible for the domestic security apparatus. The appointment was presumably a special gesture to the Palestinian majority in the country, at a time when Jordan's control of the Palestinians' fate was beginning to be seriously challenged in the inter-Arab arena, and one that was not repeated for more than 20 years. (In October 1986, another Palestinian was appointed to this position. This was in a cabinet headed by Zayd al-Rifa'i and the Minister of the Interior was another member of the Dajani family, Raja'i Dajani.)

Immediately after his appointment, from his very first news conference, Tall made a concerted effort to create the impression that his government was about to introduce far-reaching reforms, including the increased participation of the citizens in government. His government, he declared, would 'serve the people rather than rule it' and it would 'remove the barrier between ruler and ruled'. Tall promised decentralization and the strengthening of local government so as to allow the citizens to share in the 'bearing of responsibility'. He explained that his government would even welcome 'constructive criticism' from the press,[7] and emphasized its intention to act according to the principle of equal opportunity and 'positive freedom', so that the individual in the state could be a 'model citizen in a model homeland'.[8]

Tall's statements did indeed create the desired impression among the political public: that there really was a prospect for change. Tall thereby hoped to mollify the opposition on the one hand, and to enlist public support on the other, in spite of the fact that neither he nor the King had the slightest intention of changing the highly centralized style of government or of bringing about any substantial distribution of political power.

In the vote of confidence in the Chamber of Deputies on 27 February 1962, Tall's government obtained the unanimous support of the members of the House.[9]

PURGING THE BUREAUCRACY

Tall only believed in reform from above. Even as a young man he was convinced that the state was the chief instrument of reform in the Arab world.[10] It is not surprising, therefore, that immediately after the formation of his first government, Tall gave top priority to an efficiency drive in the bureaucracy. He set about his task with characteristic thoroughness and determination. At the beginning of February 1962, a committee was formed with Khalil al-Salim, the Minister for Social Affairs and Minister of State for Premiership Affairs, as chairman. The committee's mandate was to study the subject of administrative reform in the various government ministries. In mid-February the government passed a special law in parliament which invested it with wider powers than those stipulated in the Civil Service Law, and henceforth it was able to dismiss those civil servants whom it classed as either inefficient or corrupt.

At the end of February 1962, the City Council of Amman was dissolved, a number of city officials were dismissed and an appointed committee was established to run the city. During the months of March to May more than 200 civil servants were sacked. The purge of the bureaucracy, while generally popular, affected many people, some of whom were probably members of families of high standing. The purge, therefore, also apparently aroused a certain amount of discontent in influential circles and Tall decided to halt his rather drastic measures after a few months. But he had already achieved his objective. At a news conference on 21 May, Tall announced that the government's efficiency drive, conducted in accordance with the special law for the reorganization of the government bureaucracy, had been completed. Henceforth the government would only take action against officials in strict compliance with the existing Civil Service Law. He explained that action against the officials dismissed was only taken after due consideration, and officials were only dismissed after the government was convinced that this was fully justified.[11] Nevertheless, the government decided to form an appeals committee, and indeed some civil servants were subsequently reinstated. Tall, however, rejected the notion of compensation for them which, he argued, was neither economically feasible nor morally justified. Tall was a very forthright and determined individual, extremely confident in the correctness of his own decisions and certainly not one who would easily retract or back down from anything he thought was right. Irrespective of whatever he may have said about removing the barriers between rulers and ruled, on this, as on other issues, he was driven by thoroughly authoritarian political instincts. The reinstated civil servants, he thought, instead of seeking compensation for their sudden loss of income, should have been quite happy with their lot, just as one who had been passed healthy after a medical examination.[12]

Tall did not encounter any serious difficulties in his actions regarding the civil service, but he collided with the army's Commander-in-Chief, Habis al-Majali, who, like Tall's good friend Hazza´ al-Majali, came from an exceptionally powerful family from the town of Karak in the south. Habis al-Majali was a veteran officer, who had already commanded a battalion at Latrun in the 1948 war. He simply would not resign himself to Tall's efforts to interfere in the appointment of officers. Relations between the two men reached a very low ebb in the summer of 1962, while Husayn was away on a visit to Britain. On his return, the King succeeded in effecting a reconciliation between them, and Tall was requested to reduce his interference in military matters.

## THE AMNESTY LAW

Even if the regime did not intend to allow any real freedom of action to the opposition, its greater sense of self-confidence in early 1962 provided for a more conciliatory and magnanimous attitude towards some of the opponents of the regime who had been imprisoned or exiled.

As part of the 'new phase' policy and in honour of the birth of his firstborn son, ´Abdallah, King Husayn instructed the government on 30 January 1962 to prepare a General Amnesty Law. At the beginning of February, the new law was passed by both houses of parliament. Wasfi al-Tall described the law as a product of Jordan's political stability and as the first of a series of measures which were intended to permit political exiles to return to the country, to become 'useful citizens' and to participate in 'the building of the homeland'.[13]

Like all political parties, the Communist Party was banned, and the hostility between the regime and communists was mutual and extreme. There was even special legislation in Jordan dealing specifically with the war on communism. Even so, the communists, who continued their clandestine operation, showed impressive staying power. The new Amnesty Law was applicable to many exiles and detainees, but it did not apply to those arrested for communist activity, apart from a few who were released from

41

time to time after they had agreed to denounce communism. The Jordanian Communist Party continued to complain that it was being harassed by the government. However, in December 1962, it was reported that about 120 communists had been released during the past few months, while about another 100 remained in prison. It did seem that the government had decided on both the carrot and the stick to curb communist activities and influence.

Among the more prominent personalities released in the General Amnesty, was Mahmud al-Rusan, of Irbid, one of the senior officers implicated in the conspiracy of the former Chief-of-Staff, 'Ali Abu Nuwar, against Husayn in 1957. In February 1960 Rusan had been sentenced to ten years' imprisonment for plotting against the regime, but was released on 10 May 1962. At the same time, Tall announced that the government had received applications from a number of political exiles to return to Jordan and that some had been granted. Later, several exiles returned from Syria. These included figures such as 'Abd al-Rahman Far'un, a former member of Sulayman al-Nabulsi's National Socialist Party. This party, founded in 1954, had rapidly become a leftist anti-Western, anti-Hashimite and pro-Egyptian force. It was declared illegal in 1957 together with all other political parties. Dr Hamdi Taji al-Faruqi, a Ba'thi, was allowed to return to Jordan, despite the Ba'thi's radical pan-Arab ideology, and even though its declared aim to change the nature of the regime in Jordan remained intact. The Ba'th, like other parties, was still illegal.

Tall and emissaries on his behalf contacted political exiles in Egypt in an attempt to persuade them to return to Jordan and to co-operate with the regime. But those approached rejected his overtures.

ELECTIONS UNDER CONTROLLED LIBERALIZATION

The release of political prisoners was one of the symptoms of the tranquil atmosphere which prevailed in Jordan during 1962. The heavy hand of the domestic security forces was relaxed, and the public also enjoyed considerably greater freedom of speech than heretofore. There was no imminent danger to the regime from the local opposition which was, in the main, disorganized, and the continuous state of disunity in the Arab world increased

Jordan's room for manoeuvre and Husayn's sense of security. In these circumstances, Husayn ordered new elections to be held for the Chamber of Deputies. The existing Chamber, which had been elected in October 1961, was not widely accepted among the political public in Jordan.[14] The elections had not been democratic even in the opinion of observers who were not particularly ill-disposed towards the regime. Candidates undesirable to the government had not been allowed to run. Pressure to stand down was brought to bear on them by the security services, or they were denied the required authorization from the Ministry of the Interior, without which no prospective candidate could stand for election. No more than some ten per cent of the eligible voters participated in the elections, and two-thirds of the candidates were elected unopposed.[15] In reality the elections were a farce.

One of the demands that the Jordanian opposition made of Tall's government was to have the Chamber of Deputies dissolved and to hold impartial elections. By the summer of 1962, Husayn and Tall had come to the conclusion that the time was ripe for such an experiment, and on 26 September Husayn issued a decree dissolving the Chamber of Deputies as of 1 October. Consequently, Tall submitted his resignation, but the King requested that he remain at his post until after the elections.[16] During the election campaign, Tall repeatedly emphasized the commitment of his government, in accordance with instructions from Husayn, to hold free elections. He declared that it was no concern of the government if members of the opposition were elected to parliament, and that the government 'would welcome the presence of opponents to the same extent as it would welcome supporters'.[17] The government's assessment was that the number of deputies representing the opposition would be small, and that the new parliament would be co-operative. Tall apparently believed that the very fact of holding freer elections would generate wider support for the government. This, in turn, would weaken the opposition, which 'had hidden in the past behind the defects which were woven into the election process in order to justify its stands' against the regime.[18]

The Arab Nationalist Movement, which was then still radically pro-Nasserist and anti-Hashimite, called for a boycott of the elections in order to deny the regime any such gain. They main-

43

tained that it was impossible to solve the problems of the people of Jordan by means of elections alone. The root of all evil, after all, was 'the very existence of Husayn's regime'.[19] Tall vigorously rejected the contention of opposition groups who, in their endeavour to influence prospective candidates and voters to boycott the elections, argued that it was inconceivable that the government would totally abstain from electoral interference. After the elections Tall announced with obvious satisfaction that the boycott had failed. Indeed, the large number of candidates and voters spoke for itself. Tall revealed that he had been approached with suggestions to hold 'guided elections', that is, to indulge in fraudulent procedures so that the government could secure the election of certain candidates, but he had refused.[20] On the eve of the elections, he announced that the government would take stern action against anyone who attempted to tamper with the elections, and, in fact, a number of people in the southern town of Karak were sentenced to imprisonment on charges of having bought and sold votes.[21]

Tall refuted the allegations made by the Egyptian media that large-scale arrests had been made throughout the Kingdom before election day, and he declared that no election in Jordan had ever been held in such a serene atmosphere. While this may have been true, not all the allegations levelled against the regime by its enemies were unfounded. Political arrests were made during the election campaign and some members of the radical opposition parties were thus prevented from running for election. Tall made it clear that the government had no intention of deviating from its hard and fast rules, in place since 1957, of not permitting parties to organize and to contest the elections. Since the banning of party activity in Jordan, candidates in elections could only represent themselves as individuals and not as representatives of political parties, and this remained so in the 1962 election. Tall explained that the government regarded these elections as a step towards the creation of what he called a 'constructive opposition'. But, he added, the elections were not intended to grant *carte blanche* to political parties, because of what he maintained was their 'subversive' nature. Tall did not, however, entirely exclude the possibility of developing party life in Jordan after the elections.[22]

For all that, it can be said that the 1962 elections suffered from a noticeably lower degree of government interference and manipulation than was the rule in Jordan. A record number of 168 candidates competed for 57 out of the 60 seats in the Chamber of Deputies, with only three being elected unopposed (*tazkiyya*).[23] About 70 per cent of the eligible voters voted,[24] a figure which was also relatively high for Jordan. These figures attest to the amount of confidence which both voters and candidates had in the relative fairness of the elections.

The election campaign was very lively indeed. The regime was harshly criticized on various issues, including some that were particularly sensitive. Palestinian candidates openly censured the negative position of the regime towards the idea of the Palestinian entity. They were also especially critical of the government in matters pertaining to the relations between the East and West Banks, arguing vehemently (and correctly) that the regime gave preference to the East Bank over the West Bank. Symptomatic of this preference, they argued, was the fact that the regime had not accorded Jerusalem the status it rightly deserved in the Kingdom. There were those who complained, quite justifiably, that the equal representation of the two Banks in the Chamber of Deputies was unfair and not representative of the Palestinians in Jordan, who actually made up two-thirds of the population. The government was not only castigated for having deliberately undermined the Palestinian component of the Kingdom, it was also attacked for its anti-Nasserist policies, and particularly for its support for the royalists in the Yemen War (see below). The candidates held fierce public debates and dozens of meetings with voters, mainly in the coffee-houses. The freedom of expression permitted on these occasions was an indication of the more liberal atmosphere, but it was little more than an atmosphere. The government made public gestures, but it did not depart from its strictly authoritarian tradition. Intelligence agents were in constant attendance at all the election meetings and public gatherings, and, as a matter of course, sent precise reports to their superiors on everything the candidates had to say.[25]

The elections took place on 24 November. They were conducted in an orderly fashion and without incident. Foreign reporters were allowed to enter polling stations to see for themselves that the electorate was indeed voting freely. The government went out of its way to demonstrate the fairness of the elections and even ordered new elections in the town of Madaba because more ballots than actual voters were found in one of the ballot boxes.[26]

A large majority of the successful candidates were not members of the outgoing Chamber of Deputies and some of them were entirely new to politics.[27] The newly elected Chamber of Deputies was markedly different from its predecessors in that it had a large number of well-educated members: of the total (60) there were as many as 25 university graduates. Even so, most of the members did not come from the ranks of the radical opposition to the regime – the members of the Ba´th, the Communist Party or the Arab Nationalist Movement. The authorities had diligently prevented some of the potential candidates from these parties from standing for election; others preferred not to take part, fearing failure at a time when Tall's government enjoyed widespread popularity. Still others presumably boycotted the elections because of their intense ideological hostility towards the regime. As far as they were concerned, participation in the elections would have been construed as an undesirable form of recognition and legitimization of a regime they despised.

The government, though it was soon to have cause to regret the elections, was initially very pleased. At a news conference held by Wasfi al-Tall on the day after the elections, he described them as a 'moment of victory for every Jordanian citizen'. They had, he said, been an exercise in good citizenship, which would serve as the starting point for the 'strengthening of all the democratic institutions'.[28]

On 28 November, Sa´id al-Mufti, the Speaker of the Senate, the appointed upper house of parliament, submitted its collective resignation to King Husayn. Mufti explained that this step was designed to enable the King to reconsider the composition of the Senate in light of the results of the recent election. On 29 November, Husayn appointed a new Senate. In keeping with the new parliamentary spirit, almost half the members were new to the Senate, including Wasfi al-Tall.[29] The press, although subject to government control and guidance, reflected an apparently prevalent mood in the political community, especially in the West Bank, when their editorials expressed the hope that a new political era was about to dawn in Jordan, one in which a genuine opposition would be able to function in parliament. *Al-Difa'*, a Jerusalem daily, suggested that the opposition would have to be constructive, while the government, for its part, would have to understand that an opposition was part and parcel of any genuine democracy, and not necessarily a hotbed of treason. *Filastin*, also of Jerusalem, wrote with considerable naivety and unbridled optimism that the recent election campaign was a turning point in Jordanian democracy, as it would no longer be possible to hold elections less fair than those of November 1962.[30]

The hopes of *Filastin* were later to prove to have been no more than wishful thinking but, for a short time after the elections at least, cautious optimism was shared by all, including King Husayn. At the first session of the new parliament on 1 December, Husayn's praise for the Tall government was received with enthusiasm and applause. The King noted that by virtue of its actions the government had earned 'the appreciation and respect of the people'. In an atmosphere of gratification and self-satisfaction, pervaded by a feeling that all was well, Husayn told the members of parliament, in an informal conversation after the session, that Jordan was approaching a phase in which the establishment of party-like forums would be possible, on condition, of course, that these would act in the interests of the state and not serve as agents for other Arab regimes.[31] He thereby in effect disqualified the three major opposition parties which in any case were illegal: the Ba´th, the Arab Nationalist Movement and the Communists, all of whom had ties with foreign countries. But Husayn's statements did not dampen the general feeling that at the end of 1962 Jordan stood on the threshold of a new era of democracy, which, though guided and limited, could still be seen as a new experiment.

### JORDAN'S INITIATIVE ON PALESTINE

The activities of the Tall government were not confined to domestic politics. The desire to lead Jordan into a new era of political stability made it imperative to lend attention to the crucial question of the Palestinian entity.

Since the early 1950s Palestinians, particularly in Egypt, had begun to lay the groundwork for the re-emergence of the Palestinian national movement as a viable and independent political force. With the formation of Fath, in the late 1950s, this movement gathered momentum.[32] Generally the Arab states had displayed a marked ambivalence towards the Palestinians, constantly vacillating between ideological commitment and expedient restraint, or at times even outright hostility. However, in the late 1950s and early 1960s, an inter-Arab consensus began to emerge in favour of the 'revival of the Palestinian entity'.

Even though for some Arab regimes their support may well have been motivated by their intention to control or contain the Palestinian revival, what was of most immediate importance for Jordan was the fact that, from the beginning of 1959 onwards, the national organization of the Palestinians and some form of political expression for their collective identity increasingly became a focal issue in inter-Arab politics. President ´Abd al-Nasir of Egypt had come to the conclusion that the organization of the Palestinians and 'the revival of the Palestinian entity' were essential components for the effective overall Arab struggle against Israel. Simultaneously these ideas were also instrumental to the furthering of Egypt's goals in inter-Arab rivalries, which were particularly acrimonious at the time. Policy on Palestine became a vehicle in the struggle for Arab supremacy between Qasim's Iraq and the Egypt of ´Abd al-Nasir and both exploited the Palestine issue as a weapon against Jordan.

At the beginning of February 1962, immediately after the formation of his first cabinet, Tall announced that the government was considering the preparation of a 'White Paper' on Jordan's policies on the Palestinian problem and inter-Arab relations. This document was in fact published later (see below), but, in the present context, it is interesting to note that, at the beginning of March, the Egyptians published the 'Gaza Constitution'. This was the forerunner to the formation of the Palestinian National Union in Gaza, which purported to represent all Palestinians 'wherever they were'.[33] This Egyptian move to revive the Palestinian entity impelled the Jordanian government to take action sooner than it had intended.

For years Jordan's policy on the Palestinian question had been defensive and reactive to a course of events that was dictated by Palestinian organizations outside the Kingdom and by Egypt and Iraq. Tall's government now sought to seize the initiative and to prepare its own plan 'for the liberation of Palestine'. In the second half of April 1962 the government invited a number of prominent personalities who were then active in Palestinian politics to Jordan for talks. The leading figure was Ahmad al-Shuqayri, a veteran Palestinian politician who had been politically active during the latter days of the British Mandate in Palestine and who served as the Saudi Arabian Minister of State for United Nations Affairs between 1957 and 1962. Emil Ghuri, 'Isa Nakhla and Munif al-Husayni represented the Higher Arab Committee, by now an essentially defunct institution led by the Mufti, Hajj Amin al-Husayni. They were joined by 'Izzat Tanus, the Permanent Representative of the Palestinian Refugees at the UN. All four were veteran Palestinian politicians with close ties to the Mufti since before 1948. The delegation had talks with King Husayn, Wasfi al-Tall and Jordan's Foreign Minister, the Palestinian, Hazim Nusayba.

The talks with the Palestinian representatives were concluded at the end of April, and, at a news conference on 21 May 1962, Tall said that during the meetings, the Jordanians had not encountered any opposition to the principles of their plan. Moreover, he maintained that Shuqayri had submitted his own proposals for the solution of the Palestinian question, and that these essentially corresponded to the views of the Jordanian government.[34] Tall's statements were just an exercise in public relations. The truth that the positions of Tall and Shuqayri were poles apart was no secret. While in Jordan, Shuqayri had given an interview to one of the local papers in which he stated that he was in favour of the organization of the Palestinians (*al-tanzim al-Filastini*) and the preservation of their own separate national identity in an organization that would unite and represent all Palestinians. Shuqayri issued palliative statements directed at the Jordanian government, to the effect that this organization did not necessarily have to take on the form of a government or acquire sovereignty over any part of Palestine. He spoke of a 'Liberation Committee or National Front' which would only deal with those matters on which all the Arab states would supposedly agree.[35] But Shuqayri's ideas about a special representative organization for the Palestinians were totally opposed to Jordanian policy, which regarded such a notion with trepidation and viewed it as potentially dangerous to the survival of the Kingdom.

The regime did much to persuade the Palestinians in the Kingdom that a special Palestinian organization, not under its own jurisdiction or political control, was quite unnecessary. In public statements, Husayn reiterated that Jordan had a definitive Palestinian plan of its own and that it was this plan that would really be 'the Arab starting point for the liberation of Palestine', and it would be Jordan's army that would be 'the spearhead of the Arab armies'.[36]

Shuqayri did not dispute the fact that Jordan had to be the starting point for the liberation of 'the usurped homeland'.[37] However, to link this with the establishment of a separate national Palestinian organization revealed an underlying understanding entirely contradictory to Jordan's.

The Jordanian government's efforts were directed towards the incorporation of the struggle for Palestine into a plan both inspired and controlled by Jordan. Thus, according to Husayn, the Palestinians would be able to decide their destiny only after Palestine 'was recovered'.[38] The King wished to be perceived as willing to leave the future of the Palestinians up to the Palestinians themselves while co-operating in the meantime with their local representatives. But what he really sought was to postpone any independent Palestinian political activity to some distant and indefinite time in the future. In contrast to Husayn, the supporters of the Palestinian entity, including Shuqayri, strove to organize the Palestinians in Jordan within a political framework that would not be controlled by the government. Their intention was to transform the Palestinian community into a political factor in its own right, that would determine its own fate as an integral part of its national struggle.

The Jordanian regime was most intolerant of the supporters of the idea of a Palestinian entity. Opponents of Hashimite policy were constantly under intelligence surveillance. It was enough for any individual or group just to mention the 'Palestinian entity' for them to be branded by agents of Jordanian intelligence as dangerous opponents of the regime.[39]

While the Jordanian government was busy with its Palestinian plan, Dr Joseph Johnson, the representative of the UN Conciliation Commission, visited the Middle East. The purpose of this commission, which was established in December 1948, with membership drawn from the United States, France and Turkey, was to assist the parties to find a solution to the Arab–Israeli conflict. In mid-1962, Johnson was working on plans to solve the Palestinian refugee problem. He suggested to Jordan that it accept a trial plan to return 20,000 refugees to Israel. Johnson did not believe that it would be possible to persuade Israel to take in a larger number. He therefore also suggested that compensation be paid to the remaining refugees so that they could rehabilitate themselves outside Israel. Jordan hastened to take advantage of this opportunity to demonstrate its loyalty to the Palestinian cause. The Jordanians sent a note to the Arab states in which they categorically rejected Johnson's proposals. Jordan called for the convening of the Council of the Arab League to discuss its own plan for the solution of the Palestinian problem and to co-ordinate the positions of the Arab states in preparation for the forthcoming session of the UN General Assembly.[40]

While Jordan was still waiting for the Arab states to reply to its invitation, which most of them did not even bother to do, Tall convened a news conference on 2 July, on the occasion of the publication of Jordan's White Paper on the Palestinian question and inter-Arab relations.[41] Tall told the reporters that it was essential to draw up a plan of action in regard to the Palestinian question, a plan which would define the objectives which the Arabs had to attain for the sake of Palestine. He rejected the demand for an organizational framework for the Palestinian entity, and made it abundantly clear that no country other than Jordan could speak for its inhabitants. He insisted that any plans must be the outcome of a combined Arab initiative and added with undisguised disdain that 'we all know that the problem of Palestine would not be solved by arming a few hundred of its sons with rifles'.[42] By such a remark, Tall sought to belittle the Egyptian and Iraqi attempts to create a Palestinian army.

The statements made by Tall were in keeping with the contents of the White Paper and the government's plan concerning Palestine, which was drafted by Tall himself, together with a Palestinian friend, Akram Zu'aytar. The purpose of Jordan's policy, as reflected by these documents, was to avert a situation in which Jordan could be attacked in the Arab arena for neglecting the Palestinian cause, which, in turn, could ultimately result in Jordan's loss of all initiative on the issue and even of its control over the Palestinian population in Jordan.

Tall's government maintained that since the majority of the Palestinians had been absorbed into Jordan it was Jordan that had to bear the major burden of the Palestinian problem. Jordan, however, called for a joint Arab effort which it regarded as a precondition for the formation of a 'centre of power' able to stand up to 'the Zionist aggression' and regain 'the lost Arab right in Palestine'. Therefore, it was incumbent upon the Arabs to co-operate in all areas and, in any event, to abstain from exploiting the Palestinian question as an issue of contention in inter-Arab rivalries. The Jordanians laid special stress on the fact that Jordan had the longest border with Israel and was, as a result, 'the main target for the enemy's ambitions' against the Arabs. But, for the same reason, Jordan could also become the springboard for the Arabs to attain their goal of 'recovering the plundered right'.

The Jordanian government wanted essentially to make three points:

(a) That the Arabs must act with caution in all matters concerning the fate of the West Bank, because of the possible reaction of Israel.

(b) In any effective action against Israel, Jordan was likely to be a crucial factor and it was therefore advisable to co-operate with it.

(c) The mobilization of Palestinian potential ought to be implemented within the framework of the Jordanian effort, because the Jordanian entity and the Palestinian entity were, in effect, one and the same.[43]

The Jordanian plan, designed above all else to thwart the 'revival of the Palestinian entity', was not accepted by the rest of the Arab world. At the end of July 1962, the Arab League's Committee of Experts on Palestine prepared a draft concerning the formation of the 'Palestinian National Organization'. This proposal, drawn up much to the chagrin of the Jordanian government, recommended the formation of the 'Palestinian National Council' and the 'Palestinian National Front'. Though not ratified by the Council of the Arab League because of Jordan's opposition,[44] the proposal marked yet another step towards the formation of the PLO, some two years later. The rejection of the plan of the Committee of Experts allowed Tall's government to continue to hope that its own plan would eventually be discussed by the Arab League and that Jordan's standing as the spearhead of the overall Arab effort 'for the sake of Palestine' would ultimately be recognized. Initially Jordan had intended to present its plan to the conference of Arab Foreign Ministers which was supposed to have convened during the UN General Assembly session in October 1962. The conference, however, did not take place and the Jordanian Foreign Minister could do no more than express his disappointment.

The Jordanian government failed to stem the tide in an Arab world that increasingly favoured the revival of the Palestinian entity. Tall's government continued to make gestures towards Palestinians wherever they were, the object being to preserve Jordan's image as custodian of the Palestinian cause, regardless of the anti-Jordanian trend in the Arab world. Tall was even said to have suggested to Husayn that he change the name of the Hashimite Kingdom to the 'Jordanian–Palestinian Kingdom'.[45] In December 1962, Hazim Nusayba announced that his government would be prepared to absorb into its own bureaucracy the Palestinian officials that the Kuwaiti government was planning to dismiss from its service, and to grant them Jordanian citizenship.[46] At the beginning of 1963 the Jordanian government appealed to the UN, demanding that it investigate the situation of the Israeli Arabs.[47] These were all rather empty gestures which changed nothing.

### CONFRONTATION WITH 'ABD AL-NASIR

The major part of the White Paper on the Palestinian question was actually devoted to inter-Arab relations. This was evidence of the importance which the Jordanian monarchy attached to its status and legitimacy among the Arab states, as well as in the eyes of its own subjects.

On the one hand, the inter-Arab passages of the White Paper were somewhat apologetic in tone, emphasizing that Jordan was at least as 'progressive' and as 'liberated' as the other Arab states (who habitually applied these adjectives to themselves). On the other hand, its central theme was an indictment of ´Abd al-Nasir and Nasserism, although neither were explicitly mentioned. In the 1950s and early 1960s, the political and ideological worldview represented by the regime of ´Abd al-Nasir was the incarnation of the most widely held perception among the Arabs of the regeneration and rejuvenation of the Arab world, after a century and a half of subjugation to the West. The salient objectives of Nasserist policy: the advocacy of political and social revolution; the overthrow of the 'reactionary' monarchies; the achievement of overall Arab unity under Egyptian hegemony; and the reorientation of the Arab world towards the Soviet Union rather than the West – all stood in stark contrast to everything the Hashimite regime represented. King Husayn had no choice but to regard ´Abd al-Nasir and Nasserism as mortal enemies who seriously endangered his regime. Consequently, ´Abd al-Nasir's successes in the inter-Arab arena were always a cause of concern for the King and his court, while the failures and setbacks of the Egyptian president, such as the dissolution of the UAR, were events which tended to reassure and encourage the regime.

The union of Syria and Egypt (the UAR), formed in February 1958, was dissolved in the wake of yet another military coup in Syria, in September 1961. Syria's withdrawal from the UAR was, in the main, a result of Syrian disappointment with ´Abd al-Nasir's domineering style and his attempts to subject Syria to absolute Egyptian control. Syrian expectations for a partnership between equals had been dashed. The dissolution of the UAR was a fillip for Husayn who was released for the first time in three years from his isolation in the Arab arena. This setback for ´Abd al-Nasir stimulated an assertive spirit in Husayn's attitude towards Egypt, possibly at Tall's instigation.[48] Jordan immediately accorded diplomatic recognition to the new Syrian regime. The Egyptians, quite rightly, interpreted the King's move as an act of defiance and responded in kind by severing relations with Jordan.[49]

The elevation to the premiership shortly thereafter of Wasfi al-Tall, whose anti-Egyptian record was no secret, was yet another expression of Husayn's aggressive mood and renewed self-confidence. He deliberately selected a person who was both capable of devising and willing to execute a policy that would openly challenge

'Abd al-Nasir and contend effectively with the Egyptian propaganda machine which attacked Jordan without respite. Thus, the White Paper of the Tall government was intended not only to formulate Jordan's position on the fundamental questions and ideological controversies preoccupying the Arab world at the time, but also to place Jordan fairly and squarely in the camp of 'Abd al-Nasir's adversaries.

In its allusions to the Egyptian revolutionary regime, the White Paper made it crystal clear that it repudiated the assumption of power by force of arms. These coups, it argued, resulted in 'the forceful imposition of views and terror against society'. Jordan called for a substantive inter-Arab debate between the different types of regime, without having recourse to inflammatory rhetoric about 'reaction, revolution, treason and patriotism', while it supported Arab unity provided that it arose from 'the free will' of the Arab peoples. Arab unity, the Jordanians contended, was not to be conditional upon the existence of any particular type of regime, nor should it focus on any single 'transient personality', that is to say, not giving any importance at all to 'Abd al-Nasir.[50]

Tall was quick to seize upon the opportunity provided by 'Abd al-Nasir's statements, in early 1962, that Egypt was not yet ready to wage war against Israel, to attack Egypt with relish. He accused Egypt of dissociating itself from the Palestinian cause, and of taking action designed to 'liquidate the Palestinian question' by 'hiding behind the backs' of the UN forces stationed on Egyptian soil since 1957.[51] After an attempt on the life of King Husayn, during a visit to Morocco in July 1962, Tall accused Egypt of being responsible for the attempted assassination and for similar attempts he said had been made on his own life. He blamed Nasserism for having introduced political subversion as a *modus operandi* in inter-Arab relations and alleged that the immorality of Nasserism was no less than 'the greatest crime ever committed against Arabism and Arab nationalism'.[52] The Egyptians, for their part, did not conceal their disdain for Tall. The Egyptian media not only denied his accusations, but added that Tall, 'the agent of reaction', had ascribed an honour to them which they did not even claim for themselves: that is to say, the attempt to purge the Arab nation of his existence and of the existence of those of his ilk.[53] The war of words – vicious and vitriolic – continued unabated until the beginning of 1963.

55

In these circumstances, it is not surprising that in its manoeuvres in the Arab arena, the Tall government consistently and whole-heartedly sided with Egypt's adversaries. At the end of July 1962, Syria delivered a complaint against Egypt to the Secretary-General of the Arab League, accusing Egypt of anti-Syrian subversion. Tall, as a matter of course, expressed Jordan's support for Syria, and advocated that punitive measures be taken against any Arab state interfering in the domestic affairs of another. 'There is no place for custodianship, domination or the use of violence in settling conflicts' between Arabs, he explained.[54]

The Council of the Arab League convened in Shtura in Lebanon at the end of August, to consider the Syrian complaint against Egypt. During the discussions there were harsh exchanges between the Syrian and Egyptian delegates, at the end of which the Egyptians chose to withdraw from the meeting – a step which the Jordanians were quick to interpret as a defeat for ´Abd al-Nasir.

At the same time King Husayn was on a visit to Ta'if in Saudi Arabia. On 29 August, at the end of the visit, Husayn and his counterpart, King Sa´ud, announced an agreement of co-operation between the two states. On 3 November, a Royal Decree was published in Jordan ratifying a series of agreements entered into at Ta'if between the two states. Salah Abu Zayd, the Director of the Department of Guidance and Information of the Jordanian govern-ment, described the Ta'if agreement as 'a semi-union between the two states'.[55] It was obvious that this move was directed primarily against ´Abd al-Nasir, and it naturally provoked sharp Egyptian (and Iraqi) criticism. At first Jordan took a defensive posture. Radio Amman explained that the agreement was not intended as a vehicle of confrontation between rival Arab blocs, but only as a means to stand up to 'Jewish aggression'.[56] This rather apologetic tone was, however, soon to be discarded. On 2 September, Radio Amman declared emphatically:

> To the propaganda trumpets of ´Abd al-Nasir in Cairo and Beirut [where a wide selection of pro-Nasserist newspapers was published] we say: Yes: The recent Jordanian–Saudi agreement is an alliance against ´Abd al-Nasir, because we reject the Johnson plan . . . we are against ´Abd al-Nasir

because we reject [his] policy of buffoonery. We are against him because we reject the replacement of Arab forces by UN forces [referring to the UN forces stationed in Sinai and Gaza], and we refuse to open the Gulf of Aqaba to Jewish shipping.[57]

The next day, in a speech to the nation, Husayn implicitly referred to ´Abd al-Nasir as that 'suspicious infiltrator' who had penetrated the ranks of the Arabs with the intention of tearing down everything that others had built up.[58]

## SUPPORT FOR THE ROYALIST CAUSE IN YEMEN

In September 1962, a crisis erupted in Yemen. A group of young army officers, fired by Nasserist inspiration, overthrew the Imam, Muhammad al-Badr, and immediately thereafter requested Egyptian military assistance against the royalist tribal forces that continued to fight for the Imam.

Once the crisis broke out, it was only natural for it to develop rapidly into a tug of war between Egypt, on the one hand, and Saudi Arabia and Jordan, on the other. From the outset, Jordan's support for the royalists was total and consistent, except that it did not send troops to Yemen, as alleged by Egypt. The support of the royalists in Yemen aroused no small amount of criticism among the opposition in Jordan (see also below), which was not at all happy with the anti-Nasserist policy of the Hashimite regime and found it difficult to accept the alignment of Jordan with the Imam in Yemen. For them the Imam was the embodiment of backwardness and reaction, while ´Abd al-Nasir was seen as the standard-bearer of revolutionary progress. The Jordanian monarchy, however, could hardly condone the forceful change of regime in Yemen, and Wasfi al-Tall emphasized that, in Jordan, people 'do not believe that the way to develop Yemen is to carry out a military coup', with unimaginable consequences.[59]

Tall never missed an opportunity to voice his criticisms of Egypt and to reiterate the same old allegations. It was not to ´Abd al-Nasir's credit, he said, to have released his troops 'from facing the enemy of the Arabs', to have them protected 'behind the International Emergency Forces [the UN forces]', and then send them to Yemen 'to use them to impose the rule of a cabal of traitors'. He vigorously rejected Egyptian allegations regarding Jordanian military intervention in Yemen, and responded with calculated arrogance and scorn to a report in this vein from the (Egyptian) Middle East News Agency. He said that if there really were Jordanian troops in Yemen, it would not have been at all possible for the correspondent of the Middle East News Agency to send his cable,[60] reporting such Jordanian intervention on the side of the Imam.

At the beginning of November 1962, the Saudis reported an Egyptian air attack on their territory. Following the incident, Tall announced that Jordan took its stand at the side of Saudi Arabia and that it considered 'aggression against Saudi Arabia as direct aggression against Jordan'.[61] Just a few days later, the Commander of the Jordanian Air Force and two pilots defected to Egypt. The defectors claimed that Jordan was preparing to use its air force in Yemen, from bases in Saudi Arabia. A Jordanian spokesman admitted that a decision had in fact been taken to transfer Jordanian aircraft to Saudi Arabia, but only as part of a plan to exchange land and air forces for training purposes and for joint military operations, on which the spokesman failed to elaborate.[62] The Saudis refuted the statements of the Jordanian defectors, but Tall was hurriedly dispatched to Saudi Arabia to recall the rest of the Jordanian aircraft and pilots to Jordan.[63] If Jordan had any intention of using its air force in the Yemen war, it backed down from doing so because of the defection of the pilots. Their desertion was yet another sign of the widespread domestic discontent with the Jordanian government's policy towards the war in Yemen.

As a result of Jordan's disappointment with US recognition of the republican regime in Yemen, a move which Husayn and Tall criticized openly, and in order to improve its image in the eyes of its domestic and foreign critics, Tall's government began to put out feelers towards the Soviet Union, culminating in the establishment of diplomatic relations in August 1963. However, at the end of 1962 and the beginning of 1963, even publicized Jordanian–Soviet contacts would not suffice to stave off the critics of the Tall government. Opposition was growing and becoming increasingly outspoken.

## A NEW GOVERNMENT: INCREASING DOMESTIC OPPOSITION

Tall's government had gained broad-based popular support because of the political liberalization it had introduced, the gathering momentum of economic development with the commencement of a new five-year plan (1962–67), and the reforms it had made in the government bureaucracy. Tall's popularity began to wane, however, as a result of the campaign the Jordanian regime waged against 'Abd al-Nasir and its very vocal support for the royalists in Yemen. These policies evoked much opposition, and not only among Palestinians. Symptoms of this growing discontent began to appear simultaneously with the measures taken by the government to allow for greater democracy. In the election campaign of October–November 1962, which was, as already noted, relatively free, a number of candidates withdrew from the race in protest against Jordan's support for the royalist regime in Yemen. Other candidates publicly expressed their support for the promotion and preservation of the Palestinian identity and for the creation of an institutional framework for it. This idea, ubiquitous in the political atmosphere of the Arab world at the time (see above), served as yet another potential cause for friction between the West Bankers and the regime in Amman.

After the elections, on 2 December 1962, Tall formed his second government. Its composition was identical to that of its predecessor except for the addition of 'Abd al-Qadir al-Salih, a deputy from Nablus, as Minister of Development and Construction.[64] At the beginning of this government's term of office it still gave the impression that it had affairs of state firmly under control. There were even reports that it was busy preparing a bill which would permit renewed party activity. However, rumours of an intention to form a 'parliamentary bloc' in opposition to the government showed that trouble was brewing.

On 27 December, Tall delivered his government's policy statement to the Chamber of Deputies to gain its vote of confidence.[65] His speech clearly indicated that the government already understood that it would have to face significant opposition in the chamber. It was beginning to transpire that the gamble which Husayn and Tall had taken in permitting relatively free elections had not paid off. Instead of strengthening the legitimacy of the regime and paving the way for the co-opting of members of the opposition into the establishment, the democratization had only given those with anti-establishment leanings a parliamentary platform from which to assail the government.

In his speech before the chamber Tall still paid lip service to the policy of liberalization, but it was evident that the regime's initial enthusiasm was waning. Tall concentrated on domestic affairs, avoiding the contentious issues of foreign policy. However, he did make a point of issuing a stern warning to the supporters of the Palestinian entity, threatening that the government would consider any 'racial, regional or sectarian fanaticism', to be an act of treason.[66]

In the vote of confidence, on 3 January 1963, Tall's government gained a large majority, 40 against 18. But this was in fact a failure in terms of Jordanian parliamentary tradition, since almost one-third of the house voted against the government – a rare occurrence which was further evidence of the growing opposition.[67]

The debate preceding the vote of confidence was one of the longest that had ever taken place in the Chamber of Deputies, and more than 30 members took part. The Tall government was praised for maintaining 'an atmosphere of freedom and democracy' and for its intention to amend the electoral law and to permit party activity. Many deputies praised the government for its efforts to develop public services and to reorganize the government bureaucracy. However, the government was criticized on many issues, even on those for which it had received praise from others. Some deputies alleged that the government was over-reliant on British Mandatory emergency laws, which gave it extremely wide powers to limit individual freedom in the name of 'the public interest';[68] or that it made excessive use of provisional laws, laws which, according to the Constitution, the government is authorized to promulgate and to act upon when parliament is in recess. (Provisional laws are brought before parliament for ratification only when it reconvenes. See 'The Jordanian Constitution' in M. Khalil (ed.), *The Arab States and the Arab League*, Vol. I, pp. 55–75.) The opponents of the government also campaigned for greater freedom of the press. The extent of Jordan's dependence on Western aid similarly came under attack and the government was called upon to establish diplomatic relations with the states of the Eastern Bloc. However, the majority of those who opposed the government based their opposition mainly on the government's Yemen policy and on the propaganda war it waged against Egypt.

Tall's explanations that placed the blame for Jordan's poor relationship with Egypt entirely on ´Abd al-Nasir, were not accepted by many, especially those who represented West Bank constituencies. To the critics of the government's policy in Yemen he replied with characteristic disdain. The government, he said, welcomed the support it had in the chamber for its Yemen policy and it had no intention of changing it. Anyone who still opposed the policy could go ahead and 'pave the sea' (*faliyuballitu al-bahr*), as far as Tall was concerned.[69]

Tall was too straightforward, too proud and perhaps too arrogant to indulge in the wheeling and dealing of politics. Before the vote of confidence it was apparent that a significant number of the deputies were going to vote against the government. Tall was approached by some of the deputies who warned him that the chances of gaining the confidence of the chamber were slim and that he had better contact a number of deputies to ensure success. Tall refused. He had made his policy statement and the deputies could vote as they pleased. He suspected that the deputies who had approached him were trying to impose their influence on him. He would remain politically indebted to every deputy he contacted before the vote of confidence and these were bound to expect favours in return, for themselves, their relatives and their cronies, particularly in the sphere of government appointments. Tall retorted that the 'shops of favouritism' had been shut down for good.[70] He neither needed nor wanted any deals.

As the voting commenced, one of the deputies started reading a petition signed by about 30 deputies who wished to vote against the government. Tall stopped him in his tracks claiming the petition was unconstitutional. The voting was to be by a show of hands. Deputies who had anything to say should do so openly and not by hiding behind collective petitions. He told the deputies that he had no particular craving for power and the chamber could vote as it wished.[71] In fact, the number who actually voted against the government was substantially lower than the petition had suggested.

Of the 18 who voted against the Tall government, 13 were from the West Bank. Two absentees from the debate were also West Bankers. Thus, only half of the members of the house representing the West Bank had expressed their confidence in his government. The latent opposition to the Hashimite regime in the West Bank had surfaced conspicuously. The flashpoint was in Jerusalem, and all its five deputies in the chamber (Dr Da'ud al-Husayni, Khalil al-Silwani, Ishaq al-Dizdar, Antun al-Bina and Yusuf 'Abduh), voted against Tall.[72] He hastened to retaliate.

On 9 January, the government appointed Fadl al-Dalqamuni, from Tall's home town of Irbid, as governor of the Jerusalem District, replacing Anwar Nusayba. Nusayba, himself a native of Jerusalem, was transferred to the Foreign Ministry.[73] (In an interview in Jerusalem, on 13 February 1980, Nusayba told the author that he was notified by telephone that 'they [the government] had had enough of me as governor and would I accept to be ambassador'.) According to an Egyptian source one of the reasons for Nusayba's transfer was his agreement to the circulation of a speech made in the chamber by one of the Jerusalem deputies. Da'ud al-Husayni. The speech, which was critical of the government's policy on the Palestinian question and of its attitude towards the royalist cause in Yemen, had not been cleared for publication in the press.[74] Nevertheless, it would appear that the replacement of Anwar Nusayba, the Jerusalemite, who had been appointed to this post by Tall in February 1962, by an appointee from the East Bank was related to far more profound considerations. It was intended as a message to the people of Jerusalem that serious opposition to the government would not be tolerated.

Nusayba refused to accept his new position in the Foreign Ministry. The Jerusalem City Council, the Chamber of Commerce, women's organizations and the deputies for Jerusalem in the chamber sent telegrams to the Prime Minister expressing their disapproval of Nusayba's removal. The Foreign Minister, Hazim Nusayba, resigned his post in protest at the dismissal of his brother, but subsequently withdrew his resignation.

On 11 January, the day that Dalqamuni took up his post, King Husayn visited Jerusalem. The purpose of the visit was to express his support for and to give his personal backing to the new governor. The inhabitants protested: a general strike was called the same day and the city was paralysed.[75] This was as clear an expression as any of West Bank resentment and general dis-affection with their relationship with the regime on the East Bank.

The next day, 12 January, Husayn convened a meeting of all the members of the Chamber of Deputies at the royal court to make it quite clear that the regime was not prepared to tolerate any opposition that was not 'constructive'. He was particularly severe in his reference to the 'destructive' rumblings which 'we have begun to hear about the West Bank and the East Bank, and this is something that I should never ever have to hear at all'. He claimed that he welcomed the existence of an opposition, but it had to be 'constructive, one that would discuss methods with us and help us to chart the course that would lead us to our objectives. But if . . . some sick people think that this way would allow them . . . to destroy and to sabotage, I declare before you that . . . I will not permit any such thing.' Husayn warned against instability in the country, which could bring about Israeli intervention. In his reference to the events of the previous day in Jerusalem, Husayn declared that strikes were not the way to solve problems. He explained that 'there is something called the respect for the authority of government (*haybat hukm*) . . . and it is inconceivable that we will allow [strikes] to be repeated'. Husayn concluded his statement with a stern warning and sarcastic condemnation directed at the Nasserist opposition in Jordan, arguing that 'if someone would like it, [he] could employ the oppressive methods of ´Abd al-Nasir or someone else . . . I can be crueler than he, but I do not consider these to be the right methods.'[76]

On the same day there was also a regular session of the Chamber of Deputies. Husayn's harsh words served as a timely support for Tall who now proceeded to settle his own accounts with the parliament-ary opposition, that is, the group of deputies subscribing to the views of the illegal political parties. But more than anything else, the positions of this group and their criticisms of the government showed how deeply they identified with the ideas and policies of ´Abd al-Nasir.

Tall now adopted a much more aggressive and scathing tone than he had done against his critics a week before in the debate on the vote of confidence. The battle lines had been drawn, and Tall was obviously raring to enter the fray. At the outset he referred to the criticism levelled against the economic policies of his government. He scornfully rejected the calls of the opposition to nationalize the economy and to stop accepting economic aid from the West. He considered their demands to be no more than an unrealistic mimicry of the slogans of 'Abd al-Nasir, at a time when Jordan was in fact developing at a faster rate than any of the other Arab states with the exception of Lebanon (see E. Kanovsky, *The Economy of Jordan*, p. 5, for support of this assertion).[77] As to the supplanting of Western assistance with Arab aid, Tall alluded to Jordan's past experience, which showed that Arab aid was likely to be unreliable and to have a variety of political strings attached as well. Tall's statements were apparently inspired by Sulayman al-Nabulsi's failure (in 1956–57) to replace British assistance with aid from Egypt, Syria and Saudi Arabia – aid which, despite many promises, in the main never reached Jordan. Jordan was subsequently extricated from its financial distress by assistance from the United States, which from then onwards replaced Britain in this respect.[78]

Tall was particularly antagonistic towards the critics of the Jordanian–Saudi co-ordination against Egypt in the Yemen crisis. He rebuked them for not even having bothered to take the trouble to clarify thoroughly what the policy of the government really was. Part of their criticism was, in his view, simply an idle repetition of 'the buffoonery (*tahrij*) of Ahmad Sa'id', the Egyptian broadcaster on *Sawt al-'Arab*. He justified his government's support for the royalists in Yemen by arguing that it was they who controlled most of the country and that without the help of thousands of Egyptian soldiers the republicans would not have been able to hold their ground.

But as Husayn had done before him, Tall devoted the major part of his speech to the experiment in democratization and to the concept and essence of freedom, as he understood it. He was most decisive in prescribing the limits of the freedom his government had granted and thus demonstrated that in spite of his Western education and the great influence the West had had on him, as on others of his generation, Tall had not internalized the basic democratic values of the West. His political culture was deeply rooted in the predominantly authoritarian traditions of the region. In his worldview, political freedom and the right to participate in government were not enjoyed by the citizenry as a matter of course. It was the government which 'granted' freedom, and it was the government which determined its bounds. In his references to the disturbances in Jerusalem (in which several of the Jerusalem deputies had apparently been involved, and who, it will be recalled, had voted unanimously against Tall in the vote of confidence), he maintained that 'it is not an expression of parliamentary freedom to intervene in the transfer of one or another official; it is also not a form of parliamentary freedom to incite [citizens] to demonstrate or to strike . . . nor to act to split the ranks and to undermine the well being [of the state], nor to waste the time of the citizens with emotional speeches'. It was the duty of the Chamber of Deputies 'to create a model of co-operation' with the government.[79] Tall thus inferred that the Jordanian parliament did not have any inherent right to act against the government, and it seems that this is precisely what he understood to be the function of parliament in the Jordanian political system, namely – a body subservient to the government, rather than one that existed to criticize it.

The government's counter-attack did not silence the opposition. On 13 January, the Jordanian Bar Association sent a memorandum to the Prime Minister, the Speaker of the Senate and the Speaker of the Chamber of Deputies in which it called upon the government, inter alia, to cease applying emergency laws and to introduce a new electoral law.[80] These demands were not accepted. Although reports of the government's intention to amend the electoral law and to pass a law regulating party activity continued to circulate, nothing of this actually materialized. The opposition, as manifested in the Chamber of Deputies and in the events in Jerusalem, deterred the regime. It now reached the conclusion that the time had come to slow down the democratization process, if not to put an end to it altogether.

### THE BAʿTHI COUPS IN IRAQ AND SYRIA –
### HUSAYN BACK ON THE DEFENSIVE

The self-confidence which the regime had displayed towards its opponents both at home and in the Arab world, was eroded by the domestic opposition and, in even greater measure, by the Baʿthi coups in Iraq (8 February) and in Syria (8 March). The two Baʿthi coups were followed by talks held in March–April 1963 among Egypt, Iraq and Syria on the possible formation of a tripartite union. Husayn was again exposed to the isolation and the sense of political suffocation he had experienced at the time of the Egyptian–Syrian union. The bold and aggressive spirit *vis-à-vis* Egypt, which had been so commonplace before, now vanished overnight without trace. Immediately after the coups, the Jordanian government recognized the two new regimes. On the day of the coup in Syria, Jordanian broadcasts ceased their attacks on Egypt, and even began to refer to it by its then official name, the 'United Arab Republic' instead of 'Egypt', which the Jordanians had hitherto used as a deliberate slight against ´Abd al-Nasir.[81]

On 9 March, Tall convened a news conference. His tone was uncharacteristically defensive. When Tall was asked about Jordan's attitude towards the Ba´th Party, he replied in a manner reminiscent of statements by celebrated anti-Semites about their Jewish friends, and it would be safe to say that he was being equally insincere. He said that even though political parties were banned in Jordan, he personally had 'many Ba´thi friends' with whom he met daily for discussion, argument and conversation. However, with regard to objectives, it was his opinion that there was no disagreement between 'any Arab government and any Arab party'.[82] His statements duly reflected the change in the political climate in Jordan and they were a far cry from Tall's pejorative declarations about the parties, including the Ba´th, only a few months earlier.

Against the background of the talks on the tripartite union that began in mid-March among Syria, Iraq and Egypt, Husayn adopted a stand that at times looked quite pathetic, depicting Jordan as fully sharing in the aspirations of ´Abd al-Nasir and the two Ba´thi regimes.[83] At the same time, signs of renewed domestic tension began to appear in Jordan. The government's speedy recognition of the new regimes in Iraq and Syria was widely supported in the Chamber of Deputies. Broad support for the government would normally be a positive sign but in this case it was a symbol of growing internal opposition, which was pressing for a thaw in relations between the Jordanian regime and ´Abd al-Nasir. Evidence to this effect could be seen in the demand by one of the deputies that the government accord recognition to the republican regime in Yemen – a demand which was rejected by Tall.[84] While the immediate recognition of the secessionist regime in Syria in 1961 could have been construed as an act of defiance directed against 'Abd al-Nasir, the rapid recognition of the new Ba'thi regimes carried a quite different connotation. Husayn could now be seen to defer to 'Abd al-Nasir, who appeared to be on the rise once again. The opposition was duly emboldened.

The events in the Arab world introduced a drastic change in the circumstances which had originally motivated Husayn to appoint Tall as Prime Minister at the beginning of 1962. In contrast to the earlier erosion of the stature of 'Abd al-Nasir, as a result of the dissolution of the UAR and the simultaneous bolstering of Husayn's self-confidence, their respective fortunes were reversed in March 1963, with the beginning of the talks on the tripartite union. Husayn was subjected to extreme psychological pressure as 'Abd al-Nasir seemed to be regaining his lost lustre and power. It was clearly the intention of Husayn to find an opening for an accommodation with 'Abd al-Nasir and to establish positive relations with the new regimes in Syria and Iraq. This also called for domestic reassessment and reorganization to forestall any effort by the Nasserist and Ba'thi opposition in Jordan to exploit the events in the neighbouring Arab states to foment unrest.

Wasfi al-Tall was not cut out to implement a policy of appeasement towards Egypt. Furthermore, it seems that Husayn did not have complete confidence in the ability of his inexperienced Prime Minister to contend with possible internal unrest. The time had come for Wasfi al-Tall to go. On 27 March, Tall tendered the resignation of his government. In his letter of resignation Tall explained that recent events required an 'evaluation of the general situation and . . . the formation of a new government to undertake responsibility for this evaluation'.[85]

In his hour of distress, Husayn sought to rely on the old guard of the Jordanian political elite and he appointed Samir al-Rifa'i as Prime Minister. Rifa'i was a Palestinian who had migrated to the East Bank in the mid-1920s and who had served King 'Abdallah faithfully for many years. Rifa'i had already served as Prime Minister in the 1940s and had considerable experience in crisis management and in the supression of civil disobedience. The declarations by Husayn and Rifa'i to the effect that Jordan wished to associate itself with the proposed Arab Union, and the flood of reports regarding the government's desire to close ranks with Egypt, Syria and Iraq,[86] failed to convince the opposition. The idea of Arab unity had an almost mystical appeal in the Arab world. So much so that, following the Egyptian–Syrian–Iraqi announcement on 17 April of their intention to form a federal union, Arab public opinion was gripped with euphoria.[87] The popular enthusiasm did not bypass Jordan, and stormy demonstrations were held in all the main towns for several days demanding that Jordan announce its accession to the union.

The demonstrations quickly turned into riots. On 20 April, 4 people were killed and 30 were injured in Jerusalem. A large demonstration in favour of Jordan's accession to the tripartite union began at eight in the morning when high-school students started to march through the streets hoisting pictures of ´Abd al-Nasir. The Jordanian flag was removed from one of the public buildings and replaced with a four-star flag, intended to symbolize Jordan's desired participation in a union of four Arab states. When the demonstrators attacked the police, there was pandemonium. People rushed through the streets chanting 'Nasir, Nasir'. The police opened fire, and in the end the army was called in to restore order in the city. A curfew was imposed and was lifted only at the end of April.[88] Some of the members of the Chamber of Deputies were detained, suspected of having participated in the organization of the demonstrations and in acts 'incompatible with the constitution'.[89]

On 20 April, under the impact of the riots in Jerusalem, the Chamber of Deputies convened for the vote of confidence in the Rifa´i government. A majority of speakers rejected the policies of the government, and especially Rifa´i's statements on the necessity for Arab unity, which they dismissed as mere empty words. For the first, and last, time in the history of Jordan, a majority of the members of the Chamber of Deputies (31 out of 60) passed a vote of no confidence in the government, and the Rifa´i government was forced to resign.[90]

The interaction between the two processes which had begun in the days of the Tall government had come to fruition. The increased democratization as manifested in the elections of November 1962, on the one hand, and the strengthening of the opposition, especially against the background of the regime's inter-Arab policy, on the other, had wrought political havoc from the regime's point of view.

The ousting of the Rifa'i government by the Chamber of Deputies upset the traditional balance of power between the parliament and the palace. It struck a blow at one of the most crucial political prerogatives of the monarchy – the authority to control government through the appointment and dismissal of prime ministers. For Husayn this was the last straw. The termination of the process of liberalization had become an urgent political imperative. On 21 April he dissolved the Chamber of Deputies which, he said, 'did not truly express the will of the electors'. Husayn appointed his elderly uncle, Sharif Husayn bin Nasir, to head a caretaker government to oversee new elections to the Chamber of Deputies and to restore law and order.[91] Sharif Husayn was a genial old man with a temperate disposition who was even a little soft-hearted. Nevertheless, he proved to be an efficient administrator and had an excellent rapport and working relationship with the King, regardless of the latter being almost 30 years his junior.

The elections to the new Chamber of Deputies in July 1963 were not conducted in the same atmosphere of relative freedom that had characterized the previous elections, a fact that was clearly borne out by the results. Most of the opponents of the regime were not re-elected to the new chamber. Some of them preferred not to take part in the election due to pressure from the authorities, who, in various ways, made it quite clear to them that they should not run for election. In certain cases the government's message was delivered to them directly, in the form of 'advice' from the Minister of the Interior or the Director-General of his ministry. In others, the same end was achieved by spreading rumours among the notables, according to which the palace, that is to say the King, or the government, namely the Ministry of the Interior, was dissatisfied with someone; or it was simply arranged to tell the person in question bluntly that he should not offer his candidature this time as he was being punished for his negative activities.[92] The short-lived liberalization experiment, begun during the tenure of Wasfi al-Tall's government, was thus finally brought to its close.

# 5

# Confrontation with the PLO
# (1965–67)

Sharif Husayn's government soon restored public order. The army was brought into the towns and the opposition was cowed by the regime's iron-fisted policy. The emasculation of the opposition, however, was not only a result of steps taken by the regime. It was also due to simultaneous changes in the Arab world.

The Tripartite Union, proclaimed in April 1963, inflamed the imagination of the masses, who felt their cherished dream for Arab unity was about to come true. Momentarily, it gave encouragement and self-assurance to the Nasserist opposition. However, it was never implemented. Within a few months relations between Egypt, Syria and Iraq had broken down completely.[1] The inter-Arab psychological and propaganda pressure on Jordan gradually faded away. Firmness on the domestic front and the dissipation of Arab external pressure combined to extricate Jordan from the crisis it had entered in early 1963.

At the end of 1963, ´Abd al-Nasir embarked on an innovative initiative in inter-Arab relations. He called for a summit meeting of Arab leaders, the first of which was held in January 1964. This was a radically new departure. ´Abd al-Nasir's Egypt now opted for co-existence and reconciliation with all the other Arab states. The slogan of 'unity of objectives' was superceded by the 'unity of ranks'. This was an attempt to unite Arab ranks, despite the political and ideological differences between the various regimes. This novel approach allowed Jordan to return to the Arab fold and take its place alongside ´Abd al-Nasir instead of against him. But *rapprochement* and 'the summit spirit' exacted a political price: Husayn withdrew his objection to the revival of the Palestinian entity, and agreed to the formation of the Palestine Liberation Organization (PLO) and the Palestine Liberation Army (PLA). He also agreed to the formation of a United Arab Command to be headed by an

70

Egyptian commander and generally accepted the leadership of Egypt in matters pertaining to inter-Arab relations, as clearly shown by Jordan's recognition of the republican regime in Yemen.[2] During this period Wasfi al-Tall did not hold any important official post, but he remained close to Husayn and met with him often. Among Husayn's close associates there were some who thought that he had gone too far in his reconciliation with 'Abd al-Nasir, and therefore supported the reinstatement of Tall as Prime Minister as a means of checking the King's conciliatory course. There were also reports, at the time, to the effect that Husayn's policies had evoked a measure of Saudi dissatisfaction.[3]

On 13 February 1965, Husayn reinstated Wasfi al-Tall as Prime Minister.[4] He replaced Bahjat al-Talhuni, one of Tall's adversaries, who was a veteran member of the establishment despite his reputation as a corrupt intriguer. Talhuni had been Prime Minister since July 1964 and his replacement aroused speculation regarding possible changes in the direction of Jordanian policy. Instead of Talhuni, who had the public image of a personality acceptable to Egypt, there was now a Prime Minister whose anti-Egyptian record was one of his most well-known trademarks. The general impression was that Husayn was about to deviate from his policy of appeasement towards 'Abd al-Nasir.[5] A few days after Tall's appointment Husayn went on an official visit to Egypt. He took Tall with him, and in their talks with 'Abd al-Nasir, they tried, *inter alia*, to persuade him that the changes in government did not herald new departures in Jordan's policy towards Egypt. However, 'Abd al-Nasir received Tall unwillingly and their meeting – the only one between the two men – was fraught with tension. 'Abd al-Nasir remained unconvinced.[6]

In his letter of appointment to Tall, Husayn spoke of the necessity to preserve the achievements of the Arab summit conferences and to maintain inter-Arab solidarity, as well as to co-operate with the PLO. But Husayn still found it necessary to emphasize that Arab solidarity ought to be subject to the 'right of every Arab country to manage its own domestic affairs and to choose the social system that it found compatible with its conditions'.[7] Husayn thus sought to reassure friends and to make it clear to potential opponents, especially to the PLO but also to Egypt, that Jordan would not allow any impairment of its independent decision-making capacity. It is very likely that the appointment of

71

Tall, a forceful politician in his own right, was made to demonstrate precisely this point.

Husayn regarded domestic affairs as the main concern of the Tall government. In view of the prevailing domestic stability and 'the summit spirit' on the inter-Arab scene, he sought once again to take advantage of the calm situation, just as he had done in 1962. As a young and dynamic personality, Tall was to make Jordan surge forward towards rapid development and modernization while broadening the base of popular support for the regime.

However, while, when appointing Tall the first time, the King had tried to make use of the 'new era' to give the population a greater sense of participation and to consolidate the legitimacy of the regime by an experiment in controlled liberalization, no similar effort was made this time. Husayn spoke only in general terms in praise of democracy, and the duty 'to support the democratic institutions'. But the objectives which he and Tall had sought to realize in 1962–63 through the democratization experiment, Husayn now strove to achieve by the formation of an efficient mechanism for political indoctrination 'to deepen national consciousness'.[8] It is quite possible that Tall's past experience in public relations and information was also a factor in the King's choice of him to lead the government once again.

### THE MERITS OF POLITICAL INDOCTRINATION

The anticipated confrontation with the PLO was probably the main immediate motivation for the decision of the new government to focus on domestic indoctrination. At the first news conference held by Tall, on 20 February 1965, the Minister of Information Dhuqan Hindawi emphasized the importance of the government information apparatus 'as an important instrument for the consolidation of the democratic regime'. In fact the purpose of the meetings with the press was to instil a sense of participation in the process of government, without embarking upon actual liberalization. Wasfi al-Tall undertook to meet the press at least once a month. In retrospect, he did not fulfil this undertaking, but in his statement of policy to the Chamber of Deputies on 11 March he stressed the intention of his government 'to mobilize the information apparatus' to educate the populace and to deepen their consciousness (taw'iyya).[9]

As part of the effort to foster loyalty to the regime and to bolster its legitimacy, and in contrast to the popular trend of the time in the Arab world, Tall placed special emphasis on Islamic influences. At a news conference on 1 May 1965, International Labour Day, he reiterated Jordan's disapproval of all the various left-wing revolutionary ideologies. He explained that Labour Day was not commemorated in Jordan (although that changed in later years) because the Kingdom had no class consciousness and there was no place there for any but religious and national holidays. Tall's objective was to distinguish between Jordan and those Arab states and many Palestinians who considered the celebration of Labour Day as a symbol of their pseudo-Marxist radicalism (whether real or imaginary). He emphasized that Jordan was 'a Muslim, Arab country in everything related to the teachings of Islam and the heritage of Arabism', and far removed from any class or confessional fanaticism. Its concepts of social justice and consultation in affairs of government (*shura*) were firmly rooted in Islam. In the inter-Arab ideological debate, Jordan was not in the camp of ʿAbd al-Nasir and his Palestinian adherents.

Tall also justified his unswerving loyalty to Husayn and the Hashimite family through religion. That the Prophet Muhammad was a scion of the house of Hashim, he related to the recent appointment of Husayn's younger brother Hasan as Crown Prince and heir to the throne. This, according to Tall, was designed to assist Husayn's leadership and to ensure the continuity of Hashimite rule, known to the Arabs since they received 'the call of [the Prophet] Muhammad the Hashimite'.[10] Tall thus reflected a traditional Hashimite belief, the roots of which go back to the Great Arab Revolt against the Ottomans in 1916, under the leadership of King Husayn's great-grandfather, Sharif Husayn ibn ʿAli, and were founded on the acceptance of the 'natural' right of the house of Hashim to lead the Arab world.

## *SHURA* BUT NO MORE

Wasfi al-Tall maintained that his government believed in 'consultation (*shura*), liberty and the freedom of speech'. Accordingly the door was open to frank advice from any citizen and to guidance for, or even criticism of, the government. However, he added the reservation that any such popular participation must be achieved 'by legitimate means and within the framework of the law'.[11] He went on to specify that the government would grant every citizen the right and the opportunity 'to express his opinion freely through the democratic institutions, the press and other communications media, clubs, associations, unions, co-operatives and local government councils and committees'.[12] In this long list of institutions, which Tall used to illustrate the channels of free expression and participation in the political system according to the law, political parties were conspicuously absent. These remained illegal and Tall took pains to remind his listeners, 'lest anyone forget', that this prohibition was still in force.[13] Although there were reports from time to time that the government might allow party activity, nothing was actually done in this respect. The notion of *shura*, which Islamic modernists tended to view as the Islamic equivalent of Western democratic restrictions on the ruler's power, was very convenient for non-democratic regimes like that of Jordan. It allowed them to create the impression of the regime's reliance on Islamic tradition and its adherence to the principles of democracy, when in practice the essence of *shura* could amount to much less than a formal and binding limitation of the ruler's power.[14]

The laws prohibiting political parties, the supervision of the press and other limitations on freedom gave the government ample leeway to suppress any opposition, despite Tall's praise for democracy and its institutions. Within the bounds of permissible politics no real opposition to the Tall government came to the fore. Most of the members of the opposition, elected in November 1962, had been eliminated from the obliging and disciplined Chamber of Deputies which was elected in July 1963 (see above, Chapter 4). In the vote of confidence in Tall's new government, which took place in March 1965, only five deputies opposed him; and in April of the same year only six deputies voted against the budget. Reports of this period indicate the existence of a 'constructive' opposition front in the Chamber of Deputies led by ʾAbd al-Rahman Khalifa, the leader of the Muslim Brotherhood in Jordan. Those who had abstained or who had voted against the Tall government in the vote of confidence were members of this front.[15] There were also a few deputies who vented old grievances about foreign aid and administrative detention. But all this could not alter the general impression of a submissive and subservient chamber.

At the beginning of March 1965, a short while after the appointment of Tall to head the government, Husayn made what was intended to be an impressive gesture to the opposition. He ordered the burning of more than 20,000 General Intelligence dossiers (copies of which one may safely assume were preserved intact). As was the case with the amnesty after Tall's first appointment to the premiership at the beginning of 1962, this gesture, albeit empty, also helped to portray the change of government as the beginning of a new era in relations between the regime and its opponents. A commentary on Radio Amman construed this decree as the turning over of a new leaf, resulting from the cordial climate of inter-Arab relations.[16] This correctly reflected the feeling of the regime that the tranquillity on the inter-Arab front, accompanied by domestic quiet, facilitated a show of moderation towards the opposition. This was especially calculated to gain public support for a possible confrontation with the opposition on the question of the Palestinian entity and the PLO. The General Amnesty, which Husayn ordered at the beginning of April to commemorate the appointment of his brother Hasan as Crown Prince and the Feast of Sacrifice (*id al-adha*), should also be viewed in the same light. (Hasan, who had then turned 18, replaced ´Abdallah, Husayn's infant son, from his marriage with Princess Muna, who had been Crown Prince since his birth in January 1962.)

The amnesty included those accused of political offences, with the exception of espionage and contact with 'the enemy, Israel'. The Amnesty Law was passed by both houses of parliament on 4 April. In his speech to parliament, Tall declared that the amnesty would also apply to political exiles, and these were indeed allowed to return to Jordan. Among the exiles who returned were notorious personalities such as ´Abdallah al-Tall (who returned from a long exile in Egypt, after having been sentenced to death *in absentia* for his involvement in the assassination of King ´Abdallah); ´Ali al-Hiyari (the former Chief of Staff who had plotted against Husayn in 1957); Shafiq Irshidat and Na ´im ´Abd al-Hadi (who were former Ministers in the Nabulsi government); and Sulayman al-Hadidi (a veteran Ba'thi).[17]

Just in case the gestures to the opposition were misunderstood, they were accompanied by severe warnings from the King and Tall, to the effect that the regime would not, under any circumstances, tolerate any breach of public order. In a speech to political prisoners who were released on 6 April, Tall said that he hoped that he would not be required to rearrest them 'for breaking the law'.[18]

## THE PRICE OF THE 'SUMMIT SPIRIT'

The tranquillity that prevailed on the domestic scene in Jordan in the early days of the new Tall government was, to a large extent, the result of the inter-Arab 'summit spirit'. However, in exchange for inter-Arab reconciliation, Jordan had to pay a political price, which exposed it to ever-increasing pressures, especially from Egypt and the PLO.

The resolutions taken at the summits in Cairo (January 1964) and in Alexandria (September 1964) called for the diversion of the headwaters of the Jordan, with the object of obstructing Israel's National Water Carrier. It was also decided to establish a United Arab Command and to foster the Palestinian entity, the practical expression of which was the establishment of the PLO and the PLA.[19] The Jordanian government was able to view the diversion resolution favourably. It meant Arab financing for the building of the Mukhayba Dam on the Yarmuk, which in any case dovetailed with Jordan's development plans. Furthermore, the plan for the dam did not adversely affect Israel, and therefore did not arouse Israeli opposition.[20] On the other hand, the resolution to establish a United Arab Command confronted Jordan with the demand to allow for the stationing of foreign Arab forces on its soil, a course that the regime did not favour at all.

Jordan's reservations in this regard stemmed from two main sources. First, it was apprehensive that the foreign forces, particularly the Iraqis, who according to the plans of the United Arab Command were to be stationed in Jordan together with Saudi forces, might try to undermine the stability of the regime; second, the Jordanians were apprehensive of possible Israeli reaction to the deployment of outside Arab forces in Jordan. Outwardly, Jordan, for obvious reasons, underplayed the first factor and focused its grievances on the second.

At the conference of Arab Prime Ministers, held at the end of May 1965 in Cairo, Tall said that Jordan did not object to the entry of Arab forces, provided that this was done after the completion of Arab preparations for an all-out confrontation with Israel.[21] At the same time, it was disclosed that Tall had told one of the Arab foreign ministers attending the conference that the Jordanian government had reliable information that Israel would invade Jordan and 'put an end to its existence' immediately the first Arab soldier set foot on its territory.[22] Tall later denied this, and claimed that an enemy that could overrun Jordan with such ease 'had not yet been created',[23] but it was evident that Jordan was, in fact, fearful of Israel's reaction.

In September 1965, at the conference of Arab Foreign Ministers preceding a further Arab summit (this time in Casablanca), and during the summit itself, Jordan again faced pressure from Lieutenant General 'Ali 'Amir, the Egyptian Commander of the United Arab Command, to permit the entry of Iraqi and Saudi forces into Jordan. 'Amir maintained that it was necessary to assemble these forces in Jordan before the actual outbreak of hostilities with Israel because the transfer of forces to Jordan during an ongoing war would, in all likelihood, have to be carried out while Israel had control of the air. This would make it difficult to carry out Arab plans. Husayn rebuffed 'Amir, and argued that Jordan would agree to the entry of Arab forces at the appropriate time only, and when it was clear that the campaign had already begun.[24] Tall added that, in the existing circumstances, there was ample defence for the Mukhayba Dam project, and the entry of Arab forces into Jordan was unnecessary. However, Tall said that Jordan agreed that in the event of the outbreak of wide-scale hostilities the United Arab Command had the authority to decide on the movement of forces as required.[25] Husayn and Tall sought to prevent any prolonged presence of Arab forces on Jordanian territory, and wanted their assistance only in the event of total war. And, indeed, Jordan asked for reinforcements from Iraq and Saudi Arabia on the eve of the Six Day War, but these did not arrive in time and were of no avail.[26]

Tall cloaked Jordan's unwillingness to become embroiled in a war with Israel, and its reservations concerning the demands of the United Arab Command, under a veil of vitriolic anti-Israeli rhetoric. Tall publicly emphasized the commitment of his government to carry out the Arab political, military and diplomatic programme agreed upon at the summit conferences, stressing that it was Jordan which was 'the spearhead of the united Arab plan for Palestine';[27] he called for the implementation of the joint Arab plan until it achieved its objective of 'uprooting the Zionist aggression from its very foundation';[28] and he explained that the Arab summit conferences had been convened on the basis of the Arabs' unreserved realization 'that the need to purify Arab land of the Zionist bridgehead' was a fundamental imperative.[29]

Tall made a special effort to dispel any doubts about Jordan's adherence to Arab objectives in Palestine, particularly in order to disguise the fact that the highest price that Jordan was being called upon to pay for the 'summit spirit' was undoubtedly related to the Palestinian question. Far more serious than any others for Jordan were the summit resolutions concerning the 'Palestinian entity'. Shortly after the second summit conference in Alexandria, these confronted Jordan with political challenges that threatened to undermine the very existence of the Kingdom in its traditional form.

## THE CHALLENGE OF THE PLO

At the summit conference in Cairo in January 1964, it was decided that Ahmad al-Shuqayri, who represented Palestine in the Arab League, would continue his contacts with other members of the League and also with the Palestinians in the diaspora in order to lay the foundations for the organization of the Palestinian people. This resolution paved the way for a political organization of the Palestinians. Shuqayri began with a series of tours in the course of which he met Arab leaders and Palestinian personalities and addressed Palestinian gatherings. His major difficulty was to persuade King Husayn to agree to the creation of the 'Palestinian entity', since without his consent the majority of the Palestinians, who were Jordanian citizens, would be precluded from taking any active part in Palestinian organization. After Shuqayri had given a ceremonial undertaking that the organization would not take any steps to detach the West Bank from the East Bank, and would not undermine Jordan's existence, King Husayn relented and in February 1964 he announced his agreement to the 'plan for the Palestinian entity' as outlined by Shuqayri.[30]

Husayn's consent did not mean that his anxieties in regard to the organization of the Palestinians had evaporated. When Shuqayri began to prepare for the first Palestinian congress, which was to serve as the constituent assembly of the PLO, the Jordanians did everything they could to belittle it and to minimize its significance. At first Jordan pressed for the congress to be held in Amman, then at Qalya on the northern shore of the Dead Sea. Shuqayri suspected that this latter choice of venue was not accidental. By associating the birth of the PLO with the 'Dead' Sea, Jordan intended to portray the organization as an abortive enterprise. The suggestion to hold the congress in East Jerusalem met with opposition from the Jordanian security services, and a compromise was reached only after the intervention of the mayor of Arab Jerusalem, Ruhi al-Khatib, according to which the congress would convene at the Intercontinental Hotel. The Jordanians insisted that the invitation be inscribed 'al-Quds, the Hashimite Kingdom of Jordan', and not Palestine. They finally agreed to the inscription: 'al-Quds, Jordan'.

Because of the difficulties arising from the dispersion of the Palestinians throughout the Arab world, Shuqayri decided not to complicate matters by holding elections, and preferred to appoint a preparatory committee which would help to organize the congress. The committee suggested that 150 politically active Palestinians be invited. The Jordanian government demanded that the list be enlarged to include Palestinian notables from Jordan and other prominent Palestinians who filled positions in the Jordanian administration, the Chamber of Deputies and the Senate. By these means Jordan intended to pack the congress. None the less, Shuqayri acquiesced, and 422 representatives were eventually invited to the congress. Of these, 388 attended, 242 being from Jordan.[31] Prominent personages from all Palestinian communities as well as party representatives from the Ba'th and the Arab Nationalist Movement, whose activity was banned in Jordan, were also invited,[32] but the government refused entry permits to some of them. The congress convened in May 1964, in a tense atmosphere and under the strict surveillance of the Jordanian security services. Their presence was so pronounced that Shafiq al-Hut, one of the original founders of the PLO, alleged that it was difficult to tell the delegates from the informers and agents.

Shuqayri was elected chairman of the congress and also of the Executive Committee of the PLO. The congress decided to convert itself from the form in which it had been convened into the first Palestine National Council, and thus became the PLO's quasi-parliament.[33]

The second Arab summit conference, which took place in September 1964 at Alexandria, endorsed the establishment of the PLO as well as the decision of the organization to set up the PLA. The conference also laid down the commitments of the member states of the Arab League to assist the organisation.[34]

The Jordanian regime from the outset perceived the PLO as a dangerous challenge. Since the annexation of the West Bank, one of the guiding principles of Jordanian policy had been to prevent the creation of an independent power-base among the Palestinian population of the Kingdom. The danger of such a power-base was inherent in its potential to erode the regime's staying power by competing for influence and control with the mainstay of the regime – the army and the other security forces. Such an erosion could have undermined the stability of the regime and finally even have toppled it. This, in turn, would pave the way for a new order, in which the Palestinian political elite would predominate, by displacing the monarchy and the essentially Trans-Jordanian establishment.

The PLO's objectives to subordinate the Palestinian population of the Kingdom to its own authority, and even to station units of the PLA on the West Bank, were, therefore, perceived as potentially inimical to the Jordanian regime. It was clear to Husayn that there would be difficulties in the relationship with the PLO and it is quite possible that he understood from the very beginning that, sooner or later, Jordan and the PLO would find themselves on a collision course. There was a fundamental incompatibility between the PLO's ambition to exercise authority and patronage over the Palestinian population, the majority of whom were in Jordan, and the demand of the regime for complete sovereign authority over the territory of the Kingdom and its citizens.

It is reasonable to assume that the appointment of Wasfi al-Tall as Prime Minister in February 1965 was intended, *inter alia*, to place a resolute and uncompromising personality at the head of the team which would have to handle most of the contacts with the PLO. Tall was by now an experienced and very self-confident Prime Minister. He was an outspoken and sarcastic polemicist with a caustic tongue, who treated his critics with disdain as he strove single-mindedly and with unflagging consistency to secure what he considered to be Jordan's vital interests. Moreover, he was a suspicious, cunning and tough negotiator.

By appointing such a personality, Husayn sought to prepare for any impending crisis, but he did not intend to initiate one. In his letter of appointment, the King emphasized the necessity to co-operate with the PLO in Jordan and in the inter-Arab and international arenas.[35] And, indeed, when Tall presented the guidelines of his government's policy to the Chamber of Deputies on 11 March 1965 he called for 'genuine co-operation' with the PLO in every sphere.[36]

There was nothing in these public statements that could solve the difficulties in Jordan's relationship with the PLO. These became quite apparent only days after Tall's assumption of the premiership. At a news conference on 20 February, Tall explained that his government considered relations between Jordan and the PLO to be based on the Arab summit resolutions, and that the government was, therefore, committed to provide the PLO with every form of assistance. Tall, however, declined to specify exactly what such assistance would entail. He was not interested in going into detail on whether to establish one or two training camps, or whether to mobilize 'this or that'.[37] His refusal to specify the practical measures stemming from Jordan's declared commitment to the PLO exposed the limits of the Jordanian undertaking. The PLO understood the real thrust of these statements perfectly. In its response to Tall the PLO welcomed Jordan's expressed willingness to support the organization. However, the PLO statement added that the organization requested talks with the Jordanian government on 'the practical plan and the detailed programmes' for the realization of the objectives endorsed by the Arab summit conferences.[38]

## TALL AND SHUQAYRI – NEGOTIATIONS BETWEEN RIVALS

Ahmad al-Shuqayri, the chairman of the PLO, arrived in Jordan on 24 February 1965 for talks with the government. Although he declared on his arrival that Jordan and the PLO were 'two wings of the same bird', this announcement could hardly bridge the abyss that separated the two. Shuqayri came with a military plan at the crux of which were demands for the setting up of Palestinian regiments; the arming and fortification of West Bank villages along the border with Israel; military training for the Palestinians in Jordan; and the raising of 'popular resistance' units among the Palestinians there. The purpose of the plan was to transform the Palestinians along the border with Israel into 'soldiers in the army of return'.[39] In his talks with Tall, Shuqayri also demanded the collection of five per cent of the salaries of Palestinian officials in Jordan for the PLO, in addition to his demand to open a PLO office in Amman.

Shuqayri's attempt at a division of labour between the PLO and the Jordanian government, in terms of which the government would operate on the official state level while the PLO would operate on the 'popular' level, was artificial and impractical. Tall's government rejected all his requests.[40] Shuqayri issued reassuring statements, but these were probably more damaging than helpful. He claimed, *inter alia*, that 'the Jordan river cannot separate the same homeland and the same people'.[41] His statements were presumably intended to allay Jordanian fears that the PLO might seek to detach the West Bank from the East Bank. These reassuring statements, however, could not conceal the truth, that Jordan and the PLO were on an inevitable collision course. Their confrontation was rooted in a struggle for control over the destiny of the Palestinian people. Due to the large Palestinian population on the East Bank and the unique relationship between the Jordanian and Palestinian peoples that both sides recognized, the struggle for control related to both banks. The PLO subsequently tended to question the right of Jordan to exist in its present form as a political entity dominated by East Bankers rather than Palestinians, while the Jordanians similarly challenged the PLO's right to exist as the organizational incarnation of a Palestinian people with their own distinctive identity.

The PLO understood that the rejection of its demands was final, and therefore waited for a suitable opportunity to launch a propaganda offensive against Jordan. At the beginning of May, Tall reiterated Jordan's 'absolute support' for the PLO. To this the PLO responded by demanding support that would be shown in 'deeds and not . . . words'. The PLO complained that it had nothing at all in Jordan, except 'a three-floor building occupied by some administrative employees', (its offices in Jerusalem). Moreover, it went on to claim that since 'Jordan is Palestine, just as Gaza is', units of the PLA should be established in Jordan as in Gaza, and the Jordanian Chamber of Deputies should promulgate a law instituting a 'liberation tax', that is a tax to be levied from Palestinians for the PLO, just as the Legislative Council had done in Gaza.[42]

The Jordanian response was immediate. At the request of Wasfi al-Tall, a special session of both the Jordanian houses of parliament was convened on 9 May 1965 to discuss Jordan's relations with the PLO. Since the Jordanians were not prepared to tolerate any independent Palestinian power-base in their country, Tall, in addressing the house, unhesitatingly rejected the demand of the PLO to establish units of the PLA in Jordan. He called on the Palestinians to join their many brethren serving in the ranks of the Jordanian army,[43] while explaining that this did not in any way contradict the Arab summit resolutions, to which Jordan fully adhered.[44] The Jordanian press was told that the summit meetings had released Jordan from any commitments to the separate military organization of the PLO, because 'the Jordanian army was the army of the sons of Palestine'.[45]

In a speech to the nation on the occasion of 'the catastrophe of the 15th of May [1948]', King Husayn elaborated upon the central theme of Jordanian policy which was to absorb and to assimilate the Palestinians into the Jordanian state. He stated that 'ever since the two Banks joined, the two peoples merged and Palestine became Jordan and Jordan Palestine'.[46]

The Jordanians consistently strove to blur the distinctive identity of the Palestinians, in order to uphold the traditional character of the Kingdom and the supremacy of the Trans-Jordanian political elite by pre-empting the possible influence of an independent Palestinian political organization. Shuqayri's objective, however, was quite the opposite. The revival of the Palestinian entity and the attempt to restore the control of their destiny to the Palestinians themselves required PLO influence and control over the large Palestinian population on both Banks of the Jordan. Shuqayri did not object to the unity of the two Banks, but from his statement it was clear that he regarded the Palestinians and the PLO, and not the Trans-Jordanian elite, as the prospective dominant factor in the complex relationship between Jordanians and Palestinians. Reacting to the statements of Tall and Husayn, Shuqayri did not conceal his perception of Palestinian supremacy. He contended that the annexation after 1948 was actually 'the annexation of the East Bank to the Palestinian homeland',[47] and not the other way around. Furthermore, according to Shuqayri, the PLO looked forward to the day when Wasfi al-Tall and Bahjat al-Talhuni, both East Bankers, would be members of the Palestine National Council. After all, he said, 'our Jordanian brothers are in fact Palestinians'.[48]

The verbal exchanges between Husayn and Shuqayri only served to emphasize what was self-evident. Jordan and the PLO were heading for a direct confrontation, emanating from their shared perception of the Jordanian–Palestinian complex as a single unit in which both parties strove for supremacy. In practice, there was no room for compromise.

PREPARATIONS TO THWART THE PLO

Shortly after Shuqayri's visit to Amman, in February 1965, and the presentation of his demands to the Jordanian government, practical measures were adopted by the Jordanian authorities to thwart the PLO and to ensure that it made no inroads into the fabric of the Jordanian state. In March, Tall announced in the Chamber of Deputies that from the beginning of that month, in accordance with the King's instructions, the government and the military authorities had begun to integrate the National Guard (the para-military body manned mainly by Palestinians in the border areas of the West Bank)[49] with the regular army.[50] From the essence and timing of this policy, one can only conclude that this was done to forestall any penetration or control of the National Guard by the PLO or its sympathizers.

In May 1965, the King announced that he had instructed the

Prime Minister to establish popular organizations to provide military training for all able-bodied male citizens, including school-boys. Schoolgirls were to receive civil-defence training.[51] Husayn and Tall obviously wanted to deprive the PLO of the basis of its demand to establish training camps for Palestinian youth. A government decision was subsequently taken on this matter, and students actually began training. All the same, this could not dispel the impression that student training was a mere exercise in public relations and a temporary pre-emptive tactic, rather than a serious long-term plan for the military training of the masses.

Despite the serious discord and the sense of impending crisis in relations between the Jordanian government and the PLO, neither side sought to precipitate a total rupture at this stage. In mid-June 1965 talks were resumed in Amman between Shuqayri and Tall and a number of ministers and Jordanian army officers. The talks focused on co-operation between the PLO and Jordan, particularly on military matters. At their conclusion, on 19 June, Shuqayri announced that an agreement in principle had been reached on the necessity to co-operate in the military reinforcement of the West Bank border villages, that is, the villages along the border with Israel. It was similarly agreed to co-operate in the military training of young people; in the organization of civil defence; and in the upgrading of 'national consciousness'. Joint committees of the PLO and the Jordanian government were also formed, to continue the negotiations and to implement the agreement that had been reached in principle. In reality, however, despite the 'agreement in principle' they claimed to have reached, both parties continued to strive to achieve decisive control over these 'popular' activities. At exactly the same time, the government authorized a bill, the purpose of which was to reinforce the border villages with volunteers and arms. This was to demonstrate that the demand of the PLO to arm the border villages, at least in co-operation with the organization, if not under its auspices, was superfluous. At a press conference on 21 June, Tall stated that the government had already completed the arming of border villages.[52]

The deliberations of the joint committees continued inconclusively during the entire month of July. At the beginning of August Shuqayri again held talks with Tall in Amman, at the conclusion of which the PLO leader announced that the discussions

85

were still at the preparatory stage because the joint committees had yet to complete their deliberations on the agreement for military co-operation. It was obvious that the talks were going nowhere and that there was not the slightest chance that Shuqayri's demands would be accepted by the Jordanian government.

At the beginning of 1965 the Fath organization, then still outside the framework of the PLO, started to carry out sabotage operations against Israeli objectives. After an Israeli reprisal action in the Qalqilya area at the beginning of September, in response to Fath operations conducted from Jordanian territory, Shuqayri seized the opportunity to attack Jordanian inaction. He argued that, in rejecting the plans of the PLO, Jordan had actually done nothing to fortify the border areas or to arm the inhabitants. It soon transpired that the Jordanian government had not accepted PLO demands in other spheres either. In the June talks between Shuqayri and Tall it had been agreed, again 'in principle', that the so-called 'liberation tax' would be collected from all civil servants, without differentiating between Palestinians and Jordanians. But while Shuqayri represented the taxation as a levy on behalf of the PLO, Tall spoke in less specific terms, noting that the government would collect a certain percentage of the salaries of civil servants 'on behalf of Palestine' (*limaslahat Filastin*),[53] without any mention of the PLO in this context. In fact no actual steps were taken to collect these taxes, and the government had not yielded to the PLO on any issue of significance.

Fundamental problems between Jordan and the PLO remained insoluble. A number of appointments made by Shuqayri in the leadership of the PLO only exacerbated the situation. In June 1965, in line with his statement that 'our Jordanian brothers are in fact Palestinians', Shuqayri appointed Najib Irshidat, the Irbid-born chairman of the Jordanian Bar Association, as a member of the Executive Committee of the PLO. At the same time he also appointed ´Ali al-Hiyari, the Salt-born former Jordanian Chief of Staff who had just been allowed to return from exile (see above), as Director of the PLO's Military Department. The appointment of two Jordanian personalities with oppositionist inclinations was bound to cause some concern to the Jordanian authorities, who feared all along that the PLO might become an organizational framework for the opposition.

Tall's reservations about these appointments reflected the basic position of the Jordanian regime, which not only opposed the promotion of a distinctively Palestinian entity, but regarded Jordanian–Palestinian unity as a vehicle to assimilate the Palestinians within the Jordanian entity. The statements and actions of Shuqayri represented the opposite end of the spectrum which supported the eventual absorption of the East Bank and the Jordanian entity into that of the Palestinians.

These contradictions were the source of deep mutual suspicion. The appointment of East Bankers and a statement of Shuqayri at the beginning of July – that the Jordanian–PLO relationship should be similar to that between the Israeli government and the Jewish Agency – did not reassure the Jordanians, and even aroused controversy within the ranks of the PLO. Shuqayri's PLO critics accused him of undermining the exclusive identity of the Palestinians and conjuring up the danger of subjugation to Jordanian custodianship by his efforts to appease the Jordanian government.[54] These allegations were without foundation. However, it is quite possible that they influenced the resignations of Hiyari and Irshidat from their posts in the PLO, at the beginning of July. It is equally possible that the resignations were induced by pressure from the Jordanian government.

## FRUITLESS ATTEMPTS AT COMPROMISE

Relations between the Tall government and the PLO were totally deadlocked by the summer of 1965. The agreement between them had not taken shape and their contrary views led to a rupture which was already discernible during the course of the third Arab summit conference held at Casablanca in September. At the summit, King Husayn again vigorously rejected Shuqayri's demands to allow conscription of the Palestinians in Jordan for the establishment of units of the PLA there.[55] The conference, much to Jordan's satisfaction, rejected the PLO demand for freedom of action in the formation of PLA units in Arab countries without having to consult their governments.[56] The resolutions of the Casablanca conference did not oblige Jordan to do any more than continue its negotiations with the PLO.[57] The resolutions were, therefore, a sore disappointment to Shuqayri.

After the conclusion of the Casablanca conference, Shuqayri launched an all-out offensive against Jordan. He accused the Jordanians of not having allowed any PLO activity within their borders.[58] Husayn and Tall responded even more aggressively than before, arguing that PLO activity in Jordan was both unnecessary and unjustified. They systematically belittled the usefulness of the organization in the struggle against Israel. As far as they were concerned, the PLO could perhaps be helpful in organizing the refugees outside Jordan. But there was no role for the PLO in organizing the Palestinians in Jordan, since this was the task of the Jordanian regime itself, which required no prodding from the PLO.[59]

All the same, Shuqayri's propaganda attack was discomfiting to Jordan, and in mid-October 1965 Tall revealed that Jordan had been in contact with Egypt in order to put an end to the propaganda broadcasts carried by the Voice of Palestine from Cairo.[60] Husayn requested the personal intervention of ´Abd al-Nasir in this matter,[61] and Jordan also lodged a complaint with the Arab League.[62] Following the mediation of the Assistant Secretary-General of the Arab League, Sayyid Nawfal, who met with Husayn and Wasfi al-Tall in Amman in early November, Shuqayri agreed to visit Jordan.[63] According to Shuqayri's account, he had agreed to travel to Amman at the behest of ´Abd al-Nasir, but he himself did not believe that there was much to be gained from the Jordanians.[64] He arrived in Amman on 19 November and met first with Husayn. Shuqayri later recalled that he had told the King:

> If I wanted to be Prime Minister at your Majesty's side, I would rent a house in Amman, and within a week I would become Prime Minister. Your Majesty knows, after all, [and I say this] without being boastful, that your present Prime Minister, Mr Wasfi al-Tall, was a clerk of mine in the Arab Office in Jerusalem in 1946; [but] all I want is for the Liberation Organization to co-operate with your Majesty for the good of the country.[65]

After this rather pompous introduction Shuqayri began his talks with Wasfi al-Tall (see Chapter 2 for Tall's Arab Office position).

The problems between Jordan and the PLO were such that the prospects for agreement were virtually non-existent. Shuqayri's personality, his abrasiveness and pomposity did not make the negotiations any easier, particularly since his counterpart in the talks was no longer Shuqayri's 'clerk', but a powerful and no less abrasive Jordanian leader who was totally uncompromising on anything related to the PLO presence in his country. Shuqayri and Tall had a few rounds of talks in the last week of November which related to the PLO's longstanding demands for the arming of the border villages, the conscription of the Palestinians, the collection of the 'liberation tax', and PLO supervision of the popular organization of Palestinians. According to Shuqayri's account, Tall was 'manoeuvring and deceptive'. Tall insisted that all questions of defence had to be dealt with by the army, while Shuqayri contended that 'the entire people should bear arms alongside the army'. Tall retorted that the government had already distributed arms to the villages and that students were receiving military training – claims which Shuqayri treated with justifiable scepticism.[66]

The conflicting arguments of the government and the PLO in regard to the arming of the border villages arose from different definitions of what this entailed. Whereas the government considered the distribution of small arms, presumably in limited quantities, as sufficient, the PLO demanded the distribution of more powerful weapons, including machine guns and even anti-tank weapons, and in greater quantities. The PLO also demanded participation in the supervision of regional defence operations in the border villages. These were demands that the Tall government was simply not prepared to consider.

When the talks with Tall ended, Shuqayri announced their failure: all the PLO demands had been rejected, he said. The Jordanian government for its part preferred to underplay the fact that the talks had failed and to cover up Jordan's own responsibility for this. On 6 December 1965, Hazim Nusayba, the Foreign Minister, convened the heads of the Arab diplomatic missions in Jordan and explained his government's position. It was impossible to hide the disharmony between the position of the Jordanian government and that of the PLO. Nusayba tried, none the less, to disguise the fact that the government had not acceded to any of the essential demands of the organization, noting, for example, that the government had put forward a plan according to which the

PLO would even participate in the raising of new regiments in the Jordanian Army.[67]

It is hardly surprising that Shuqayri rejected the offer, which really meant the dismissal of his own plan to establish separate PLA regiments similar to those established in Egypt, Syria and Iraq (though in each of these countries the PLA forces were under the firm control of the respective general staffs). According to one source, Shuqayri had even demanded that Jordan agree to the creation of fida'i (guerrilla) bases on the West Bank along the border with Israel, under PLO supervision. It is reasonable to assume that Shuqayri did, in fact, make such a demand, in view of the change in his attitude towards Fath at the end of 1965, when he began to give public support to their sabotage operations which he had previously opposed. This demand was, of course, unacceptable to the Jordanian government, as were the rest of Shuqayri's demands, and perhaps even more so. An appreciable number of Fath operations were conducted from Jordanian territory, which resulted in Israeli reprisal action against objectives on Jordanian soil. Tall's government consequently made noticeable efforts to prevent Fath activity and to round up Fath cells on the West Bank. When important, detailed intelligence concerning Fath fell into their hands at the beginning of 1966, members of the cells of the organization that still remained on the West Bank were arrested within a few days. The Jordanians even falsified encoded messages to Fath operatives in Syria instructing them to go to Jordan, only to have them apprehended as they set foot on Jordanian soil. Tall himself took intelligence material on Fath activity in the Persian Gulf to Kuwait, and asked the authorities there to take punitive action.[68]

The Jordanian government was no less indisposed towards the idea of organizing the Palestinians in popular organizations that would function under PLO auspices. Hazim Nusayba explained to the Arab diplomats that not only were the Jordanian authorities already engaged in weapons and first-aid training for youth, but a wide range of popular organizations had already been in existence since the foundation of the Kingdom. These included the two houses of parliament, the state administration, the army, the city and village councils, the chambers of commerce, the professional associations, clubs and schools. Nusayba's statement could not be

1 Wasfi al-Tall, seated on the left, with teachers and students at the High School in Salt

2   Wasfi al-Tall with his wife Saʿdiyya.

3　Tall as Director of Jordanian Radio

4 'Turning a new leaf'; Tall sets fire to domestic intelligence dossiers

5 Tall and King Husayn

6   The end of the road – Tall's final return from Cairo

construed as anything other than a rather cynical exercise in evasion. Though Nusayba added that his government was open to suggestions for improvements in these bodies, the thrust of Jordan's policy remained obvious. Any popular organization in Jordan, he noted, had to be founded 'on a comprehensive popular basis taking into consideration *all Jordanian citizens*'[69] (emphasis added) – that is, without any differentiation between Jordanians and Palestinians.

Jordan's opposition to PLO demands for separate Palestinian popular organization was so adamant that, in Shuqayri's talks with Tall and other government officials, the Jordanians refused in principle even to discuss the subject. They alluded to the organization of Palestinians in the past in political parties opposed to the regime, and flatly refused to permit the PLO to become an organizational framework for the country's Palestinians. They had no intention of repeating their bitter experience of the mid-1950s, before the banning of the parties in April 1957, when party activity had almost toppled the monarchy.

Another request which Shuqayri made to the Jordanian authorities was to allow the holding of general elections to the Palestine National Council, in accordance with a system determined by the PLO. Nusayba contended that the Jordanian government had accepted this PLO proposal in principle.[70] But Shuqayri argued that the Jordanian government's agreement 'in principle' merely disguised the fact that it did not wish to comply with the procedure and the system under which the elections were supposed to be held. The government suggested that the Jordanian Interior Ministry approve the electoral procedure, a clear indication that the Jordanian government was not prepared to allow the elections, except under its own supervision. The government also demanded that PLO information activity be co-ordinated with the Jordanian Ministry of Information[71] – a demand which the PLO rejected. Shuqayri complained that the concessions made by the Tall government to the PLO were of no significance. Thus, the government agreed to exempt the offices of the organization from payment of telephone accounts and cables, postage and customs duties, and had authorized the PLO to establish a radio link between its offices in Jerusalem and those outside Jordan. Since the Tall government had refused to allow the PLO any real scope for activity among the

Palestinian population in Jordan, all that remained was to state the obvious, that is, that the PLO had no role to play in Jordan. Accordingly, it had to concentrate on 'organizing [the] Palestinian people dispersed in the various [other] Arab countries and the [rest of the] world'.[72] Since the majority of the Palestinians resided in the Kingdom of Jordan, government policy there was designed to transform the PLO into an empty vessel that could be controlled or at least effectively neutralized. Shuqayri had accused Tall of wanting to gain control of the PLO[73] and there was more than a grain of truth in this accusation. Since the inception of the PLO, Jordan's intentions had repeatedly been exposed, for example, when it attempted to bolster its influence in the Palestine National Council by increasing the number of Palestinians from Jordan in the council (see above).

Although Jordan did not gain control of the organization, it did prevent the PLO from gaining a foothold on Jordanian territory. The Jordanians also made it their business to harass the PLO. Shuqayri raised a series of complaints on this score. He alleged that the Jordanian government had issued passports to persons operating against the PLO outside Jordan; that government-inspired sermons were preached against the PLO in the mosques after Friday prayers; that members of the organization operating in Jordan were subject to security surveillance and were unable to visit refugee camps without the prior permission of a district governor; that the Jordanian Interior Ministry forbade the distribution of PLO pamphlets or notices without its approval; and even that listening devices were installed in Shuqayri's office in Jerusalem.[74] There is no reason to assume that these complaints were not well founded. The Tall government's opposition to the activities of the PLO was part of its simultaneous upholding of Jordanian sovereignty and its outright disapproval of the very notion of the revival of the Palestinian entity. Shuqayri criticized Jordan's use of the term 'Jordanians of Palestinian origin', alleging that this was a deliberate attempt to obliterate the Palestinian identity. 'The word Jordanian is a new one which was introduced during the British occupation,'[75] and in any event 'this word does not exist in Arab history. [The] Jordan is known to be a Palestinian river and that is the end.'[76] Shuqayri's assertions are not historically accurate (at the time of the Arab conquest of Palestine, the areas west of the Jordan and some to the east were divided between *Jund Filastin* and *Jund al-Urdunn*), but this had no bearing on their political significance – that the Jordanian state was a creature of British imperialism and, as such, had no right to exist.

## THE MARCH 1966 AGREEMENT

Despite the fact that the positions of Jordan and the PLO were poles apart, both parties preferred to postpone a total severance of relations for as long as possible. Husayn chose to preserve his self-styled image as the protector of the Palestinians, while the PLO preferred to keep the door ajar for the possible establishment of even a curtailed political presence in Jordan.

At the end of February 1966, after efforts at mediation at the Arab League, talks were held in Cairo between a Jordanian delegation led by the Interior Minister, ´Abd al-Wahhab al-Majali, one of Tall's confidants, and a PLO delegation headed by Shuqayri. On 1 March 1966 the parties arrived at an agreement. The Tall government conceded nothing at all in the military field, but it was agreed that the subject be left open for future discussion.

A comparison of the demands raised by Shuqayri when the talks began on 21 February with the contents of the final agreement shows that the PLO did not gain much on any other issues, such as popular organization, the 'liberation tax', or information matters. The government agreed to allow the PLO to broadcast for one hour on Jordan radio, but only under the supervision of the Ministry of Information. It also agreed to the collection of the 'liberation tax', but from all citizens and at a lower rate than initially requested.[77] In so doing, the government had merely reaffirmed what it had already agreed to during the talks in June and November 1965, which the PLO had then rejected as inadequate. On the day after the signing of the agreement, Shuqayri commented that had it not been for King Husayn's last-minute intervention the agreement would not have been reached.[78] This remark deserves attention since, on another occasion, after the failure of the November talks, Shuqayri had singled out Tall for criticism and had made no reference to his talks with the King. He had explained that he did not wish 'to drag King Husayn into the differences between us and the Jordanian government'.[79] One gains the impression that Shuqayri regarded Husayn as a more amenable negotiator than Tall and the Jordanian government. There is no conclusive evidence that this was in fact the case, although it is possible that Tall's direct and aggressive approach appeared less flexible than that of Husayn. However, Husayn and Tall may have differed in style and temperament but not in their understanding of the essence of the Jordanian–PLO relationship. Indeed, Shuqayri may have only been trying to create an impression of real differences of opinion in the Jordanian leadership, perhaps as a tactic to damage the mutual trust and confidence between the King and his strong and forceful Prime Minister.

At the end of March, Shuqayri had talks with Husayn and Tall in Amman on the implementation of their new agreement. Understanding was reached on a number of clauses, such as the collection of the 'liberation tax', the one-hour PLO broadcast on Jordan radio and the establishment of summer youth camps for military training and national guidance. However, the March agreement did not bring the parties any closer, and it was probably not even intended to do so. It only postponed the head-on collision and made it possible to conduct some more fruitless negotiations in a more cordial atmosphere. Yet, even this modest achievement was not lasting. Within two months, contacts were broken off altogether, the two sides were as far as ever from any solution and on the brink of total rupture and outright confrontation.

### THE SUPPRESSION OF THE OPPOSITION AND POPULAR PLO SUPPORT

The March 1966 agreement put off the confrontation between Jordan and the PLO, but it was probably clear to both sides from the outset that the clash could not be prevented. At the end of March, shortly after the signing of the agreement, a source close to the PLO reported that the Jordanian National Security Council (a body consisting of army officers and personnel from General Intelligence and the Ministry of the Interior) had come to the conclusion that Jordan could not allow the agreement to be construed by the PLO as having altered the status of the organization in Jordan, and that the time had come for the regime to crack down on the PLO's local base of popular support. A

number of officers of questionable loyalty were reportedly dis-
charged from the army and some senior Palestinian civil servants
were similarly removed.[80] These reports accurately reflected the
atmosphere that prevailed at the time in the upper echelons of the
Jordanian establishment. Tall confirmed later that there were
many who had criticized the government for its agreement with the
PLO.[81] As the government prepared for its offensive, various
opposition groups made contact, with the object of forming a
united front. These groups, associated with the political parties
banned since 1957, were the natural recruiting ground for active
supporters of the PLO. They shared many ideas, especially those
related to the need to change the nature of the regime so as to
transform Jordan into the vehicle of Palestinian liberation. It is,
therefore, not at all surprising that many members of these illegal
parties subsequently joined the PLO, and even assumed leadership
roles in the organization. At the beginning of 1966, meetings were
held in Beirut between Shuqayri and other Palestinians, representing the Arab Nationalist Movement and the Ba´th, in an effort
to co-ordinate Palestinian political activity.[82]

All these developments coincided with the gradual dissipation
of the 'summit spirit' which had existed in the inter-Arab arena
since the beginning of 1964. The atmosphere of reconciliation
which the Arab leaders had tried to maintain was a major factor in
restraining Jordan and the PLO, prompting Husayn and Shuqayri
to avoid an explosion. However, by the end of March 1966, as the
'summit spirit' increasingly became a thing of the past, both sides
were well advanced in their preparations for a decisive showdown.

In early April the Tall government landed the first blow by
initiating a wave of arrests of people connected with the Arab
Nationalist Movement, the Ba´th and the Communist Party, as well
as of members of professional groups (mainly those of lawyers,
engineers and doctors) who were associated in varying degrees with
the PLO.[83]

The Minister of the Interior, ´Abd al-Wahhab al-Majali, denied
that there was any connection between the arrests and the PLO.
He maintained that the arrests were carried out against members
of the banned political parties who had been involved in illegal
party activity. Their objective, he said, was to create a unified front
to 'sow dissension, create anarchy and make repeated attempts to

stage a revolution'.[84] Sharif ´Abd al-Hamid Sharaf, the Minister of Information, took the same line and declared immediately after the arrests that these measures were not related to the PLO, and that mutual understanding and co-operation continued to prevail in relations between Jordan and the PLO, in accordance with the March agreement.[85] On 1 May, the Voice of Palestine began broadcasting from Amman, as previously agreed, and it was even reported that the Jordanian Treasury was making preparations for the collection of the 'liberation tax' for the PLO. The Jordanians were clearly trying to maintain a 'business as usual' posture. But the reality was quite different. A Lebanese daily with good connections in Jordanian government circles reported at the time of the arrests that Jordanian General Intelligence had been aware for quite a while of the activities on behalf of the PLO of members of the illegal parties, and that many of these party activists had filled various positions in the PLO's branches in the country. Once the authorities had received information that this activity was also being conducted in accordance with instructions obtained from outside Jordan, they decided to arrest those involved, whether they were PLO functionaries or not.[86] However, it is possible that not only PLO activists were arrested, and that the blow struck against the Arab Nationalist Movement and the Ba´th was also intended to undermine Egyptian and Syrian support in Jordan. All the same, it was the PLO that immediately felt itself to have been the target, and it was the PLO office in Beirut that was the first to make a public issue of the arrests.[87]

MOUNTING TENSION WITH THE PLO

It was clear that tension between the authorities and the PLO was increasing. At the beginning of May, the government announced that it had decided to postpone 'Palestine Week', which was supposed to have been held in mid-May. Since the March agreement, no progress had been made on any of the more substantial and problematic issues. After the PLO demand for the conscription of Palestinians into the PLA had been rejected yet again, Shuqayri complained that Jordan had not even agreed to introduce general conscription for the Jordanian army.[88] Jordan had agreed in March 'to study the subject' of general conscription,[89] but during negotiations with the PLO on the matter, it rapidly became apparent that the government had no intention of conscripting thousands of Palestinians, and thereby undermining the mainstay of the regime. Tall gave administrative reasons for Jordan's opposition.[90] He did not, of course, delve into the sensitive political question of the inclusion of Palestinians in the front-line formations of the army. The government, after all, was at pains to assert that the Jordanian army was a Palestine Liberation Army since so many Palestinians were already serving in it (though not in front-line infantry and armoured units).

The government was by now firm in its resolve not to show any leniency at all towards the PLO or towards the activities of the opposition parties – the principal potential source of public support for the PLO. The government had anticipated the symbiosis between the parties and the PLO. This was one of the main reasons for its dismissal of PLO demands on the question of 'popular organization' (see above) and it was the chief motivation behind the wave of arrests in April.

On 7 May, Wasfi al-Tall held a news conference, which dealt, in the main, with the question of the party members under arrest. Tall's 'strong man' credentials had been solidly established, and he made no bones about using the full power of the state to suppress the opposition. All the same, having returned to government a year before with the symbolic turning of a new leaf in the regime's relations with the opposition (the General Amnesty and the demonstrative burning of the General Intelligence dossiers – see above), Tall felt a special need to explain, but not to apologize for, the recent steps taken by his government. He admitted that about 200 people had been arrested – a much higher figure than had previously been announced by the Jordanians – but he explained that those arrested had simply broken the rules of the game. The Jordanian regime was guided by 'the ideal of the General Amnesty', which was a 'genuine democratic ideal that permits freedom of opinion, within the framework of law and order'. However, according to Tall, certain groups had decided 'on their own' to act 'against the law and the intention of the amnesty'. He accused the members of the 'destructive parties' of having acted in a manner that was contrary to Jordan's 'religious and national concepts of ethics'. He even bothered to add that they had not been arrested because of their opinions, but because they had tried to implement their ideas 'by unethical and illegal means'. Tall argued that it was clear to anyone that 'unethical means must necessarily lead to the attainment of unethical objectives'. While the Arab world was on its guard against the 'Zionist invasion', the Arabs, because of the party activists, were also forced to contend with 'ideological invasions', which were designed to 'divide [the Arabs] into classes, sects and groups in order to disseminate weakness and doubt in [the Arabs'] ranks'.[91]

Tall's statements on the 'destructive' activity of the party members were clearly directed against the PLO, particularly after Shuqayri himself had sprung to the defence of the detainees. However, Tall continued to abstain from an untimely frontal attack on the PLO. It was easier to attack the opposition parties as divisive elements – a tactic which had been employed for years by other regimes, including that of ´Abd al-Nasir. The PLO, the organizational incarnation of the budding revival of the Palestine national movement, was a far less convenient target for such disparaging remarks.

Tall's argument was a clear elucidation of the fact that he, and the regime as a whole, equated opposition with subversion. Tall's declaration and the arrests themselves indicated to the PLO and to its supporters in Jordan that their activities, or for that matter any other political activity carried out without permission, would not be tolerated. The government was adamant on this score. When the Jordanian Bar Association sent a note of protest to Tall after the arrests, Tall demanded that the president of the association, Shafiq Irshidat, a veteran member of the opposition and a PLO sympathizer, withdraw the note and even dissociate himself from its contents. Irshidat refused, and a bitter feud between the two men ensued.[92]

Signs of an impending confrontation with the PLO were noticeable not only in the steps taken by the Tall government to deny any foothold in Jordan to the PLO. They were also apparent in the attempts of the government to bolster its own influence within the organization by pressurizing the PLO to increase the representation of Palestinians from Jordan in its institutions. In preparation for elections to the Palestine National Council, Shuqayri decided that 60 of the 150 seats would be allotted to

Palestinians from Jordan. Tall complained that this was not consistent with the fact that the majority of Palestinians lived in Jordan. He contended that they ought to have a majority in the council as well. Shuqayri dismissed Tall's argument on the grounds that no one outside the PLO had any right to interfere in the affairs of the organization.[93] (In the event, the elections were never held.)

While rejecting Jordanian attempts to interfere in PLO affairs, the PLO nevertheless continued to strive to secure freedom of action for itself in Jordan. At the third session of the Palestine National Council, held in Gaza at the end of May 1966, the demand for 'Palestinian freedom of action' was the rallying cry of the council's resolutions. These stated, *inter alia*, that the PLO would not oppose anyone in the Arab world 'except whoever challenged' its freedom of action. The resolutions went on to point out that the arrest and banishment of, and violence against, many Palestinian nationalists in the 'places of Palestinian concentration', namely Jordan, were 'an attempted challenge of this kind'. The organization therefore demanded the immediate release of the 'imprisoned nationalists', and insisted that Jordan should finally accede to all the demands previously made by Shuqayri.[94]

## CRISIS AND RUPTURE

The hostility towards Jordan, vented at the Gaza meeting, and the alliance between the PLO and the archenemies of the regime in the illegal political parties heralded an imminent rupture between Jordan and the organization. No holds were barred any more. There was no longer any political choice but to respond to the PLO if Jordan did not wish to lose face. The exchange of invective led very quickly to a total breakdown in Jordanian–PLO relations. Having already prepared the ground by discrediting the parties, Tall now assailed Shuqayri directly for having added numerous party members to the Palestine National Council in Gaza 'without permission from anyone' and for having devoted the Gaza meeting to an 'onslaught of recrimination, party fanaticism and the splitting of Arab ranks'. Shuqayri had 'turned the meeting into a rabble-rousing party demonstration instead of a demonstration of mobilization'.[95] According to Tall, the Gaza meeting was a demonstration against Jordan, instead of one for Palestine, and it was the designs of the party members against the Hashimite regime which had unleased 'Shuqayri's insane trumpets'.[96]

Jordan accused Shuqayri of having set up a clandestine organization of party members at the Gaza meeting with the object of operating in Jordan to overthrow the regime.[97] Tall said that matters had come to a head and it was 'in the interest of Palestine and its cause and even in the interest of Shuqayri himself' to foil the designs of the party activists against Jordan.[98]

It is difficult to believe that Tall really hoped to convince many people to give credence to his assertion that Jordan's actions against the PLO supporters were in Shuqayri's interest. But there were no bounds to his capacity for distortion and attempted deception in order to justify the steps taken by Jordan on the Palestinian question, which was potentially so dangerous to the regime.

Shortly after the conclusion of the Gaza meeting, Shuqayri resumed his attack on Jordan. On 9 June, in a speech to a unit of the PLA in Syria, Shuqayri accused Jordan of having carried out only a minor part of its agreement with the PLO and complained that Husayn had also refused to meet him to discuss the arrests of the party activists in Jordan. Shuqayri insisted on the right of the PLO to intervene on behalf of the Palestinians in any place in the Arab world because, he said, the PLO was responsible for all Palestinians.[99] The PLO's claims to bear responsibility for a majority of Jordan's population and to have the right to intervene in its domestic affairs in the extremely sensitive area of internal security, coupled with Shuqayri's public support for the opposition to the regime, were the last straw for Husayn. Encouraged by Tall,[100] he replied with a ferocious rejoinder. In a speech in ´Ajlun, on 14 June, Husayn flatly rejected the PLO leaders' attempts 'to appoint themselves as [Jordan's] custodians', and declared that there was no hope at all for Jordanian co-operation with the PLO in its existing form.

Husayn, directing his remarks both to the PLO and to Fath, also issued a stern warning against any ill-considered activity, which might 'expose our front to aggression before the completion of our plans, in accordance with the directives of the United [Arab] Command', and might drag the Arabs into an untimely war. He condemned those who sought to drive a wedge between Jordanians and Palestinians, and warned very forcefully that 'any hand maliciously raised against this united and struggling country, we will sever; every eye that glances at us with a look of hate, we will gouge out. From now on we shall not be negligent nor shall we make even the slightest concession.'[101]

In the wake of King Husayn's speech, the Tall government initiated a further series of measures against the PLO. The Voice of Palestine, from which the PLO had already withdrawn its own personnel, continued to operate from Amman, calling for the dissolution of the PLO and for its replacement by a different organization to represent the Palestinians. One of the reasons given by the radio was that Shuqayri had gone 'insane'.[102] Tall ordered the dissolution of the election committees, established in Jordan by the PLO to prepare the groundwork for the proposed elections to the Palestine National Council, and he warned political figures in the West Bank that anyone who participated in the Executive Committee of the PLO would be considered a traitor by the government.[103] The government decided to stiffen the penalties for illicit arms possession and there were also numerous reports, at the end of June and during July, of more arrests of PLO and party activists and supporters.

The attack by the regime naturally drew a riposte from Shuqayri who, in a speech to Palestinians in Cairo on 17 June, restated his denial of Jordan's right to exist in its present form. Shuqayri's speech was punctuated with the rhythmic chanting of the audience: 'Amman revolt, revolt and let Husayn catch up with Nuri', or 'Amman revolt, and let Wasfi catch up with Nuri!'[104] (Shuqayri's listeners were thus expressing their wish for Husayn and Wasfi al-Tall to meet the same fate as Nuri al-Sa'id, the Iraqi leader, who was murdered in Qasim's revolution in July 1958).

Shuqayri appealed to the Palestinian ministers in the Tall government to resign from their posts. He alleged that

the principal foundations of statehood were lacking in the Jordanian government, because it existed on aid and support given to it by imperialism. . . . The final conclusion we have reached is that both Banks of Jordan are under the colonialist rule of the Hashimite family, and it is therefore incumbent upon the Jordanian people, with the Arab nation behind them, to free Jordan from this colonialism, as an essential step towards the liberation of Palestine.[105]

101

For those who may have required further clarification, Shuqayri noted that when he spoke of Jordan he spoke of 'Palestine, the boundaries of which begin with the Mediterranean Sea in the west and end with the Iraqi and Syrian deserts. This is where our people are and all of this country is the starting point of liberation.'[106]

## TALL'S ASSAULT ON 'SHUQAYRI'S PLO'

Tall convened a news conference on 4 July at which he replied to Shuqayri's aggressive rhetoric with some of his own propagandistic hyperbole. Tall's pungent response was directed against the PLO under Shuqayri's leadership and against Shuqayri himself. The Hashimites, he contended, had done their very best for the Arab cause and, as opposed to Shuqayri and his ilk, they had not 'made a living from [the cause] and had not engaged in land profiteering' in Palestine.[107] Tall attributed the propaganda attacks against Jordan to the 'subversive' parties with 'foreign destructive principles', who were guided by the desire for 'peace (*sulh*) with Israel'. According to Tall, Shuqayri was still preoccupied with the implementation of this plan as a follow-up to 'his many assignments in New York'. Shuqayri had in fact served as Saudi Arabia's representative to the UN before his activities on behalf of the PLO, but he had not taken part in any negotiations for peace with Israel. Tall's object was to tarnish Shuqayri's reputation. As far as Tall was concerned, all means to this end were justified, including what he knew to be total fabrication. The labelling of Shuqayri as a negotiator with Israel served as a basis for the contention that it was not Shuqayri who was the protector of Palestinian rights, but rather Jordan which was really acting to 'revive the Palestinian entity so that it would become a positive factor that would uphold the plan for Arab mobilization'. Tall added that, in the interests of Jordan and the Palestinian cause, it was imperative to foil Shuqayri and 'to strike at his clownish programme with an iron fist', because, under the influence of the Arab Marxists, its purpose was to enter into a peace settlement with Israel.

Tall repeated a demand he had made previously for an Arab summit conference to define the precise nature of the Palestinian entity, as this had not been done before. In his first attempt to obtain such a future discussion of the PLO role, Tall emphasized that Jordan had serious reservations about Shuqayri and would actually like to see him removed, because 'the present organization [of the PLO] has become Shuqayri's [private] apparatus'.[108]

The PLO responded in similar vein to Tall's assault, in broadcasts from the Voice of Palestine in Cairo, with the object of tarnishing his reputation and patriotic credentials. For this purpose it claimed that the Arab nation knew Wasfi al-Tall very well, 'ever since he was an officer in the British Army. His dubious relations and his suspicious contacts with foreign imperialists are known to all . . . the PLO does not expect to be praised or eulogized by agents and hirelings.'[109]

A special session of the Jordanian parliament was convened in Amman on 16 July to discuss relations with the PLO. Tall argued that once Shuqayri had revealed his intentions towards Jordan in his radio broadcasts, which asserted that 'the destruction of the Jordanian entity is the road to Palestine', the government had no alternative but to sever its relations with the organization and to reiterate its demand that an Arab summit must clearly define 'the [Palestinian] entity and its authority'.[110] After Tall's speech, the Chamber of Deputies passed resolutions expressing the loyalty of the entire people to Husayn and their complete support for his policy. The resolutions stated that since the majority of the Palestinians lived in Jordan, and because of Jordan's 'position and [the nature of] its entity, this Kingdom is the only . . . practical starting point for unified Arab action to retrieve the Arab right in Palestine'. The Chamber of Deputies also determined that the Palestinian entity should serve as a support for the Arab states, particularly for the Hashimite Kingdom of Jordan, and it ought not to pose as 'a substitute opposing the Jordanian entity'.[111] Thus, with ease, the regime obtained the authorization of a subservient parliament to recognize the polarity between Jordan and the PLO, and to sever all political ties with it.

## THE DISINTEGRATION OF THE 'SUMMIT SPIRIT'

The disruption of Jordan's relations with the PLO coincided with the gradual disintegration of the 'summit spirit' and the attempted inter-Arab reconciliation which had begun at the first Arab summit in Cairo, in January 1964. The first signs of disintegration began to appear after the third summit conference in Casablanca in September 1965. One of its symptoms was the stepping-up of the attack by the PLO on Jordan. But the principal cause for the eventual dissipation of the 'summit spirit' was the renewed tension between ´Abd al-Nasir and King Faysal of Saudi Arabia, following their failure to come to an agreement over the Yemen crisis. The Arab world began to re-divide along 'revolutionary' and 'conservative' lines, with ´Abd al-Nasir at the head of one camp and King Faysal at the head of the other. The renewed division of the Arab world was discomfiting to Jordan. The more conciliatory atmosphere, now vanished, had relieved Jordan from its difficult struggle with ´Abd al-Nasir. It had assisted the regime to improve its image both at home and abroad, and had enabled Husayn to steer clear of the need to choose friends in a divided Arab world, choices which inevitably made enemies as well.

The rupture with the PLO supplied Egypt with a convenient opportunity to attack Jordan again, but this was no more than a pretext. The real reason was Husayn's decision to support King Faysal in his increasingly acrimonious struggle with the Egyptian president.[112] Jordan supported Faysal's appeal for Islamic solidarity and his initiative to convene an Islamic conference. However, as far as the Egyptian and Syrian regimes were concerned, this was immediately construed as an attempt to form a conservative bloc directed against the 'revolutionary' states. In order to achieve his objective, Faysal began a series of visits to Muslim countries, particularly to those whose relations with Egypt were, at best, cool. He started off in December 1965 with a visit to the Shah of Iran who was known to be an implacable opponent of ´Abd al-Nasir. In January 1966 he visited Jordan, and thereafter Turkey, Sudan, Pakistan, Morocco and Tunisia (whose President Bourguiba was also a well-known rival of ´Abd al-Nasir) as well as countries like Guinea and Mali, whose Muslim presidents were on good terms with ´Abd al-Nasir. Although Jordan and Saudi Arabia consistently denied that Islamic solidarity was aimed against ´Abd al-Nasir, the very fact that Islam was emphasized as the basis for solidarity created the impression that the intention was to form an alliance within the Arab world, with the support of some non-Arab, pro-Western Muslim states, to counteract the secularist revolutionary ideology which ´Abd al-Nasir again began to promulgate openly at the end of 1965.[113] Even during the period of inter-Arab compromise, when the summit conferences were held, 'Abd al-Nasir still harboured reservations about co-existence between the 'revolutionary' and the 'conservative' regimes. The former never really relinquished their desire to 'export' revolution to the rest of the Arab world, while the latter were forever on their guard to stave off the revolutionary tide with every resource at their disposal.

At the end of 1965, 'Abd al-Nasir restated his former position that only the Arab revolutionary forces could effectively stand up to the 'Zionist peril'. During the course of 1966, 'Abd al-Nasir's contention exacerbated the tension and rivalry between the so-called 'progressive' and conservative regimes in the Arab world. In these circumstances, it was only natural for Jordan to realign itself with Saudi Arabia against the self-styled radicals.

Usually, reorientation of this nature in Jordanian policy would have been accompanied by a change of government, but in Wasfi al-Tall's case this was uncalled for. His views and past experience were such that Husayn could hardly have found a better candidate to implement a policy of realignment with Saudi Arabia, and probable confrontation with 'Abd al-Nasir and the Syrian Ba'th, with unswerving determination and conviction. During Tall's first term as Prime Minister, these were precisely the guidelines of Jordan's inter-Arab policy, manifested on the one hand by the ongoing propaganda war with 'Abd al-Nasir's Egypt, and on the other by the signing of the Ta'if agreement of co-operation with Saudi Arabia (see Chapter 4).

The visit of King Faysal to Jordan, at the end of January and the beginning of February 1966, was generally perceived as a sign of an emerging camp based on Islamic solidarity. Indeed the joint communiqué, published at the end of the visit, called for the revival of the Ta'if agreement in order to combat 'deviation and atheism'.[114] The leaders of Arab conservatism thereby clearly expressed their ideological opposition to the secularist, revolutionary and socialist ideas expounded by the regimes of 'Abd al-Nasir and the Syrian Ba'th. However, at this stage, Jordan still preferred to avoid an open, head-on confrontation with 'Abd al-Nasir. It firmly rejected allegations, made by the Egyptian and Syrian media, that Faysal's visit was intended to establish an

105

'imperialist' alliance, similar, in essence, to the Baghdad Pact. During the visit, Tall had gone to the trouble of inviting a number of Lebanese reporters to his office for a special briefing on Jordan's position. Tall had explained that the meeting between Husayn and Faysal was intended solely to strengthen the support of the Muslim world for the Arab cause. This, he added, was in line with Arab summit resolutions. He denied any intention of forming an Islamic alliance because Jordan did not support 'the policy of pacts and special alignments'.[115] There was nothing in Tall's statements to the Lebanese reporters that could have pacified ´Abd al-Nasir, much less Salah Jadid's neo-Ba´th regime which came to power in Syria in February 1966. This regime was more energetic than its predecessor in its effort to bring to an end the 'summit spirit' and the peaceful co-existence with the 'reactionary' regimes.[116]

On 9 May, Tall paid a five-day visit to Saudi Arabia. In his talks with the Saudi leadership, the principles of the Ta'if agreement were discussed, with special emphasis on economic co-operation between the two countries.[117] The political objective, however, was to demonstrate Jordan's support for King Faysal in the inter-Arab dispute with Egypt and Syria.

By now the lines of the dichotomy in the Arab world had been clearly drawn. At the end of May 1966, the Syrians demanded not only the abolition of the notion of a general Arab summit, but also the convening of a mini-summit of the 'progressive' Arab states. Egypt responded favourably to the Syrian initiative and, on 22 July, ´Abd al-Nasir announced that Egypt would not participate in the general Arab summit conference, scheduled to take place in Algeria in September. He explained that he could no longer sit with the 'reactionaries' unless they mended their ways and abandoned their anti-Egyptian policies.[118]

Syria's strident tone failed to have any effect on Jordanian policy. The Jordanians continued to support the Saudis and 'Islamic solidarity' and insisted on the continuation of the all-Arab summit conferences. The Syrians now assumed the leading role in the propaganda war against Jordan. The exchange of invective between them reached such a height that, at the end of May, the Syrians and the Soviets (who, for reasons of their own, also opposed the formation of a pro-Western alliance in the Arab world) accused Jordan of concentrating its forces in a threatening posture on Syria's southern border. The Jordanians denied this allegation.[119] However, at a news conference at the beginning of July, Tall assailed the Syrian Ba'th regime. He argued that they had begun levelling accusations against Jordan following the arrest of Ba'th Party members in Jordan in April (see above). Tall went on to question the moral right of the leaders of the new regime in Syria to criticize the behaviour of the Jordanian government,[120] for, he explained, they had seized power by force of arms in February 1966 and, in so doing, had caused the death of hundreds of innocent bystanders in the streets of Syrian cities. They had even shelled the home of Amin al-Hafiz, who was president at the time.[121] Tall took great pride in the Jordanian legal system and in the fact that the regime did not use violence against its opponents, as the Syrians had done.

True enough, the treatment of the opposition in Jordan was far less brutal than in Syria, but Tall's self-righteousness was not totally justified. When the party members were arrested in April 1966 there was not much evidence of due process as generally practised in countries governed by the rule of law and the separation of powers. A rather routine and matter-of-fact statement by 'Abd al-Wahhab al-Majali, Minister of the Interior, was particularly revealing in this respect. Majali said that all detainees 'proved to be guilty' during their interrogation would be 'brought to trial'.[122] If 'guilt' had already been 'proved' under interrogation by General Intelligence agents, it is not at all clear what role remained for the courts to play, other than to rubber-stamp the conclusions of the interrogation. This was a far cry from due process and further evidence of the lack of tolerance towards opponents of the regime.

At the end of August and the beginning of September 1966, as Jordan began to take more of the initiative in its confrontation with Syria, its relations with Egypt also reached a new low. Thousands of people took part in anti-Egyptian demonstrations in Jordan, orchestrated by the government in protest against the execution of three members of the Muslim Brotherhood in Egypt. The Jordanian press was also harnessed to conduct a scathing propaganda campaign against 'Abd al-Nasir's regime. The Egyptians responded with seditious broadcasts. Radio Cairo quoted an article from the Lebanese newspaper *al-Muharrir* which appealed to the Jordanian people to overthrow the regime for the sake of the struggle for Palestine because 'the road to Amman . . . is more than half the road to Haifa, Jaffa and occupied [western] Jerusalem'.[123]

While Jordanian–Egyptian relations continued to deteriorate, an abortive coup in Syria, on 8 September 1966, brought about a complete rupture in Jordanian–Syrian relations. The leader of the coup, Major Salim Hatum, who in February the same year had led the force which attacked the home of Amin al-Hafiz, now attempted a coup against his former cohorts. The attempt failed and traces pointed to Jordanian involvement.

Hundreds of those implicated in the abortive coup, led by Hatum himself and Colonel Talal Abu ´Asali, escaped to Jordan where they were given political asylum.[124] Syria accused Jordan of involvement in the coup and, after Talal Abu ´Asali left Jordan for Egypt, the Egyptians joined the Syrian propaganda attack against Jordan. Muhammad Hasanayn Haykal, the editor of al-Ahram, published an interview with Abu ´Asali in which he stated that Jordan and Saudi Arabia had been behind the abortive coup. Abu ´Asali said that Salim Hatum had been in contact with Wasfi al-Tall and the director of Jordan's General Intelligence, Muhammad Rasul al-Kaylani, both on the eve of the abortive coup and after its failure. Abu ´Asali alleged that Tall had asked for assistance from Syrian officers who had obtained asylum in Jordan to 'bring about stability in Damascus'.[125] Jordan, of course, vigorously denied these charges. It was impossible to verify whether Tall and others in the Jordanian regime had made contact with Salim Hatum before the coup attempt. However, in the light of Tall's declared hostility towards the Syrian regime, including a statement on the need for action to overthrow it,[126] such a possibility could not be ruled out. After the abortive coup, threats that the Jordanians would use force against Syria if the latter were to close its border with Jordan were attributed to Tall.[127] The Syrians, for their part, continued their subversive activity against Jordan and dispatched teams of saboteurs to strike at Jordanian objectives.[128] Further incidents to widen the breach between Jordan and its enemies in the Arab world followed in rapid succession. By the end of 1966, the 'summit spirit' had vanished without trace.

## THE IMPACT OF THE SAMU´ OPERATION

By the late 1950s the embryonic movement for independent Palestinian political organization had begun to take shape. Its purpose was to enable the Palestinians themselves to regain control of their destiny and, at the same time, to organize military activity against Israel. An important landmark in these formative years was the founding of the Fath organization. At first, Fath was a clandestine organization with its headquarters in Kuwait, led from the very beginning by Yasir ´Arafat. In the early 1960s, after the dissolution of the UAR, ´Abd al-Nasir's messianic appeal began to wane. Moreover, it became increasingly apparent that he had no intention, at that time, of going to war with Israel. Palestinian nationalists, including ´Arafat and his associates, concluded that self-reliance was the real key to liberation. The successful precedent set by the Algerian war of liberation was widely regarded as the example to follow. It was believed to be essential to embark upon the immediate establishment of independent Palestinian organizations and a Palestinian military force.

Numerous organizations were established. They all adhered to a formula which, in one way or another, combined the idea of the 'Palestinian entity' with the 'Algerian model'. Most of these organizations disappeared within a short time, due to inaction, but the few that survived, together with Fath, were later to become the backbone of the PLO and the Palestinian national movement. The Fath leadership was convinced of the necessity to prepare for military action, and not to repeat the mistake made by most other Palestinian organizations in the past, who had exhausted themselves on fruitless political and propaganda activities. During 1964, Fath established ties with the Syrian Ba´thi regime, which allowed the organization to establish training camps in Syria. Apart from their identification with the theory of 'popular liberation war', the Syrians recognized the possibility of using Fath as an ancillary weapon in inter-Arab struggles, just as ´Abd al-Nasir had used the PLO under the leadership of Shuqayri.[129]

Fath began its military operations against Israel in January 1965 with an attempt to sabotage the National Water Carrier. This was followed by dozens of other sabotage operations on Israeli territory, mostly carried out by small groups which had infiltrated from Jordan. Fath emerged, at first, as a competitor with the PLO, and Shuqayri initially expressed reservations about Fath operations. However, the Fath operations attracted a great deal of attention, and spurred the formation of similar fida'i organizations. In the PLO, the more militant members began to prevail,[130] and they gradually prompted Shuqayri to give public support to the Fida'iyyun and then, finally, to engage the PLO itself in sabotage operations against Israel.[131]

The renewal of the power struggle in the inter-Arab arena, between Egypt and Syria on the one hand, and Jordan on the other, was manifested *inter alia*, in the encouragement given by Egypt and Syria to fida'i groups to conduct operations from Jordanian territory (but not from their own). By the end of 1966, Shuqayri was actively assisting the Fida'iyyun and operating fida'i organizations under the auspices of the PLO. Shuqayri and his Egyptian supporters also tried to exploit the Fida'iyyun to subvert the Jordanian regime, while simultaneously competing with Fath militancy by independently promoting acts of sabotage in Israel.[132] The change in the PLO's mode of operation and the competition that developed between the PLO and Fath led to a marked increase in the number of operations against Israel during the last months of 1966. Many of these operations were planned and organized in Jordan and carried out from its border with Israel. The efforts of the Jordanian security authorities to prevent these operations were only partially successful.

On 11 November 1966, an Israeli army vehicle travelling on a dirt road near Arad struck a mine and three soldiers were killed. The Israeli Army retaliated with great force. On 13 November, in broad daylight, a large-scale punitive operation was carried out against the village of Samu´, south of Hebron. According to the Officer Commanding of Israel's Southern Command, the objective was 'to force Jordan to seal off Mount Hebron to Fath operations'. This was the largest punitive action carried out by the Israeli Army since the Sinai Campaign of 1956, and it included armoured forces, infantry, artillery and engineers, as well as an element of air support. The Israeli Army demolished 41 houses in the village of Samu´. According to a Jordanian source, 15 Jordanian soldiers and 5 villagers were killed in the operation.[133]

Contrary to Israeli expectations, the Samu´ operation had no significant influence on the intensity of sabotage operations across the Jordanian border, not even on those conducted from the Mount Hebron area. Nor did it affect the prestige or strength of the fida'i organizations. On the other hand, its impact on the domestic scene in Jordan had a very unsettling effect on the regime.

The relative ease with which the Israeli army had succeeded in gaining control of a village and demolishing a large number of its houses was a shocking revelation to the inhabitants of the West Bank in general, and to those of Mount Hebron in particular. The operation also accelerated the process of total disintegration of the 'summit spirit', and exposed Jordan to a propaganda offensive by Egypt, Syria and the PLO combined. They could now claim with somewhat greater credibility that their previous demands for the stationing of foreign Arab forces in Jordan, for PLO and PLA activity there, and for the arming of the border villages were justified. Had they been accepted by Jordan, the Israeli army action in Samu´ might have been prevented.

The sense of shock among the population, the Arab propaganda and the clash between the 'revolutionaries' and the 'reactionaries' in the Arab world converged to produce a major confrontation between the regime and the inhabitants of the West Bank. Demonstrations and violent clashes between West Bankers and the Jordanian security forces rocked the area for two weeks.

Since the annexation of the West Bank to Jordan, one of the main causes of tension between many Palestinians and the regime was the policy towards Israel. The regime preferred to preserve the status quo with Israel, and quiet along the border was therefore essential. Jordan's attitude was a function of weakness and of the fear of having it exposed by Israeli punitive action or of even losing the West Bank, in the event of an all-out confrontation. The Palestinians, however, demanded that Jordan be transformed into the staging ground for 'the war of liberation'. The Samu´ operation revealed this latent tension very acutely. It showed the regime in a bad light: it was incapable of defending the West Bank and could hardly be expected to become the vanguard of the struggle against Israel.

In the second half of November, the West Bank was in turmoil as a wave of unrest shook the towns of Jerusalem, Nablus, Hebron,

Ramallah, Jenin and Tulkarm. Beginning on 19 November, Nablus was the scene of four days of violent demonstrations. The army was called in to restore order and a number of demonstrators were killed before a curfew was clamped down on the town. Violent demonstrations broke out in Jerusalem on 23 November. Hebron was cut off by road-blocks which stopped traffic to and from the city, and on 24 November news arrived from Ramallah of violent demonstrations in a nearby refugee camp. The demonstrators blocked the road to Jerusalem with stones and were finally dispersed by the army. The most serious demonstrations were in Jerusalem. Initially the government had ordered the closure of all schools in the city, but on 25 November a curfew was imposed after more than 1,000 demonstrators had taken to the narrow streets of the Old City, calling for the overthrow of the monarchy. On the following day, the riots were renewed within the walls of the Old City. Four people were killed and 15 injured. The funeral of one of the persons killed turned into a massive demonstration against the government. Four thousand people chanted slogans against Husayn and the Tall government as the funeral procession marched towards the East Jerusalem police headquarters, where it was dispersed by police wielding batons and whips. The curfew imposed on Jerusalem was extended to cover the other unruly towns of Nablus, Hebron and Ramallah, and additional flashpoints of unrest, such as the Jalazun refugee camp near Ramallah. In all the demonstrations, appeals were made to the government to distribute arms to the populace and to allow the entry of the PLA and other Arab forces into Jordan. The demonstrations also demanded that Jordan take action against Israel. The regime was accused of being unable and unwilling to defend the West Bank, and the demonstrators, inspired by the PLO, condemned the government's policy of non-cooperation with the organization. While the demonstrators shouted support for Shuqayri, pictures of Husayn were torn to shreds. The unrest gradually petered out, and on 29 November Husayn announced that order had been restored.[134]

On the day of the Samu´ operation, Shuqayri noted immediately that the obvious lesson was that 'the people must be organized, trained and armed . . . We are confident that if this had been the case this morning, the people and the army would have brought about the ruin, destruction and extinction of the enemy.'[135] Radio Damascus accused Jordan of having abandoned the Palestinian population to face 'bestial, treacherous raids, without organization or arms'.[136] On 19 November, in order to silence the criticism and to persuade the public that the regime was taking action to improve the security situation, Husayn instructed Tall to take all the necessary measures to introduce conscription. This was a very shrewd move by Husayn. It was certainly good tactics to conscript disorderly youngsters, so that the government could keep a watchful eye on them, instead of having them imprisoned, to achieve essentially the same effect. Husayn himself hinted at this motive when he warned that anyone who evaded service 'to carry out sabotage actions, or to follow the deceivers . . . will be severely punished'.[137] As for the scope of conscription, Wasfi al-Tall said that it was the intention of the government to ensure that it did not affect the economy, as the strength of the economy was as important as that of the army.[138] One can only conclude that the conscription was meant to be limited, and that the government had no intention of altering the prevalent composition of the Jordanian Army – in which the Bedouin and other Trans-Jordanians predominated in the key formations – by conscripting an exceptionally large number of Palestinians. It is, therefore, not surprising that the conscription law, published on 26 November 1966, limited service to 90 days only, after which the conscripts were transferred to the reserves, without being integrated into units of the standing army. [139]

As a result of the severe censure of the government, both at home and in the Arab world, because of its inept response to the Israeli raid on Samu´, Tall held a news conference, on 21 November, to defend his government. To do so, Tall gave a distorted picture of the events which had hardly any basis in fact. Thus, for example, he claimed that Israel had used such large forces in Samu´ that they reached the size of 'almost half the force it deployed in the Sinai invasion [in 1956]'. He went on to argue that, at the time of the Samu´ operation, Israel had also assembled forces in other sectors along its front with Jordan. The Jordanian High Command assumed that Israel was about to carry out a full-scale invasion of Jordan, and that the Samu´ operation was intended solely as a diversion. The army, therefore, refrained from concentrating its full power at Samu´. Even so, Tall declared, the Jordanian Army had won 'an overwhelming victory' at Samu´, inflicting heavy losses on the Israelis, whom, he said, had lost more than 35 men in the operation (in the Samu´ operation, one Israeli was killed).

However, the major thrust of Tall's defence came in the form of a counter-offensive against his Arab critics. Tall accused the Arab states of having failed to live up to the founding principle of the United Arab Command which held that an attack on any one of the countries bordering on Israel would be considered as an attack on all of them. Concerning Egypt, he said sneeringly that Jordan understood the restricted availability of Egyptian ground forces because of the UN presence in Sinai and the Egyptian deployment in Yemen. Nevertheless, he added, Jordan had at least hoped for Egyptian air cover over Samu´, which, he said, was within the sphere of Egyptian Air Force responsibility according to the plans of the United Arab Command. As for Syria, he said, tongue in cheek, that Jordan also appreciated the particular 'political and military conditions in fraternal Syria'. The Syrian army, he suggested, had been disabled by the arrest and dismissal of hundreds of officers in the ongoing struggle for power in Damascus. Nothing much could be expected from Jordan's Arab brethren, and Tall concluded that the Samu´ operation had proved that Israel could afford to abandon its other fronts because of its assurance that no hostile action would be launched from there. In order to show Egypt in a particularly unfavourable light and to portray Jordan as being more committed than any to the struggle for Palestine, Tall scornfully rejected the notion of stationing UN forces on Jordanian territory, as had been done on the Egyptian border. He explained that this would have meant the acceptance of the fact of Israel's existence 'and that as far as we are concerned the Palestine question has drawn to a close. We would prefer to die than do such a thing.' Continuing with this super-patriotic, but hollow, hyperbole Tall asserted that the fact that Jordan was striving to avoid an untimely war did not mean that 'if a battle was imposed on us we would sit and watch', thereby alluding disparagingly to the inaction of his Arab brethren during the Samu´ operation. He admitted, however, that during and after the Samu´ operation some in the Arab world had suggested dispatching forces to Jordan. But, in line with Jordan's own reservation about such assistance, Tall argued that this was not the way to help. It would have been much better, he contended, had they opened fire, or at least carried out some manoeuvres, on the other fronts to deflect Israeli pressure from the Jordanian front.

Another point made in the Arab world was to assert that Jordan was trying to prevent fida'i activity from its territory. Tall candidly admitted that this was, in fact, the case, but he justified Jordan's stand, explaining that the pre-emptive measures against the Fida'iyyun had been carried out according to the instructions of the United Arab Command. The Command, he said, had recommended 'striking with an iron fist in all incidents of infiltration and fida'i operations' which were likely to drag the Arabs into an untimely war with Israel, before the necessary preparations had been completed. The United Arab Command had, in fact, issued such instructions[140] and had sent numerous memoranda to the various general staffs requesting them to prevent incursions into Israel. Tall flatly rejected the logic according to which Jordan was obliged to permit such actions while, as he put it, 'the Fida'iyyun are thrown in jail and disarmed' in the Gaza Strip and in Syria. To Shuqayri, who had decried Jordan's ineptitude, he suggested that if he was really concerned about Jordan, he could go ahead and open a front in Gaza.[141]

Tall's statements exacerbated the already tense relationship between Jordan, on the one hand, and Egypt, Syria and the PLO, on the other. After his news conference, a Radio Cairo commentary condemned Tall as 'a fully committed agent of British imperialism . . . who has sold the honour of his country and betrayed his Arabism on the altar of cheap personal gain'.[142] In early December 1966, demonstrations were staged in Syria in support of 'the struggle of the Jordanian people for freedom from the rule of the treacherous regime'. On 7 December, President Nur al-Din al-Atasi declared in an address to a popular rally in Damascus that 'the liberation of Jordan means the liberation of Palestine' and, therefore, the regime in Jordan had to be overthrown and the monarchy removed.[143] On 23 December, after prolonged restraint, ʿAbd al-Nasir himself joined in the fray against Jordan. In a speech at Port Saʿid, he accused the King of

Jordan of being 'ready to sell the Arab nation', just as King 'Abdallah and Nuri al-Sa'id had done.[144]

The increasingly bitter confrontation between Wasfi al-Tall's government and the Arab world did not make the restoration of order in Jordan any easier. On 23 November, the PLO called upon the ministers in the Tall government to resign, to save their honour, their reputation and even their lives: 'All of you should resign leaving Tall alone to meet his fate.' Another PLO statement appealed to the Jordanian security forces not to intervene in demonstrations because 'the people's revolution is your revolution'.[145]

The ministers did not resign and a harsh crackdown by the security forces restored a measure of tranquillity towards the end of November. The intensity of the demonstrations declined and the violence abated, but the hot coals of disaffection continued to smoulder. At the beginning of December, a popular conference, which was expected to draw many participants from both Banks, was scheduled to take place in Jerusalem. The purpose of the conference was to discuss the developments which had taken place in Jordan since the Samu' operation. At first Husayn authorized the conference but when he realized that it was intended to serve as a platform for the pro-PLO opposition to assail the Tall government, the King withdrew his consent and ordered its cancellation.[146] The banning of the conference and the house arrest imposed on many of its prospective participants did not prevent the publication (outside Jordan) of the statement which was to have been issued by the conference. The statement was a rather vicious indictment of Wasfi al-Tall and his tough, uncompromising attitude towards Palestinian opposition on the West Bank. Tall's outspokenness after the Samu' operation against the introduction of Arab forces into Jordan and against fida'i operations from Jordan, and his strong-arm tactics against the opposition, made him and his government the target of militant Palestinian criticism.

The events in Jordan after the Samu' operation were typical of a regular phenomenon of Jordanian politics. The government and the prime minister often served as a sort of 'lightning conductor',[147] deflecting and absorbing criticism of policies for which the King was actually responsible, whether he had laid them down or implemented them, or both.

## OPPOSITION WITHIN THE ESTABLISHMENT

Discontent with the Tall government was not confined to the Palestinian opposition. In the establishment itself, rumblings of disapproval mounted steadily. Bahjat al-Talhuni, one of Tall's longstanding rivals in the establishment (see above),[148] took advantage of the circumstances that arose after the Samu´ operation to step up his efforts to undermine the Prime Minister. Talhuni and his supporters opposed the policy of estrangement from Egypt as well as the confrontation with the PLO. They approached Husayn to have these policies moderated or changed and to persuade the King to replace Tall.

The opposition within the establishment had begun to crystallize in June 1966, after Husayn's speech in ´Ajlun when he announced the severing of all ties with the PLO. The total rupture with the PLO invited fierce criticism, not of the King, whose support the critics needed, but of the Tall government, which they wanted to see replaced. Their next move was the founding of an opposition bloc under the direction of Bahjat al-Talhuni and other key personalities of the Jordanian establishment, such as the Speaker of the Chamber of Deputies, ´Akif al-Fa'iz, who was later to become a prominent supporter of the PLO,[149] Salah Abu Zayd, a former Minister of Information in the Talhuni government, and Ahmad al-Lawzi, a member of the Chamber of Deputies.

The statement attributed to Tall in October, to the effect that Jordan would use force against Syria if the latter should close their common border (see above), supplied more ammunition to Tall's rivals at home. Under pressure from Husayn, Tall retracted the statement but his retraction did not prevent Talhuni from persisting in his effort to drive a wedge between Tall and Husayn. Talhuni's attempt was unsuccessful. Nevertheless, he and his associates began to spread rumours of an impending change of government, according to which Tall was about to be succeeded by Talhuni. Tall responded to this rumour-mongering with charac-teristic scorn and contempt, dismissing his opponents as 'aspirant ministers' (*mustawzirun*) and 'new agents'.[150]

Talhuni and his cohorts were not deterred by the King's defence of his Prime Minister, nor by Tall's contempt for them, and they continued to connive for his dismissal. They had a long list of complaints against Tall and his government which they made known to anyone who was prepared to listen. These ranged from steps he had taken to raise taxes, customs duties and the prices of basic commodities, to the rejection of his policy towards the PLO and the alignment of Jordan with Saudi Arabia in the struggle against Egypt and Syria. They also complained that Tall reserved too much authority for himself and failed to consult with any other leading political personalities, with the exception of senior members of the security establishment. Tall's critics were referring to Sharif Nasir bin Jamil, Husayn's uncle, who was then Deputy Commander-in-Chief of the army, Chief of Staff 'Amir Hammash, Radi 'Abdallah, Director of General Security (the police), and Muhammad Rasul al-Kaylani, head of General Intelligence. It was only natural for Tall to have developed a close working relationship with the security hierarchy. The regime invested much effort in the area of domestic security, having to deal with PLO or Syrian-inspired subversion, while simultaneously trying to clamp down on fida'i activity from Jordan. Moreover, there was every reason to believe that the security leadership fully identified with Tall's uncompromising views in respect of the PLO presence in Jordan and the need to keep a close watch over every movement of the opposition.

The stormy aftermath of the Samu' operation was also keenly felt in parliament. At the beginning of December more than 40 members, that is, a clear majority of the Chamber of Deputies, decided that they would not express their confidence in the Tall government in the forthcoming session of parliament. At the same time, the West Bank deputies met with King Husayn and requested the dismissal of the Tall government. Acceding to such a request, originating from public pressure, would have created an intolerable precedent and Husayn turned them down.

On 22 December Wasfi al-Tall submitted his resignation to the King. Husayn accepted the resignation of the government, but immediately called upon Tall to form another.[151] Not only did Husayn reaffirm his unwavering confidence in Tall, but he also dissolved the Chamber of Deputies on the same day thereby preventing an undesirable confrontation in parliament which could have erupted between Tall and his opponents when a vote of confidence was taken or when the budget for 1967 was brought before the Chamber of Deputies for approval. Husayn's manoeuvre removed an immediate source of pressure on the government and defused the tension. He also laid the groundwork for public expectation of change by his proclamation of new elections to the Chamber of Deputies, to be held on 15 April 1967. (The constitution stipulated that new elections had to be held within four months of the dissolution of the Chamber of Deputies.)

The domestic situation stabilized at the beginning of 1967. Apart from an isolated demonstration in Nablus in the middle of January, there were no further instances of mob or police violence. The internal opposition had been silenced. However, the Syrians and the PLO, with the backing of ´Abd al-Nasir, intensified their campaign against Jordan, initiating acts of sabotage in Amman, Jerusalem and other towns. Egyptian propaganda against Jordan continued relentlessly, accusing Jordan of having failed to fulfil its commitments to the United Arab Command. All the same, it was clear that the failure of Egypt, Syria and the PLO to destabilize the Jordanian regime after the Samu´ operation was reassuring to Husayn. Shortly after the formation of Tall's new government, Jordan launched a vigorous counter-attack.

## JORDAN'S COUNTER-OFFENSIVE

On 3 January 1967, the government closed down the PLO office in Jerusalem and arrested its staff. At the end of January the Jordanian government notified the Arab League that it had withdrawn its recognition of the PLO 'under its present leadership' because this leadership had made the overthrow of the Hashimite regime its principal objective.[152]

On 7 January, Wasfi al-Tall held a news conference in which he delivered a scathing attack on the 'revolutionary' regimes and the PLO in typically pugnacious style. He blamed them for the division in the Arab world – which they hoped would divert attention from their domestic predicaments. The people living under these regimes 'were promised everything, but attained nothing except charlatanry and hollow slogans'. These states had promised 'to wage the war of liberation [and] rescue Palestine', but instead of doing so they had chosen to occupy themselves in 'fighting Arabs, engineering coups, concocting plots . . . everything but Palestine'.

119

Tall even accused ´Abd al-Nasir of having come to a 'gentlemen's agreement' (he used the English expression) with Ben Gurion after the Sinai campaign, through the intermediary, Dag Hammarskjold, Secretary-General of the UN, according to which Egypt's forces in Sinai were to be limited and UN forces were to be stationed along the border with Israel, all as an interim step towards a peace agreement with Israel. Tall concluded, 'as far as ´Abd al-Nasir is concerned, the question of Palestine actually ended after that'. As for the PLO, it was simply 'one of the bombs with which the Arab revolutionaries tried to blow up the summit conferences', and Tall contended that the Jordanians had known all along that 'Shuqayri and his group' were no more than 'one of the arms of Egyptian intelligence'.[153]

The anti-Egyptian tone of Jordanian policy was confirmed in a strongly worded speech by King Husayn in Jerusalem at the end of January;[154] and at the beginning of February, Husayn and Tall went on a series of visits to the Gulf states and Saudi Arabia, apparently to garner political and financial support for Jordan's anti-Egyptian policy.

Following a cabinet meeting on 18 February 1967, during which Husayn's visit to the Gulf and Saudi Arabia was reviewed, Jordan announced that it had withdrawn its recognition of the republican regime in Yemen. On 23 February, Jordan withdrew its ambassador from Cairo. On 27 February, it resumed diplomatic relations with West Germany, which had originally been severed in May 1965 in compliance with the wishes of ´Abd al-Nasir, following West Germany's establishment of diplomatic relations with Israel.[155]

Concurrent with government action to restore order, and as a supplementary measure in the war of words against Egypt and the PLO, Tall took advantage of the dissolution of parliament to enact a new 'provisional' press law, designed to tighten government supervision of the press.[156] At least some of the newspapers had been reluctant to co-operate with the government in its struggle against Egypt and the PLO.[157]

The law was approved by the government on 4 February. It revoked the licences of all newspapers and permitted their reopening only upon the fulfilment of specific financial conditions, one of which was that the government would hold a 50 per cent share of the ownership. When the law came into effect at the end of

March only two daily papers in Arabic were published (*al-Dustur* and *al-Quds*), as opposed to the five appearing previously (*al-Manar, Filastin, al-Jihad, al-Difa´*, and *al-Urdunn*). *Al-Difa´* resumed publication a few months later, and *al-Urdunn* reappeared at the beginning of 1970. This, however, was not the case with *Filastin* and it is quite possible that its demise was an intentional government policy which did not favour public enhancement of the Palestinian entity.

Sharif ´Abd al-Hamid Sharaf, Minister of Information, explained that the purpose of the law was to ensure freedom of the press, but his explanations were not convincing.[158] Tall and Sharaf were concerned that the relatively small distribution of the papers and their stiff competition for the limited advertising revenues might have exposed them to tempting offers of financial support from outside the country, as was the case with the Lebanese papers which were generally 'bought' by the highest bidder in the Arab world.[159] The government, therefore, did seek to ensure the freedom of the local press, but only from potential outside influence, by reinforcing its own control.

The newspaper owners protested against the new law – which, in fact, was not approved by the Chamber of Deputies when brought before it at the end of 1967.[160] Subsequently, however, private ownership of the press was gradually reinstated. Government control and supervision were never completely abandoned, but they were relaxed somewhat during the 1970s and early 1980s, when Jordan enjoyed exceptional economic prosperity and political tranquility. However, following the rather serious economic recession of the mid-1980s, and with growing Islamic fundamentalist opposition, measures similar to those taken by Tall in 1967 were implemented by the government of Zayd al-Rifa´i in 1986. (Ironically, one of those to be removed from his post in this press shake-up was Wasfi al-Tall's brother, Muraywid, chairman of the board of directors of the daily *Sawt al-Sha´b*.[161])

On 4 March 1967, shortly after completing the preparations to put the press law into effect, Tall submitted his resignation to King Husayn. Tall's reason for resigning was that some of the members of his government had decided to run in the forthcoming elections. As his government had been appointed, *inter alia*, to supervise the elections, he thought it proper to resign to prevent a possible

121

conflict of interests. This, however, was not the true reason for the change of government for when the Tall government had supervised relatively free elections in 1962, only those members of the cabinet who actually ran in the elections resigned, and not the entire government. Moreover, Tall's resignation was no guarantee of fair elections nor even of his own non-interference in the election process. The Ministry of the Interior, which was directly responsible for the supervision of the elections, remained in the hands of Tall's appointee, Wasfi Mirza. Sharif Husayn bin Nasir, who was known to have a good rapport with Wasfi al-Tall, was appointed as the new Prime Minister. Hajim al-Tall, Wasfi's cousin and close friend since childhood, continued to hold the post of Director-General of the Interior Ministry, a position he had held in all the Tall governments. Tall himself was not removed from the heart of the political scene. On the day he resigned, he replaced Sharif Husayn bin Nasir as Chief of the Royal Court, an intimately close adviser to the King, and was thus at the centre of events and at the highest level of decision-making.

The replacement of Tall as Prime Minister was apparently dictated by the King's desire to placate the Palestinians without appearing to be submitting to immediate pressure. Husayn probably assumed that such a change, just before the elections, would create an atmosphere conducive to the election of government-favoured candidates without removing Tall from the inner councils and without curtailing his influence, even in the election process itself. The Tall government had succeeded in restoring domestic stability but Husayn had come to the conclusion that on the question of relations with Egypt things had gone too far. The replacement of Tall was, therefore, intended to pave the way for an improvement in this sphere as well.

# 6

# Behind the Scenes (1967–70)

TALL AND THE SIX DAY WAR

In his capacity as Chief of the Royal Court, Wasfi al-Tall had regular access to the King, and he remained at the centre of events. Nevertheless, in the crucial and critical weeks of May–June 1967, Tall's efforts to persuade Husayn not to join Egypt in a war with Israel were of no avail.

Tall firmly opposed Jordan's entry into the war. He was not the only one of Husayn's confidants who advised caution. Sharif Nasir bin Jamil, Husayn's uncle and Deputy Commander-in-Chief, and Zayd al-Rifaʿi, Husayn's very close friend, similarly had their doubts.[1] But Tall alone had the courage publicly to criticize the Jordanian–Egyptian co-operation in June 1967. After the war, he revealed that he had never favoured the pro-Egyptian tilt in Jordan's policy that followed his resignation from the government. 'I had a premonition of what would happen,' he noted.[2]

On the eve of the war Tall openly expressed his deepest fears of the consequences for Jordan if it joined the Egyptian bandwagon. While Arabs everywhere rejoiced euphorically over the impending victory, Tall grieved as if the weight of the entire world rested on his shoulders. He feared for Jerusalem and the West Bank and told his friends and acquaintances that he was convinced that the Arabs were heading for disaster. If there were any others at all who foresaw the catastrophe as clearly as he did, they kept their views to themselves. No one spoke up like Tall. But no one heeded his advice either. Moreover, there were those in Jordan who were much too quick to dismiss his scepticism as 'the cock and bull stories (*khuzaʿbalat*) of Wasfi al-Tall'.[3]

Just a few days before the war Tall begged Husayn not to join the fray. The King contended that he had no choice. He could not afford to be branded as a traitor to the Arab cause. Now convinced that war was inevitable, Tall suggested to Husayn that the

Jordanians concentrate their forces in Jerusalem and make an effort to capture the Israeli side of the city. The Jordanians, he proposed, should transform the city into a well-armed and well-supplied fortress where they would fight in the streets and hold out 'like the Israelis had done in 1948', until the UN imposed a ceasefire. The Israelis, he argued, would not be able to make effective use of their air superiority in Jerusalem which had such a large Jewish population and would thus be distracted from an all-out offensive on the West Bank. (The idea of cutting off Jewish Jerusalem, 'Operation Tariq' in the Jordanian Army's war plans, had been a central facet of Jordanian planning since 1949. The Jordanians believed that if they could seize Jewish Jerusalem it could be used as a vital pawn to recover all the Jordanian territory Israel might have occupied when a cease-fire was imposed; see Mutawi, p. 115.)

Husayn explained that such operational decisions were no longer his own. In accordance with the defence pact that Husayn had already signed with ´Abd al-Nasir, Major General ´Abd al-Mun´im Riyad, Chief of Staff of the United Arab Command, had arrived in Amman in early June to assume command of the Jordanian front. It was for Riyad to decide, the King concluded.[4] Tall's advice was not taken and the Jordanians were subsequently very critical of Riyad for having failed to implement longstanding Jordanian plans to take Jewish Jerusalem.[5]

After the débâcle, Tall could do nothing but lament that he had 'warned everybody, but no one would listen. I didn't think we were ready for war . . . We could easily have avoided this premature war. Of course, we hardly expected such a devastating defeat. But with the information we had, we didn't believe in the possibility of victory either.'[6] Husayn's final decision to commence hostilities against Israel was taken just before 9a.m. on 5 June in the underground operations room of Jordanian general headquarters. Wasfi al-Tall was there at the time, but still alone in his opinions, and, on that occasion, he kept them to himself.[7]

Tall, not surprisingly, blamed ´Abd al-Nasir for Jordan's catastrophe. He accused the Egyptian President of having 'over-estimated his ability as a politician' and of deliberate deception. 'He wanted to push things to the limit, to poke around in the crack, but not to the point of rupture.'[8] Tall, of course, did not mention that Jordanian propaganda broadcasts were one of the factors which had pushed ´Abd al-Nasir to the brink. The propaganda campaign on the eve of the war, initiated and planned by Tall,[9] had urged ´Abd al-Nasir to dismiss the UN emergency forces from the border area and to close the Straits of Tiran, so as to demonstrate the seriousness of his intention to go to war with Israel.[10] Since the late 1950s, when Tall had been the director of Jordan radio, he had accused Egypt, on innumerable occasions, of having no intention of really going to war with Israel, citing the presence of the UN forces in Sinai as evidence (see Chapter 3).

Tall did not criticize Husayn's decision to enter the Six Day War, even though he had opposed it. He even justified Jordan's actions in the same terms used by Husayn when he explained that: 'We were prodded into joining the others in the 1967 war not by the fear of public opinion or a desire to be in on the spoils, but by our honour, which demanded that we observe our mutual defence agreements.'[11] The decision to participate in the war did not emanate from considerations of honour. On the eve of the war, Husayn admitted to his confidants that no matter what happened on the battlefield, he would be placed in a sorry state of affairs. If the Israelis did not defeat Egypt, ´Abd al-Nasir's power would be enhanced to such an extent that he would be able to sweep Husayn from his throne. If the Israelis crushed ´Abd al-Nasir and Husayn had not taken part, Jordan's position would become untenable as Husayn would be denounced throughout the Arab world as a traitor like his grandfather, ´Abdallah; but if the Israelis defeated ´Abd al-Nasir and Husayn had taken part, he would probably lose the West Bank.[12]

The impact of the anti-government riots in Jordan in the wake of the Samu´ operation and the anti-Jordanian subversion, promoted by Syria and the PLO at the time, were still fresh in Husayn's mind in the summer of 1967. Egypt's closure of the Straits of Tiran in May 1967 had a destabilizing effect in Jordan: Egypt's challenge to Israel boosted ´Abd al-Nasir's prestige in the eyes of the Palestinians, and gave rise to mounting euphoria and a rekindling of hope for the imminent liberation of Palestine. Popular emotions rose to fever pitch. Husayn began to sense that the charged atmosphere, coupled with the traditional hostility towards him from a considerable segment of the Palestinian community, might soon become a serious threat to his regime. He felt compelled to extend his co-operation with Egypt, Syria and Iraq, even though these states had initially rejected his overtures. The relentless Egyptian propaganda attacks against Husayn apparently gave rise to his conclusion that ´Abd al-Nasir might very well exploit the mounting nationalist enthusiasm, as well as his own ever-increasing prestige in Jordan, to overthrow the Hashimite regime.[13] Further- more, in the aftermath of Samu´, it is possible that Husayn believed that Israel, after dealing with Egypt and Syria, might launch an offensive against the West Bank, whether Jordan played a role in the war or not.[14]

When Husayn returned to Amman with Shuqayri, after having concluded a defence pact with Egypt, shortly before the outbreak of hostilities in early June, Amman was overcome with popular excitement. Surging mobs filled the streets – an alarming experience for the King. The excited popular mood had great effect on his final decision to go to war.[15]

Husayn's concerns and considerations were not shared by Tall. Husayn was always deeply anxious about the legitimacy of his regime in the eyes of the Arab world in general, and the Palestinians in particular. As a result he was prepared to make even costly compromises for the sake of his long-range objective of consolidating the regime at home and abroad. Husayn was thus prepared to make concessions to Egypt and to the Palestinians in order to enhance the legitimacy of his regime, or at least to forestall serious damage to it. That did not change the fact that he trusted neither the Egyptians nor the Palestinians.

Tall's considerations were different. He had less finesse, was less complex and less sophisticated. He could not see beyond the immediate dangers of Jordan entering a war, dangers which Husayn had not overlooked. However, the King weighed these dangers against others, which seemed to have greater and more serious long-term ramifications. Tall's considerations were short term if not shortsighted, and were founded on his implacable distrust of Egypt and Syria. Husayn sought, above all, to avoid yet another confrontation with Palestinians in the Kingdom. His self- confidence had once more been shaken and he loathed the idea of having to use force against them, and, in so doing, to jeopardize his relentless quest for legitimacy. Tall was less sensitive and less flexible on this point, as would clearly be demonstrated in the confrontation between the regime and the Fida'iyyun three years later (see Chapter 7). On the eve of the Six Day War, Tall was prepared to pay the price both of confrontation with the Palestinians and of isolation in the Arab world. Not so Husayn.

Their differences in approach and style were also apparent in their respective treatment of certain specific questions of minor import. Thus, for example, Shuqayri recalled a meeting with Husayn and Tall in Amman at the beginning of June, after Shuqayri and Husayn had returned together from Cairo, following the signing of the Jordanian–Egyptian defence pact. Shuqayri had again presented his demand for the deployment of PLA forces in Jordan. Tall had replied with a flat 'no', which, according to Shuqayri, was given with 'every bit of arrogance'. Husayn, who opposed the idea no less than Tall, had suggested that the entry of PLA forces might arouse 'sensitivities between the Jordanian Army and the Palestinian Liberation Army'.[16] Shuqayri's efforts to persuade the Jordanians were unavailing. The attitudes of Husayn and Tall were identical, but their tone and style were totally different. (A few days later, the Iraqi controlled PLA Battalion 421 entered Jordan, without the prior consent of Husayn, on the heels of the Iraqi force which had come to fight on the Jordanian front; Kamm, p. 16.)

There was a similar appreciable difference in the manner in which Husayn and Tall related to General ʿAbd al-Munʿim Riyad, the Egyptian Chief of Staff of the United Arab Command, who commanded the Jordanian front. Though Riyad was unfamiliar with this front the Jordanian General Staff, for the most part, tended to accept his authority without question.[17] Husayn's comments on the war occasionally imply that Riyad acted on his own initiative, but Husayn does not blame him for the defeat. Husayn even commends him by contending that, in the prevailing circumstances, 'he [Riyad] could not have done better'.[18] However, Tall and a number of high-ranking army officers were openly critical of Riyad, arguing that, had he allowed the Jordanians to conduct their own defence, the result might have been very different.[19] Tall had grave complaints against Riyad and against Egypt in regard to their conduct of the war. He accused Riyad of making some very serious mistakes:

The first was to believe Egypt's statement: 'We have crushed the enemy air force and are crossing the Israeli frontier.' We did not have a single Jordanian liaison officer in Egypt! It's incredible! Thus we were at the mercy of whatever false information Egypt decided to give out. On the first day of the battle Riyad was totally ignorant of what had actually happened to the UAR Air Force, until late in the afternoon or evening . . . when a telegram from Cairo admitted the real facts.

Riyad's second serious mistake was the manner in which he had moved the Jordanian armour on the West Bank, ordering them to proceed to the western front, completely exposed to Israeli air power.

Even if our information on the destruction of the Israeli Air Force, had been accurate, in no way did it justify Riyad's decision to shift the tank brigades. Strategically, it was nonsense. Moreover, because the Jordanians' tanks did not know there would be no allied air cover and wanted to execute the order as fast as possible, they made their moves fully exposed. Thus they were at the mercy of the enemy air force, whose unexpected size convinced everyone that there had been Anglo-American intervention. I never believed it for a moment.

Tall maintained that Riyad's Jordanian deputy, Brigadier ´Atif al-Majali, had strongly opposed some of Riyad's decisions, as did some of the officers in the field. 'But Riyad wouldn't listen and, in the end, what he decided was done.' Tall was so convinced of Egypt's deep-seated hostility towards Jordan that he ascribed Riyad's obstinacy to 'disinterest: he didn't much care'.[20]

Tall's animosity towards Ba´thi Syria was no less fervent than that which he harboured towards Egypt. In the trying days of the June war, when Arab forces had clearly been routed, Tall still had the presence of mind to become involved in a plot to overthrow the Ba´thi regime in Syria. Syria's behaviour towards Jordan before and during the war was deplorable. As tension steadily mounted in late May, a truck loaded with dynamite exploded at the Jordanian border post of Ramtha, killing 21 Jordanian bystanders. During the war itself, the Syrians also failed to meet their commitment to send troops to reinforce the Jordanian front.[21] The Jordanians had every reason to feel extremely bitter towards the Syrians, who bore the major responsiblity for the deterioration of the situation into war in June 1967 and, thus, for Jordan's calamity as well.

In September 1968, the trial of 77 officers and civilians began in Damascus, where they were charged with involvement in the abortive coup of Salim Hatum in September 1966, and in a subsequent attempted coup by Hatum in June 1967. Hatum and his supporters had fled to Jordan after the abortive coup of September 1966, where they obtained political asylum (see Chapter 5). At the trial, the principal witnesses alleged that Salim Hatum, the architect of the plot who was executed in June 1967, had received support from Wasfi al-Tall, Radi al-'Abdallah, Director of Jordanian General Security (the police) until April 1967 and Minister of the Interior until October 1967, and from Muhammad Rasul al-Kaylani, Director of Jordanian General Intelligence until the beginning of 1968.

One of the witnesses testified about his ties with Salim Hatum and the contacts made with Jordan. Tall was said to have been present at a number of meetings and, according to the witness, Tall was 'sponsoring and directing the conspirators' activities'. He said that Tall had sent a cheque, signed by Radi al-'Abdallah, for over 40,000 Lebanese pounds to Salah al-Din Bitar, a veteran leader of the Ba'th who was in exile in Lebanon and was also involved in Hatum's plot. During the June 1967 war, the witness said, a number of meetings with Tall were held in Amman when he urged the conspirators to exploit the opportunity presented by the war and, at a meeting between Tall and Hatum on 10 June, it was decided to carry out the plot under the pretext of rescuing Syria from Israel. Hatum and his supporters,who were housed in a military camp in Mafraq in northern Jordan, crossed the Jordanian–Syrian border on the next day but, as they failed to make contact with their supporters in Syria, the plot failed. They were captured by Syrian security forces as they tried to escape back to Jordan[22] and were brought to trial in September 1968.

On 14 June, a few days after the end of the war, Tall resigned from his post as Chief of the Royal Court. On 1 August Husayn appointed an Advisory Council which included a number of prominent people representing a wide spectrum of political opinion in Jordan, from Wasfi al-Tall on the right, to Sulayman al-Nabulsi on the left.[23] The purpose of this council was to create the impression that the regime enjoyed wide public support in the time of crisis that followed the war. The council, however, soon lost its political significance. On 31 October 1967, Husayn appointed a new Senate which included Tall. But, in practice, Tall was now excluded from the small and intimate group that bore the real responsibility of government.

In the first few years after the war, Tall was, for the most part, in the political wilderness. He spent a considerable amount of time on public speaking, largely about the lessons he thought the Arabs ought to draw from the defeat of June 1967. True to form, he delivered scathing attacks on the Arabs themselves for their shortcomings in the confrontation with Israel.

Strongly criticizing the revolutionary regimes of Egypt, Syria and Iraq, where the military had assumed power, Tall condemned army involvement in politics. The politicization (*tasyis*) of Arab armies, he contended, had resulted in the loss of thousands of officers, who had been dismissed on political grounds, and was, therefore, a major cause of the defeat.[24] But the main thrust of his argument was that the Arabs had learnt nothing from their past errors. They suffered from serious weaknesses of national character and intellect (*khulq wal-'aql*), which had prevented them from developing the required collective motivation to fight. War, he argued, was above all a struggle of wills and, though the Arabs had the potential to wage a successful war, they lacked the rudimentary willpower. (Much of what Tall had to say in these lectures had already been published in a book he had written before the war under a pseudonym – *Filastin: Dawr al-khulq wal-'aql fi ma'rakat al-tahrir* (Beirut: manshurat dar al-abhath wal-nashr, March 1967), see Sulayman Musa, *A 'lam min al-Urdunn*, p. 146.)

Too many Arab leaders indulged in what he called, the 'politics of the rabble', proffering opportunistic, machiavellian and irresponsible slogans and slander instead of rational and scientific analysis and appraisal. If Arabs would only adopt a purely rational approach, planning and mobilization for liberation would become a matter of course. Tall dismissed as 'totally naive' the view, so widely held in the Arab world, that time was ultimately on the Arabs' side. The Arabs, he maintained, could not wait for their society to develop gradually, and, in the meantime, sink into a stupor of false self-confidence and procrastination. Arab society had to be mobilized from above in order to develop its potential power to the full. Tall's study of Nietzsche during his student days at the AUB had clearly made a lasting impression.[25]

As for Israel, Tall contended, it was not an invincible, 'fierce colossus', but only seemed so because of the Arabs' own ineptitude. He urged the Arabs to acquaint themselves with Israeli society, suggesting, as he had done after the 1948 débâcle, that the Arabs could use this knowledge to defeat Israel. Tall saw the secret of Israeli military prowess in their motivation, their devotion to their cause and their will to fight. It was these factors, he pointed out, that were more important than numbers of men and weapons. Tall was correct in according such importance to motivation and the collective will to fight as factors in the Israeli victory. He was mistaken, however, in ascribing Israeli motivation to the teachings of the Torah and the Talmud. These, he said, inculcated a 'hatred for the other', inner discipline and a belief in being God's chosen people which were the foundation of the Israeli faith and the source of their inspiration.[26] Not only was this a distorted perception of Jewish religious teachings, but it was also a misconstrued understanding of the role of religion as a motivating force in contemporary Israeli society. The vast majority of Israelis who serve in the army are irreligious. Their motivation is primarily a product of their education in a secular environment founded on the values of the Zionist ideal of Jewish national, and not religious, inspiration.

Nevertheless, on the basis of his understanding of the sources of Israeli motivation, Tall suggested that the Arabs should develop a collective will to fight on the basis of their own national and religious beliefs. The people ought to be motivated by their religious duty of jihad (holy war). The Arabs, Tall argued, should forget 'illusions and fairy tales' about peaceful solutions. Israel would not withdraw voluntarily from the occupied territories and Arabs, therefore, had no choice but to overcome their fragmentation and make rational and calculated preparations for an all-out war against Israel. The fight for Palestine, Tall contended, had to be the core of all Arab action. But the cause of Palestine should not be allowed to serve as an instrument of inter-Arab propaganda warfare,[27] that is, to be used by other Arab states or the Palestinians against Jordan. This latter remark is particularly noteworthy, and central to the understanding of the interaction between ideology and self-interest, as it appeared in the political make-up not only of Wasfi al-Tall but of other Arab leaders as well. Tall's ideological commitment to the struggle against Israel was genuine and not just lip-service to the Arab cause in Palestine. However, this ideological commitment was never his sole consideration. In Tall's view, neither ideology nor commitment must be allowed to infringe upon the national interest of the Jordanian state. In this respect he did not differ from Husayn or other Arab leaders. When the active pursuit of the armed struggle with Israel conflicted with the national interests of each and every state, invariably the latter prevailed.[28] Tall only differed from many others in his candour, his outspokenness and his rather narrow and, at times, shortsighted definition of Jordan's national interest. This, however, was but a matter of degree. Nevertheless, as a result the inherent contradictions in ideology and practice were considerably more pronounced in Tall's character and political behaviour.

As a stalwart of the Hashimite regime and the embodiment of the Trans-Jordanian political elite, Tall instinctively opposed any policy which he believed to be damaging to Jordan's immediate national interest. Tall's opposition to Jordan's entry into the Six Day War was a perfect example of this conflict between his sincere belief in the necessity to confront Israel and his loyalty to what he construed as Jordan's immediate supreme interest. His attitude to the fida'i presence in Jordan before and after the Six Day War was yet another case in point. Though he himself became a proponent of guerrilla warfare against Israel after the 1967 war, under no circumstances was he prepared to tolerate fida'i action that infringed upon the sovereignty of the Jordanian state and undermined its domestic stability. Since this was precisely what happened in Jordan in the late 1960s, Wasfi al-Tall was quick to become the archenemy of the Fida'iyyun.

## THE ARCH-ENEMY OF THE FIDA'IYYUN

Tall's exclusion from the inner councils of government after the Six Day War was no accident. At a time of co-operation between Jordan and Egypt in the Arab arena and collaboration between the Hashimite regime and the Fida'iyyun in Jordan, there was no room for Tall in the upper echelons of Jordanian decision-making. In the aftermath of the Six Day War, the Fida'iyyun consolidated their forces in Jordan. Hostilities on the border with Israel intensified and, as a result, Israeli reprisal actions increased. The prestige of the Fida'iyyun, as the chief standard-bearers of the struggle against Israel, reached new heights, particularly after the Karama operation in March 1968. In this operation, a large Israeli force attacked the town of Karama in the Jordan Valley, with the object of striking at fida'i bases. About 90 Fida'iyyun and some 100 Jordanian soldiers were killed and more than 100 Fida'iyyun were captured. The Israelis also suffered relatively high casualties – 28 killed and 90 wounded – and damaged Israeli equipment was abandoned on Jordanian territory and paraded in Amman a few days later. Fath portrayed the battle of Karama as a glorious victory for the organization and a vindication of the doctrine of protracted popular war, particularly when compared with the humiliating defeat of Arab regular armies in the Six Day War.

The enhanced status of the fida'i organizations, and Fath in particular, was also evident in the changing balance of power between them and the PLO. After the June war the fida'i organizations such as Fath and the Popular Front for the Liberation of Palestine were glorified by Arab public opinion. The PLO was compelled to establish a new form of *modus vivendi* with the fida'i organizations. The PLO chairman, Yahya Hamuda, who succeeded Shuqayri after the 1967 defeat, decided to convene a new Palestine National Council designed to reflect the changes in the Palestinian arena. Bargaining began, mainly with Fath, on the allocation of seats in the council. Once agreement was finally reached, it became clear that the fida'i organizations were now dominant factors in the council. The council that convened in Cairo in July 1968 differed radically from its predecessors. The hundreds of notables who used to appear at national councils in the Shuqayri era were gone and a younger generation of Fida'iyyun had taken control of a recon-structed PLO.[29] Fath went on to transform the PLO into an umbrella organization for fida'i groups but did not discard the PLO framework, which was maintained to safeguard the Arab and inter-national recognition it had already gained. At the meeting of the Palestine National Council in Cairo in February 1969, Fath took full advantage of its large representation to complete its takeover of the PLO, and Yasir ´Arafat, the leader of Fath, was elected chairman of the PLO's Executive Committee.[30]

In the immediate aftermath of the 1967 war, influenced by the defeat of the Arab regular armies and the rising stature and prestige of the fida'i organizations, Tall became an advocate of guerrilla warfare against Israel. He argued that until such time as the regular Arab forces were made ready for an overall confrontation with Israel, the Arabs ought to harass Israel by mounting guerrilla operations in the territories it occupied. He even suggested that parts of the regular Arab armies be converted into fida'i units.[31] In theory this should have created a common ground between Tall and the Fida'iyyun. In practice, it did not.

Fida'i activity conducted from Jordanian territory drew Israeli reprisals, forcing the Fida'iyyun away from the border area and deeper into Jordanian territory. In the populated areas of the Kingdom, particularly in Palestinian refugee camps in Amman and other towns, the Fida'iyyun soon established their own 'state within a state' which eroded and, indeed, flouted the authority of the central government. For Wasfi al-Tall this was an intolerable threat to the Jordanian state. While supportive of the principle of guerrilla warfare, he contended that it could succeed only as an underground operation in the occupied territories themselves. Moreover, it had to be co-ordinated with the Jordanian government and armed forces. Fida'i actions, he argued, should not be allowed to jeopardize Jordan's national interests by providing Israel with opportunities to strike at Jordan. Nor could the Fida'iyyun be allowed to create a state of anarchy in the Kingdom. Tall did not believe that Jordan, or any state for that matter, could possibly tolerate a variety of organizations within the state, each with its own military force, which did not obey the law of the land.[32] Tall was quick to come to the conclusion that, notwithstanding his support for the notion of guerrilla warfare, the Fida'iyyun in Jordan had to be crushed.

Since the Palestinian refugee camps in Jordan had been transformed into fida'i strongholds, Tall suggested dismantling the camps and the resettlement of refugees elsewhere.[33] His advice was not taken. Resettlement of refugees had always been regarded by a Palestinian and overall Arab consensus as an unacceptable concession to Israel and a denial of their right to return to their original homes in Palestine. Though the refugees in Jordan had accepted Jordanian citizenship and many participated in various rehabilitation schemes, this was based on the understanding that they were in no way compromising their right to return (see Avi Plascov, *The Palestinian Refugees in Jordan, 1948–57*, London: Frank Cass, 1981, pp. 44–6, 61–72, 161.)

Tall and others in the Jordanian establishment remained concerned about the ever-increasing influence of the PLO in Jordan. During 1968, while Husayn still refrained from restricting the fida'i presence, Wasfi al-Tall and Husayn's uncle, Sharif Nasir bin Jamil, resorted to various devious means to undermine fida'i influence. They created their own fida'i organizations whose purpose was to provoke and antagonize the population, so as to discredit the Fida'iyyun.[34] When this objective was not achieved, Tall drew up a detailed plan of action which he presented to King Husayn in August 1968.

On 4 August, a few days after an Israeli Air Force retaliation strike on the town of Salt, Tall met Husayn to assess Jordan's position. He sought to convince the King that Israel intended to destroy the regime in Jordan and to crush Palestinian and Arab resistance. In order to contend with this danger it was necessary to strengthen the Jordanian front with air and armoured forces, to raise a national militia, to reorganize the regular army into small, self-sufficient combat units, and to integrate fida'i activity into the general military effort. According to Tall's plan, this effort was to be focused on waging a 'real guerrilla war', which would hurt and weaken Israel, force it to overextend itself, and eventually bring about its collapse. The ultimate objective of this campaign was the liquidation of Israel and thus its execution was conditional upon a rejection of any political settlement which would recognize the sovereignty of Israel over any part of Palestine. To ensure success, Tall demanded that Arab society be transformed into a 'fighting society', in which everyone would be obliged to contribute to the general national effort. But execution of the plan was subject to a further condition – that the Fida'iyyun be brought under the control of the Jordanian Army.[35] The sting of Tall's plan was in its tail. His political objective was to force the Fida'iyyun to co-operate with the government and thereby to restrain the PLO and to arrest the process of erosion of state authority.

135

Tall's plan was not adopted. Although Husayn recognized the inherent danger of continued unrestricted fida'i operations, he was initially opposed to precipitant action, hoping that he would eventually reach some form of *modus vivendi* with the PLO.[36]

Tall's genuine concern for the stability of the regime did not affect the progress of his personal rivalry with Bahjat al-Talhuni, who served as Husayn's Prime Minister for most of the period from 1967 to 1970. From his seat in the Senate, Tall habitually attacked Talhuni's corruption and that of his government. At a closed session of the Senate in March 1969, Tall criticized Talhuni's policies towards the Fida'iyyun and Egypt,[37] which were far too soft for Tall's taste. Tall organized a parliamentary campaign against Talhuni,[38] and demonstrated his displeasure with government policy by voting against the budget when it was presented to the Senate for approval in March 1970.[39]

Tall refrained from making extreme statements against the Fida'iyyun during the period preceding the civil war of September 1970,[40] but his hostility towards them was well known. In October 1969, at a time of increasing tension between the PLO and the Jordanian regime, there were rumours in Amman that Tall would be recalled to head a military government that would crack down on the PLO.[41] The PLO reacted strongly to these rumours. There were reports to the effect that fida'i leaders had warned Husayn that the appointment of Tall as Prime Minister could spark a civil war.[42]

As the Fida'iyyun consolidated their position in Jordan, so their demands on the regime increased. As a result of fida'i pressure, Muhammad Rasul al-Kaylani, one of their staunch opponents, was removed from his post as Minister of the Interior in February 1970.[43] In June of that year Husayn acceded to their demand to remove Nasir bin Jamil, Commander-in-Chief of the Jordanian Army, and Zayd bin Shakir, Commander of the Third Division, from their posts. The Fida'iyyun continued to demand the removal of other personalities from positions of influence, including Wasfi al-Tall,[44] who was often with the King during this period, urging him to take a more resolute stand against the Fida'iyyun. Husayn's apparent readiness to submit to the dictates of the Fida'iyyun aroused the indignation of key figures in the Hashimite family, in the Trans-Jordanian political elite and in the senior officer corps.

They began to exert ever-increasing pressure on Husayn to take decisive action and put an end to the anarchy in the Kingdom by crushing the Fida'iyyun.[45]

At the end of July 1970, Jordan and Egypt announced their acceptance of the US initiative for a ceasefire in the war of attrition with Israel which had been waged mainly on the Egyptian front. Jordan and Egypt also expressed their readiness to enter into negotiations with Israel on the basis of UN Security Council resolution 242, under the auspices of the UN envoy to the Middle East, Gunnar Jarring. This new departure in Egyptian and Jordanian policies was unacceptable to the fida'i organizations. They flatly rejected resolution 242 and regarded Jordanian and Egyptian policy as a threat to themselves and to their fundamental objective of 'liberating Palestine'. The more radical factions of the PLO sought to defeat the American initiative by creating chaos in Jordan and, if possible, by overthrowing the regime altogether.

### 'BLACK SEPTEMBER'

On 1 September, Husayn's motorcade was ambushed as it passed through an area in Amman controlled by the Popular Democratic Front for the Liberation of Palestine. Though the Fida'iyyun denied it, the Jordanians were convinced that an attempt had been made on Husayn's life. The Popular Democratic Front made the unlikely assertion that the shooting was government-inspired provocation. On 6 September, the Popular Front for the Liberation of Palestine landed three hijacked passenger aircraft on a deserted runway near Zarqa. By holding the passengers hostage, the Fida'iyyun humiliated the Jordanian Army, which seemed helpless. (The hostages were only freed by the army two weeks later, during the fighting in the civil war.)

The fida'i stronghold in Jordan appeared most formidable during the summer months of 1970, particularly around the northern town of Irbid. In mid-September the Fida'iyyun proclaimed 'a liberated area' in the north.[46] The King's authority was being totally undermined. Now, after the loss of precious time, Husayn finally made up his mind to smash the Fida'iyyun in an all-out confrontation. On 15 September, the King's confidants and advisers, including Wasfi al-Tall and Zayd al-Rifa'i, Chief of the

Royal Court, assembled at the Hummar Palace in Suwaylih, north of Amman, together with senior army officers such as the King's cousin, Zayd bin Shakir, who had been appointed Deputy Chief of Staff after having been returned to service in August, Major-General Qasim al-Mu´ayita and Brigadier Mazin al-´Ajluni. These men, who had favoured decisive action against the Fida'iyyun for some time, persuaded the King that the time had come. They believed that the army would be able to force the Fida'iyyun out of the towns in two or three days. Husayn's indecision suddenly evaporated. The uncertainty and frustration of the past few weeks was gone. The atmosphere at the Hummar Palace on the night of 15 September was like that of a command post on the eve of battle. Operational plans were prepared on the assumption that a show-down was inevitable within hours.[47]

On the morning of 16 September, Radio Amman announced that King Husayn had appointed Brigadier Muhammad Da'ud, a Palestinian from Abu Dis near Jerusalem, to head a military government. Although the title was given to a Palestinian, real authority remained in the hands of Husayn and a few intimate associates in the army and the political elite, and, most promin-ently, Wasfi al-Tall. Tall, in uniform, remained at the King's side for the entire course of the September campaign.

The army began its attack on 17 September. Patton tanks of the 60th Armoured Brigade, supported by armoured personnel carriers, entered Amman on all sides and attacked the fida'i strong-holds, especially those in the refugee camps in Jabal al-Hashimi, Jabal Husayn and Jabal Wahdat. Fighting also took place in Suwaylih, Zarqa and Salt, and in the 'liberated area' near the town of Ramtha on the Syrian border and, later, in Irbid as well. Amman airport was closed and communications with Beirut and Damascus were cut.

The Jordanian Army assessment that it would be possible to defeat the Fida'iyyun and remove them from the towns within three days proved to be mistaken. As time elapsed, the likelihood of inter-Arab pressure to stop the fighting, and of outside inter-vention on behalf of the Fida'iyyun, increased. On 18 September, Syrian armour began to penetrate into northern Jordan. The intention of the Syrian force was to prevent the Jordanian Army retaking the 'liberated area' and disrupting fida'i supply routes from Syria. On 20 September, the main Syrian force, consisting of two armoured brigades, entered Jordanian territory and on the following day the Syrian force was increased to divisional strength. It was confronted by the Jordanian 40th Armoured Brigade. The Jordanians had control of the air in the armoured battles and the Syrian advance was halted on 22 September. The Syrians had suffered heavy casualties and, on 23 September, they retreated and evacuated Jordanian territory. The Syrian withdrawal was brought about by a combination of factors: the effective opposition of the Jordanians on the battlefield; an Israeli show of force in the area facing the concentrations of Syrian forces in northern Jordan; and Israeli Air Force overflights of the Syrian invasion force. The Israeli posturing dissuaded the Syrians from intensifying their intervention. Had the Syrians continued fighting, they would have had no alternative but to launch their air force into the battle against Jordan. The Syrians considered such a move with trepidation, especially in view of the Israeli threat.[48] The Syrian Minister of Defence and commander of its air force, Hafiz al-Asad, who according to Patrick Seale was then already 'master of Syria in all but name', had no intention of committing himself to unequal combat with Israel.[49] Moreover, his intervention had been rather half-hearted from the outset. The Syrians were also deterred, one may safely assume, by American resolve and by American pressure on both Syria and the Soviet Union to have the Syrian forces withdrawn from Jordan.

The Syrian withdrawal left the Fida'iyyun in desperate straits. In the days preceding the withdrawal, the Fida'iyyun had come under heavy attack in Amman. Their strongholds were being shelled and houses from which they fired were hit by tank and artillery fire.

The Fida'iyyun agreed to a ceasefire on 24 September, their power almost shattered after a week of ferocious fighting and thousands of casualties. But the army was still not in complete control. The Fida'iyyun retained control of a number of northern towns, especially Irbid, and of some areas in the capital. Although the Jordanians had a clear military advantage, Husayn was compelled to accept the ceasefire because of mounting inter-Arab pressure. Jordan was condemned throughout the Arab world. Vigorous protests were staged against Husayn in the West Bank censuring the actions of the 'Hashimite Nero' and the 'butcher of

Jordan' and calling for the severing of all ties with the Jordanian regime.[50] Libya and Kuwait ceased their financial aid to Jordan.

Against this background of criticism, a conference of Arab leaders was convened in Cairo to put an end to the bloodshed. On 27 September, in total isolation, Husayn was compelled to accept an agreement, worked out in Cairo, which enabled the Fida'iyyun to maintain a presence in Jordan. The agreement also called for the stabilization of the military situation as it had existed on 24 September when the ceasefire came into force.

Tall and many of the generals were not happy with the concessions made in Cairo.[51] In fact, neither was Husayn. From the moment he had made up his mind to fight, his intention had been to evict the Fida'iyyun. The way was paved for the return of Wasfi al-Tall to the premiership. There was no candidate better than he to direct and implement a policy designed to root out the Fida'iyyun.

# The Final Eviction of the Fida'iyyun (1970–71)

On 26 September, after the resignation of Muhammad Da'ud as head of the military government, Husayn appointed Ahmad Tuqan, also a Palestinian, as Prime Minister.[1] His was no more than a caretaker government, and having yet another Palestinian to head it was intended to play down the anti-Palestinian character of the regime's action against the Fida'iyyun. It was a further attempt by the King to convince the public that action against the Fida'iyyun had been taken only to restore order in the Kingdom, and was not directed against Palestinians *per se*.

The Tuqan government resigned on 28 October, and Husayn reappointed Wasfi al-Tall as Prime Minister. The King no longer had any need for delaying or diversionary tactics. The appointment was an indication of his renewed self-confidence after the blow his army had dealt the Fida'iyyun a few weeks before. His self-assurance was reinforced by the death of 'Abd al-Nasir at the end of September. 'Abd al-Nasir's death left a void in the leadership of the Arab world and Husayn concluded that conditions were ripe for the launching of a comprehensive policy of reconstruction. The Fida'iyyun would not be able to oppose it, and an Arab world in disarray would not be able to interfere in its execution. The cardinal precondition for the implementation of this policy was the gradual, but final, eviction of the Fida'iyyun from Jordan, to pave the way for a rehabilitation of government, the restoration of regular economic activity, and the institution of a policy of rapid development.

This was not the first time Husayn had appointed Wasfi al-Tall to lead a government that was to implement a new and ambitious political programme, but on this occasion, perhaps more than any other in the past, Tall was the man for the job. As a firm believer in law and order, Tall would brook no fida'i challenge to government authority. Furthermore, he was an experienced and incorruptible administrator, thorough and efficient, and also less sensitive, even indifferent, to inter-Arab criticism and pressure.

The significance of Tall's appointment was not lost on the Fida'iyyun, who accused him of having directed the 'September Massacre'. They were obviously afraid that he would not hesitate to continue the war against them.[2]

Tall's anti-fida'i image and his well-known hostility towards Egypt also alarmed Cairo. The day before the publication of the official notice of appointment, President Anwar Sadat recalled his ambassador from Amman for consultations. When the ambassador returned to his post, he met King Husayn and then returned to Cairo with a message for Sadat which stated that Tall's appointment did not herald any significant change in Jordanian policy. The Egyptians were not convinced and their ambassador did not return to Amman. The Egyptian daily, *al-Ahram*, explained that 'although the UAR had no right to interfere in the domestic affairs of any Arab country . . . [it] could not minimize the importance of what was taking place in Jordan'. From the UAR's point of view, 'Wasfi al-Tall had previously adopted notorious political attitudes and . . . had recently been the most prominent manipulator of the bloody crisis in Jordan'.[3]

Wasfi al-Tall was not unduly perturbed by the criticism levelled against his appointment, and it had no effect on the actions of his new government. On 7 November Tall held a news conference in which he stressed that the prime concern of his government was to guarantee stability, government authority and the rule of law and order. Tall, seasoned and experienced in public relations, sought to justify the forceful policy of law and order in acceptable ideological terms, linking it to national objectives, particularly to the struggle with Israel. Tall argued that in order to wage this struggle, which, he said, was a fundamental principle and the very essence of the 'Jordanian existence', Jordan had to remain united and stable. To ready oneself for battle required the consolidation of 'law and order, on the one hand, and production, on the other', because 'without law and order it is impossible for any society in this world to guarantee its citizens real security'.[4]

There was a great deal of rhetoric in Tall's statements praising the partnership with the Fida'iyyun. But in reality this was no more than a cover designed to prepare public opinion for the final showdown. He described his government as being eager to co-operate with the Fida'iyyun, but also intimated that there were certain factions of the PLO who did not intend to honour the agreements they had reached with the government. In a well-calculated manner, Tall was preparing the ground for the prosecution of a war against the Fida'iyyun to the bitter end. On the surface, this was portrayed as a development which was undesirable to the government; it was solely the fault of extremists of the radical left in the fida'i camp. These, the government suggested, had chosen to prevent any genuine co-operation between the army and the major faction of the PLO – Fath.

On 2 January 1971, Wasfi al-Tall appeared before the Chamber of Deputies to obtain a vote of confidence in his government. His policy statement was similar in style and content to his statements at his news conference of 7 November 1970.[5] The Tall government received a vote of confidence without any difficulty, by a majority of 40 against 1.[6] The government thus appeared to have received the stamp of broad public approval. Despite the fact that the Chamber of Deputies was not representative of all sections of the public, and even though many of the Palestinian deputies remained on the West Bank and did not attend the session, the vote nevertheless reflected a pervasive mood of weariness with anarchy and a strong public desire to return to normality. Attempts by the parliamentary opposition at the time of the vote to organize an expression of disapproval of government policy were unsuccessful.[7]

The government's resolve to guarantee law and order, that is, to bring the Fida'iyyun under government control and to uproot their autonomous enclaves, made a continuation of the armed confrontation between the army and the Fida'iyyun a foregone conclusion. The Cairo agreement of September 1970, which was meant to regulate relations between the government and the Fida'iyyun, did not solve the fundamental problems between them. Like its predecessors, it was never implemented. It laid down that fida'i freedom of action was to be guaranteed without infringing on the sovereignty of the state – a total contradiction in terms. The Arab leaders deliberating in Cairo were not unaware of this contradiction. Accordingly, they also stipulated that certain exceptions to the rule of law

143

should be allowed in Jordan to facilitate fida'i activity.[8] But Wasfi al-Tall left no room for doubt as to his interpretation of the Cairo agreement, the Amman agreement and the Amman protocol (the last two were signed in Amman in October 1970 and detailed the commitments of the parties, on the basis of the general agreement in principle reached in Cairo). In Tall's view, these agreements were meant, above all else, to ensure the sovereignty of the Jordanian state and only thereafter to allow for the freedom of fida'i action. The first principle was a precondition for the application of the second.[9] In fact, the application of the first ruled out the second altogether. Needless to say, Tall's formula was unacceptable to the fida'i organizations, and in particular to the more extreme factions, such as the Popular Front for the Liberation of Palestine, led by George Habash, and the Popular Democratic Front for the Liberation of Palestine, led by Na'if Hawatima. They opposed any agreement with the Jordanian regime. Their attitude and their activities against the regime thus provided a convenient pretext for the government to take action against the entire fida'i presence in Jordan, irrespective of factional affiliation.

In his speech in the Chamber of Deputies on 2 January 1971, Wasfi al-Tall outlined 'the philosophy of government' on which the Jordanian regime was founded. In traditional Hashimite fashion he noted that Jordan's Arab mission was inspired by the Great Arab Revolt. He went on to revive the slogans of the early 1960s concerning the struggle to achieve 'unity, freedom and a better life' (see Chapter 4), which particularly reflected Jordan's conservative and anti-revolutionary point of view, a view founded on pragmatism and the rejection of any form of class ideology. Tall spoke in favour of clearly defined objectives, untainted by what he regarded as static or even fossilized ideology which, he argued, could bring about the disintegration of any state as a result of 'corruption, the spread of opportunism . . . and the predominance of deviation'.[10]

The message was crystal clear – Jordan would strive for progress in its own pragmatic way and it had no need of fida'i radicalism, especially not that of Marxists and pseudo-Marxists. On another occasion, Tall emphasized that 'it was not the task of the Fida'iyyun to revolutionize Jordan'.[11]

The deep chasm between the Jordanian regime and the Fida'iyyun was also manifest in all matters relating to their respective attitudes

144

towards the Arab–Israeli conflict. In his speech on 2 January 1971 in the Chamber of Deputies, Tall maintained that the fact that Jordan had accepted UN Security Council resolution 242 and the initiative of the American Secretary of State, William Rogers, was not to be construed in any way as an agreement to concede the rights of the Palestinian people.[12] This disclaimer, however, could not conceal the differences between the government and the PLO, which had flatly rejected both the Security Council resolution and the Rogers initiative. Furthermore, one of Jordan's motives in its open conflict with the Fida'iyyun, ever since September 1970, was precisely to ensure freedom of action for itself in this area of the political process, which the Fida'iyyun opposed and which Tall justified as a legitimate means to eradicate 'the traces of the June 1967 aggression'.[13]

Jordan's desire to maintain room for manoeuvre in determing the political destiny of the Palestinians also dictated its fierce opposition to the idea of a Palestinian entity or state. This had been suggested at the time by some West Bankers as part of a local initiative for a negotiated settlement with Israel. Tall condemned this idea as 'a blow to the significance of the holy unity [with Jordan] . . . and a step towards the liquidation of the Palestinian question', in accordance with 'the destructive schemes' of Israel. The Jordanian government, he said, would fight against them with all the means at its disposal.[14] The identical views of the PLO and the Jordanian government on this particular point arose because of the opposition of both to any form of independent political initiative on the West Bank, and not from any shared interest. Each of the parties sought to decide the political fate of the Palestinians, to the exclusion of all others. This point of 'agreement' was, therefore, only another facet of the deep-rooted hostility and fierce competition between the Jordanian regime and the various factions of the PLO.

### RELENTLESS PRESSURE

In early November 1970, shortly after Tall's appointment, incidents involving an exchange of fire between the Fida'iyyun and the Jordanian security forces increased, particularly in Amman. At times, these incidents were initiated by the Fida'iyyun, especially

145

the more radical factions of Habash and Hawatima, and at times they were provoked by Jordanian security forces. In any event, they provided the government with the required pretext for widespread action to restore law and order and to expel the Fida'iyyun, initially from the towns and subsequently from the entire country. According to the Cairo and Amman agreements of September and October, both sides were to withdraw their military forces from Amman and other towns. The Fida'iyyun, however, were allowed to maintain militia forces in the towns and under this guise they were able to preserve a military presence there, despite the agreements. Tall's objective was still to eliminate every fida'i stronghold.

The transition period laid down for the implementation of the Amman agreement expired on 9 November. On that very day, Tall announced that henceforth the carrying of arms and the storage of explosives and heavy weapons in populated areas were forbidden. Personal weapons could only be kept by militia personnel in their homes. One may safely assume that Tall did not really believe that the battle would end with the Fida'iyyun simply complying with his orders. All the same, these were good tactics, especially since he probably expected the Fida'iyyun not to obey his orders, and in so doing to provide him with the pretext he needed to use force against them. Shooting incidents continued in Amman and other towns despite all the agreements. As a result, government troops were reinforced in all the main towns, particularly in Amman and Irbid.

A further agreement between the government and the Fida'iyyun was signed on 14 December – positive proof that the previous agreements had not been carried out. Now, however, because of their deteriorating performance in the field, the Fida'iyyun were compelled to accept terms they had previously rejected. Thus, for example, they agreed to collect the weapons of their militia forces and keep them in central stores. Though these stores were to have fida'i protection, this step by the government was designed to weaken the Fida'iyyun seriously in the towns by cutting them off from their personal weapons. Tall now declared that henceforth it was strictly forbidden to keep weapons in the home. The Fida'iyyun were supposed to have understood from this warning that the government really did expect them to carry out the agreement on the collection of weapons from their men, or else face the violent consequences.

At the beginning of January 1971, after the supremacy of their forces in all the towns had been assured, the government launched an offensive against fida'i bases along the road between Amman and Jarash. Some 3,000 fighting men were stationed there – mainly from Fath, but also from other organizations, such as the pro-Syrian al-Sa'iqa, the pro-Iraqi Arab Liberation Front, the Popular Front for the Liberation of Palestine and the Popular Democratic Front for the Liberation of Palestine. This campaign was planned in order to isolate the Fida'iyyun from the main towns and to establish government control of roads connecting the various fida'i concentrations outside the towns. Brigadier Ahmad 'Abd al-Hamid Hilmi, the Egyptian head of the inter-Arab ceasefire observer corps which was established by the Arab states after the outbreak of the civil war, alleged that this action was contrary to assurances he had received from Wasfi al-Tall not to use force against the Fida'iyyun. In an apparent reference to Tall, he complained that there were those in the Jordanian leadership who ignored the observer corps. At a news conference in Amman on 11 January, Ibrahim Bakr, the spokesman of the PLO Central Committee, alleged that when the Fida'iyyun became aware of the army's intention to seize an abandoned police station on the Amman–Jarash road and to patrol along the road, they appealed to the Supreme Arab Follow-up Committee (the main inter-Arab body which was to supervise the execution of the agreements between the Fida'iyyun and the Jordanian government, and under whose auspices the ceasefire observers operated) and requested its intervention. Bakr said that a meeting had taken place between fida'i representatives and Wasfi al-Tall on 6 January, in which Bahi al-Adgham, the Tunisian chairman of the Follow-up Committee, also participated. At this meeting, Bakr said, it was agreed that the Fida'iyyun would occupy the police station for 'supply' purposes, and that the army would not patrol along the Amman–Jarash road.[15] It is impossible to verify whether Tall had promised what Hilmi and Bakr attributed to him, but there can be no doubt whatsoever that he had no intention of leaving it to the Arab observers, or to the Fida'iyyun, to determine where, how and against whom the Jordanian armed forces would be deployed.

Tall made no secret of his opinion that there was no need at all for the Arab observers. He contended that the agreements between the government and the Fida'iyyun were enough to regulate their relations, and that external supervision was not only superfluous but an infringement of Jordan's sovereignty. After the inter-Arab observer corps had ceased to function and had left Jordan in March 1971, Bahi al-Adgham accused the Tall government of being responsible for the failure of the Follow-up Committee. He said that the government had expressed reservations about the committee's intervention in Jordan's affairs, and that Tall had even notified the committee of his wish that the Arab ceasefire observer corps should leave the country. When the observers did not comply with this demand immediately, the government imposed restrictions on them which effectively prevented them from carrying out their tasks.[16]

The fighting at the beginning of January in the area north of Amman was inconclusive, but it prompted tension and clashes in Amman itself. On 13 January, Tall and Ibrahim Bakr signed yet another agreement, the last in the long series of agreements between Jordan and the Fida'iyyun which solved nothing and were never fully executed. The agreement set out in detail the manner in which the weapons of the fida'i militia in Amman and other Jordanian towns were to be collected and stored. A timetable for the agreement set 22 January as the deadline for the completion of the collection of militia weapons.[17] On 25 January Tall announced that, since the period allowed for the collection of the weapons had ended, any exchange of fire in any area would result in 'special measures' being taken against the entire area in question. He also gave warning of the severe punishment which would be meted out to those in illegal possession of arms. These announcements paved the way for punitive action by the security forces against the Fida'iyyun, particularly in Amman. Henceforth there would be absolutely no compromise.

The Fida'iyyun, well aware of government intentions, preferred not to concentrate all their weapons in the central storehouses and continued to conceal secret stores of heavy weapons in Amman and other towns. The government, equally aware of fida'i tactics, did not evacuate all its forces from the capital, keeping them there in the guise of police. Shortly after the expiration of the deadline for the implementation of the January agreement, and following a number of incidents in Amman in February, the regime decided to make a final push to drive the Fida'iyyun out of the large cities of Amman and Irbid for good.

On 26 March, after the discovery of an illegal cache of weapons in Irbid, heavy fighting broke out between fida'i and army forces in the town. The authorities imposed a curfew the following day, during which some Fida'iyyun in the city were arrested and the rest were driven out. The fida'i presence in Irbid thus came to an end. The events in Irbid led to mounting tension in Amman in late March which was exacerbated by the flow of government reinforcements to the capital. There were a few exchanges of fire between fida'i and government forces and an attempt by the Fida'iyyun to enlist public support by organizing student demonstrations in their favour was foiled by the security forces. In order to prevent any further attempts to stage demonstrations, Tall forbade students and workers to leave their schools and places of employment should any incidents occur in the city – ostensibly in the name of order and public safety.[18]

At the beginning of April, Husayn met fida'i leaders in an attempt to persuade them to leave the capital. Husayn warned that if they failed to do so, the government would have no choice but to do everything in its power to restore calm.[19] In view of the overwhelming superiority of government forces, and with the events in Irbid fresh in their minds, the Fida'iyyun recognized the resolve of the government and finally agreed to withdraw from Amman.

On 10 April, Tall ordered searches for illegal weapons throughout the capital. During the course of these searches, which continued for a few weeks, numerous caches of arms and explosives were discovered. Fida'iyyun and fida'i sympathizers were arrested, and even the theoretically legal weapons stores of the fida'i militia were shut down. By May, there was nothing left of the fida'i presence in Amman, and Tall declared, with obvious satisfaction, that the situation was 'very good', and that law and order had been fully restored.[20]

On 15 May, under the terms of an understanding reached with the Fida'iyyun before their withdrawal from Amman, the Jordanian authorities began to release detainees under a provisional

General Amnesty Law. However, the amnesty was only carried out after a parliamentary ploy by Tall and Husayn designed to reduce its scope. On 10 April an extraordinary session of parliament was convened by royal decree to debate the approval of the budget and a number of other laws, including the General Amnesty Law. At its meeting on 11 May, the Chamber of Deputies debated a number of amendments submitted by the Judicial Committee of the Chamber, aimed at broadening the application of the amnesty law, which had originally related only to persons arrested on the specific charge of illegal possession of weapons or explosives. Tall opposed the amendments and suggested to the Chamber of Deputies that it should adopt the bill in its original form and that it should recommend to the government the initiation of another law with broader application. Tall thus sought to ensure a limited amnesty. His suggestion, however, was not accepted and the chamber decided to refer the bill back to the committee for amendment.

The Chamber of Deputies was due to reconvene on 16 May to debate the law and its amendments,[21] but on 12 May the extraordinary session of the Chamber of Deputies was prorogued by royal decree. On the following day Husayn approved the Provisional General Amnesty Law ('provisional' indicating a law authorized by the government and the King while parliament is in recess) in its unamended form. This did not apply to the many detainees held for various kinds of general (and political) offences against the security of the state or against public safety. The new law therefore allowed the government to carry out a very selective release of fida'i detainees, keeping in custody those whom, from the very outset, it had no intention of freeing.

## THE FINAL EXPULSION

Concurrent with the eviction of the Fida'iyyun from the large towns, the army continued to harass fida'i bases in the countryside. Their bases were intermittently shelled, their supply lines disrupted. The pressure was unremitting. Fida'i morale was being steadily sapped as they were driven to despair and a sense of helplessness.[22] After their eviction from Amman and Irbid, the Fida'iyyun were prevented from regrouping in the Jordan Valley.

The government wanted to ensure that they would be unable to take any action against Israeli objectives. Jordan feared Israeli retaliation which would have severely hampered the efforts to rehabilitate and repopulate this important agricultural area, or which could possibly have deteriorated into full-scale war. The Fida'iyyun were therefore forced to concentrate most of their forces in the wooded highland area between Jarash and 'Ajlun. The army controlled their supply lines from Syria and, since they were hemmed into a relatively small area, the Fida'iyyun were at the mercy of the government forces which began to prepare for their final expulsion from the whole of Jordan.

On 2 May, Tall issued a particularly cynical statement, according to which 'all intruders' on archaeological sites throughout the Kingdom were required to vacate them within a month. The statement authorized the Minister of Tourism and Antiquities to seek the aid of the security forces if the order was not complied with.[23] The purpose of the order was to evict the Fida'iyyun from archaeological sites in the Jarash–'Ajlun area, ostensibly to safeguard tourism.

On 16 May, 'Abdallah Salah, Jordanian Foreign Minister, himself a Palestinian, informed the ambassadors of the Arab states in Amman that the Jordanian government had solid evidence that Fath was planning the assassinations of a number of leading Jordanians and other acts of violence.[24] The note was clearly part of a calculated effort to prepare Arab public opinion for a large-scale army offensive against Fida'iyyun of all factions, including Fath. Fighting between the army and the Fida'iyyun resumed in earnest at the end of May and the beginning of June, particularly in the area of 'Ajlun and Jarash. In an attempt to minimize its seriousness, Tall alleged that the Fida'iyyun did not have full control of their men and that there were, therefore, isolated incidents 'here and there'.[25] However, it was obvious that the army was moving in on the last strongholds of the Fida'iyyun, as the Jordanian propaganda offensive against the Fath leadership gathered momentum.

On 2 June, King Husayn sent a message to Wasfi al-Tall, in which he praised him and his government for the measures taken to 'safeguard the homeland'. Husayn said that 'if there is on our soil today a handful of people who make plotting their profession and treachery their vocation . . . then we wish our opposition to them to be firm, decisive and valiant, allowing no room for hesitation, tolerance or compromise'. Husayn added that one could not leave the fate of the Palestinians in the hands of those who had 'made it their mission to commit daily crimes in the name of the people'. In his reply to Husayn, Tall emphasized that 'we shall . . . purge the ranks – all the ranks – of those professional criminals who pose as Fida'iyyun, to save fida'i action itself from the evil designs against it'.[26] This was the green light given publicly by Husayn to Tall to strike at the last redoubt of the Fida'iyyun, without any discrimination between their various organizations. 'All the ranks', meant just that – Fath and the various Marxist factions, without any distinction.

Simultaneously with the military preparations for the final onslaught, Tall strengthened his direct control over the army by giving his own operational orders without the prior approval of the Commander-in-Chief, Habis al-Majali. Tall also systematically undermined the validity of the agreements signed by the government and the Fida'iyyun. He contended that the Cairo agreement and the Amman protocol had guaranteed the sovereignty of the state as well as the freedom of 'genuine fida'i action'. But according to the pronouncements of Husayn and Tall, no existing fida'i organization, nor Fath, qualified as 'genuine'. Moreover, Tall intimated that the agreements, as formulated, were, in fact, no longer binding. He argued that the conditions under which these agreements had originally been made 'no longer existed'.[27] Tall even added that the Cairo and Amman agreements had been 'temporary arrangements',[28] thereby suggesting that their validity had actually expired. On 19 June, the Central Committee of the PLO submitted a counter-memorandum to the Arab ambassadors in Amman, in which the PLO maintained that, at meetings at the beginning of June between fida'i representatives and senior army officers, a map had been presented to them which indicated alternative deployment areas for the Fida'iyyun. These, they complained, were in desert areas, without water, roads or means of communication; yet they were forbidden to maintain their present bases. The Fida'iyyun naturally rejected the Jordanian plan for their redeployment.

The army siege of the 'Ajlun–Jarash enclave began to tighten. At the end of June, in conjunction with overt military preparations for a large-scale offensive, the Jordanian media briefly reverted to the tactic of distinguishing between Fath and the more radical Marxist organizations. This was apparently an attempt to give Fath a last chance to cut itself off from these organizations and to accept the authority, and indeed the control, of the government; or possibly an effort to erode the mutual trust between the different factions in the PLO. The media, therefore, found fault with 'certain resistance organizations' but not with all. If 'the resistance' really wanted co-existence with the government it had to expel from its ranks 'advocates of . . . class struggle and world revolution'. The door was still open 'to those who [had] abused the nation's trust' to rejoin the Jordanian forces 'in one front against the enemy and against those who directly or indirectly support him'. It was suggested to the Fida'iyyun that they should opt for action within the framework of Jordanian sovereignty on the grounds that 'there is no difference between a Palestinian and a Jordanian'. Since 'Palestine is Jordan with its two banks' and because 'Jordan is Palestine, east and west', there was 'no reason for the fida'i action to become an independent entity within the framework of Palestinian–Jordanian unity'.[29]

Fath's response to this suggestion was quick and defiant. An unidentified source in the organization retorted at the beginning of July that 'if some think that fida'i action should become the humble servant of the regime in Jordan, and that the revolution should come under so-called Jordanian sovereignty', they were mistaken because 'we would rather die honourably than submit and collapse once and for all'.[30] At the same time, the PLO's quasi-parliamentary body, the Palestine National Council, convened in Cairo. At the council, the move towards a total rejection of any form of co-operation with the Hashimite regime, which had been gathering momentum since the civil war, was reiterated with even greater conviction.[31]

On the morning of 13 July 1971, the expected, full-scale offensive on the last fida'i strongholds was launched. Government armoured and mechanized forces, infantry and artillery attacked with a vengeance. The fida'i situation was hopeless. Two days later, on 15 July, a Jordanian spokesman announced that all the Fida'iyyun in the Jarash–'Ajlun area had been evacuated 'to the new areas agreed upon'.[32] In actual fact, there were no such 'agreed' areas. Most of the Fida'iyyun in the Jarash–'Ajlun area were captured by the army, while the rest fled to Syria or to Israel. Within a few days, all the remaining pockets of resistance were overpowered. The fida'i presence in Jordan had finally been uprooted. At a news conference on 17 July Husayn said that Jordan was 'completely quiet' and that there was 'no problem' now.[33]

On 19 July, Wasfi al-Tall held a news conference to sum up the recent events. He explained that after the Fida'iyyun had assembled in the Jarash–'Ajlun area, this region had become 'an occupied area subject to the harshest conditions of evil and terror', as though it was 'part of another country, far from Jordan'. He accused the Fida'iyyun of having taken over roads which were of military importance, and of having turned down suggestions by the government to move to alternative areas. On 13 July, in an operation which took 'no more than four hours', the army occupied a number of fida'i positions. It then ceased operations to notify the Fida'iyyun that this was just an example of what the army was capable of doing and that it would be preferable for them to move to 'the agreed areas'. (As already mentioned, there never had been such an agreement, but the government consistently claimed the contrary to justify its actions, as though they had been taken in consequence of a breach by the Fida'iyyun of the so-called 'agreement'.) Tall went on to explain that the Fida'iyyun chose not to heed the warning of the government and, as a result, the army drove them out of a few more of their bases on 15 July. On the same morning, Tall said, Yasir 'Arafat had declared 'war on us officially' when he appealed to all fida'i bases to attack the army, which was in consequence, compelled to evict the Fida'iyyun from all their bases. Serious fighting had ceased by midday on 15 July and thereafter the operation became one of simply 'rounding up the Fida'iyyun'.[34]

As for the future, Tall said, the Jordanian government would seal 'every channel of evil regardless of how small it may be . . . We shall not tolerate the chaos of the past, undisciplined commands and attacks on our citizens and soldiers.'[35] After 'a real sifting of the good fida'i elements from the bad', it would be possible to discuss the question of prospective areas of operation for them.[36]

It was not long before Tall's words were translated into deeds. Many of the more than 2,000 Fida'iyyun who had been captured by the army were released between 20 and 22 July. Most of them were expelled from Jordan, while others were released to their homes in the country. Of those who remained in Jordan, 39 were to be allowed to conduct 'real resistance to the Israeli enemy'.[37] This was a true reflection of the minor, if not immaterial, role the regime was prepared to accord to fida'i action in Jordan. Tall was not deterred by Arab censure or by the economic sanctions that some Arab states imposed on Jordan because of its treatment of the Fida'iyyun. Tall made it clear that the Arab states would have no impact on the government's policy. He declared emphatically that he would 'never sell the stability, security and tranquillity' of Jordan 'for any kind of political, financial or economic consideration. That must be clear. Security, stability, sovereignty and tranquillity must come first.' Everything else was secondary.[38]

Tall still maintained that Jordan adhered to the principles of the Cairo agreement and everything that emanated from that agreement. However, beyond the general and rather vague commitment to the principle of freedom of fida'i activity, which was open to very different interpretations, both Tall and his Minister of Information, 'Adnan Abu 'Awda, tended to dismiss other, more specific, elements of the agreements as inessential and as mere procedures for which there was no longer any place.[39] These statements referred to the particulars of the Amman agreement and the Amman protocol, which had defined the locations of fida'i deployment. Once the Fida'iyyun had been evicted from these areas, the Jordanians had no intention of ever allowing them to return by virtue of some defunct agreement.

Shortly after the expulsion of the Fida'iyyun from Jordan, Egypt and Saudi Arabia initiated talks between representatives of Jordan and Fath in a vain attempt to heal the breach between Jordan and the PLO. The negotiations, which took place on neutral ground in the Saudi city of Jedda, were doomed from the outset. The Fath representatives demanded that Jordan reinstate and implement the previous agreements. The Jordanian delegation, led by Riyad al-Muflih, who was a veteran Trans-Jordanian politician with a firm anti-fida'i predisposition, insisted on a new agreement that would be based on the existing situation in Jordan. The negotiations began in September and soon reached the inevitable impasse. All the same, they were renewed at the beginning of November.

155

The Jordanians now suggested amendments to the Amman agreement, the gist of which was an offer to establish two fida'i bases in Jordan, under the supervision of the Jordanian Army. Their principal purpose was to serve as bases for penetration into Israeli territory for fida'i operations there, without transforming the East Bank into a haven to which the Fida'iyyun would return after their operations. These suggestions were vigorously rejected by the Fida'iyyun who, quite rightly, maintained that they emptied the Amman agreement of any content.[40] There was no basis for agreement and the Jedda talks were discontinued.

The Jordanian design to wipe out every trace of the PLO presence was consistent and uncompromising. From early August, the government took over or closed down offices of the PLO, Fath and the Palestinian Red Crescent, and other offices operated by organizations which belonged to the PLO or acted on its behalf. Though a PLO office was allowed to remain in Amman, this was no more than an empty gesture. To all intents and purposes, no form of genuinely independent Palestinian activity existed in Jordan any more.

### POLITICAL REHABILITATION OF THE KINGDOM

The prolonged presence of the Fida'iyyun in Jordan had left its mark on all walks of life. Concurrent with their gradual eviction, the Tall government made a concerted effort to restore the Jordanian state to its traditional form. When he was appointed to head the government, Tall noted that one of his principal goals would be to carry out a complete and radical reform of the state bureaucracy.[41] And, indeed, a few days after his appointment, the government approved a provisional Civil Service Law which gave it special powers to dismiss and to retire civil servants. During his first term of office as Prime Minister in 1962 Tall had taken similar action (see Chapter 4). However, this time there were distinct political objectives for these measures which went far beyond considerations of efficiency and economy. Tall strove, with typical resolve, to remove from government service anyone whose loyalty to the regime was questionable, or who had previously shown sympathy towards the Fida'iyyun. Many, probably most, of those removed were Palestinians.

In January 1971, Hasan al-Kayid, a former Minister of the Interior and a sworn enemy of the Fida'iyyun, was appointed head of the Civil Service Commission. (One of the concessions Husayn had previously made to the Fida'iyyun was the dismissal of Kayid in April 1968 from his post as Minister of the Interior. See *Middle East Record*, 1968, p. 587.) In the four months from November 1970 until March 1971 when the provisional Civil Service Law was in force, hundreds of officials were dismissed. Yasir ʿArafat, and other sources hostile to the regime, accused Tall of implementing a policy of 'Jordanization' (*Ardanna*).[42] Tall refuted the allegation. In a letter to a personal friend on the West Bank, he explained that he wanted all the West Bankers to know that the wave of dismissals was only designed to rid the administration of corrupt personnel, whether Palestinian or Trans-Jordanian. He contended that, all in all, no more than 250 officials had been dismissed, of whom 160 were Jordanians and only 90 Palestinians.[43] It is difficult to accept Tall's version at face value. This is particularly so since Husayn himself admitted later that it had been essential to rid the bureaucracy of those 'whose conduct [was] besmirched by evil or deviation',[44] terminology which suggests a lot more than corruption or inefficiency. On the other hand, those who regarded Tall's policy of dismissal as calculated 'Jordanization' seem to have misinterpreted the dismissals of many Palestinians as a purging of Palestinians *per se*. Officials were not removed just because they happened to be Palestinians. Those who were not dismissed as a result of a genuine need for reform or economy were dismissed because their loyalty was suspect, as part of the general policy of the Tall government to eradicte every vestige of fida'i influence in the country. This may well have affected Palestinians more than others, but it must also be borne in mind that some of those who filled important roles in the implementation of the purge were themselves Palestinians, such as the Minister of Information, ʿAdnan Abu ʿAwda, and the Minister of Labour and Social Affairs, Mustafa Dudin. The army, of course, was not ignored during the purge and Palestinian officers and soldiers suspected of fida'i sympathies were dismissed.

The Tall government similarly took steps to reduce fida'i influence in the Jordanian press. When Tall was Prime Minister in early 1967 he had introduced legislation designed to reinforce government control of the press (see Chapter 5). However, as a by-product of the consolidation of the fida'i 'state within in the state' after the Six Day War, government press control was severely eroded. With his return to government Tall strove energetically to complete what had been left undone.

The newspaper *Fath* which began to appear without a licence in mid-1970, when the Fida'iyyun were at the zenith of their power, was forced to cease publication in Jordan in January 1971 (it then appeared in Damascus instead). At the end of December 1970, the government temporarily suspended publication of the weekly *'Amman al-Masa'*, after it had published what was defined as material damaging to 'the public interest'.[45] This weekly, which in the past had been rather sympathetic towards the Fida'iyyun, was edited by a Palestinian, 'Arafat Hijazi, who oddly enough had been associated with Wasfi al-Tall in the early 1950s in the publication of another newspaper, *al-Hadaf* (see Chapter 3). Now, however, Hijazi was active in an opposition organization called the Professional Gathering (*al-tajammu' al-mihni*), a grouping of professionals which was an offshoot of the opposition organization *al-tajammu' al-watani* (the National Gathering) led by Sulayman al-Nabulsi. *'Amman al-Masa'* was allowed to reappear a few months later, but another weekly, *al-Sabah*, which Hijazi began to publish in August 1971 and which was supposed to present the views of the members of the Professional Gathering, was closed down two weeks after its first appearance and had its licence withdrawn. The licences of the long-established daily *al-Difa'* and the weekly *Akhbar al-Usbu'* were also withdrawn, after their publication had already been suspended by government decree in May 1971. The editors of these two papers, Ibrahim al-Shanti and 'Abd al-Hafiz Muhammad, were both Palestinians. *Al-Difa'*, like Hijazi's paper, had occasionally shown sympathy for the Fida'iyyun or had ventured to criticize government action against them.

Simultaneously with the eradication of PLO influence in the press, the Tall government set up the Jordanian Press Establishment, which began publication of the daily *al-Ra'y* (Opinion) in June 1971. Wasfi al-Tall himself chose the name of the paper which was to become the semi-official mouthpiece of the regime. Tall had also chosen the same name for the paper of the Arab Nationalist Movement with which he had been associated in the early 1950s (see Chapter 3). Tall had come an exceptionally long way since then. The editor of the new *al-Ra'y* was the former Director-General of Jordan Radio, Nizar al-Rafi'i, who also served as Director-General of the Jordanian Press Establishment. His career in the information field and his appointment as editor of *al-Ra'y* were clear signs of his unflinching loyalty to the regime.

It was this criterion which also dictated the course of government action against other institutions in the country, particularly the trade unions. In the trade union elections held in July 1970 many fida'i supporters had been elected.[46] Their influence in the unions was most conspicuous when, in January 1971, trade unions issued a statement censuring government measures against the Fida'iyyun.[47] However, shortly afterwards the government began to exert pressure on undesirable trade union leaders to resign. One of them, Fathi al-Naji, fled to Damascus in August where he complained that he had been hounded by the Jordanian authorities. In September a number of members of the Executive Committee of the Federation of Trade Unions succumbed to government pressure and submitted their resignations.[48]

Tall also resorted to stern measures against West Bankers in an effort not only to deter but even to punish fida'i sympathizers or other critics of the government. A blacklist was compiled of people whose entry into Jordan was forbidden or who were to be detained for interrogation immediately upon entry. It was reported that West Bankers were even required to sign a statement of loyalty to King Husayn and condemnation of the Fida'iyyun when they crossed the Jordan River bridges into Jordan.[49]

The General Amnesty Law which was promulgated in May 1971 (see above) also applied to 93 West Bankers against whom detention orders had previously been issued. Tall had initially objected to their inclusion in the amnesty, and they were pardoned probably only by virtue of Husayn's intervention.[50] Moreover it is also possible that it was because of the King's insistence that Tall should instruct the General Security and General Intelligence personnel to be more hospitable towards West Bankers coming to Jordan. Tall, in an apparent effort to improve the image of his government in the eyes of the West Bankers, sent a message to notables in East Jerusalem and Nablus at the beginning of June, asking them to explain to the public that the government measures

159

against the Fida'iyyun on the East Bank had no effect on the civilian population and were only in direct response to fida'i provocation.[51]

All the same, in Tall's order of priorities, the well-being of West Bankers was relatively less important than the relentless effort to restore law and order and to revitalize the economy. Thus, in June 1971, the government decided to suspend the salaries of Jordanian civil servants on the West Bank as they also received salaries from the Israeli authorities.[52] (The necessity to cut expenditure had arisen because of the suspension of economic aid by Kuwait and Libya in the aftermath of the civil war.) Tall had proposed stopping the double salaries of West Bankers in December 1970, but Husayn had objected, possibly because he still hoped that Kuwaiti aid would be resumed and because of his unwillingness to take action that would be damaging to the West Bank population. But in the budget for 1971 the funds allocated to the West Bank were specifically linked to the receipt of Libyan aid, which the Jordanians certainly did not expect to be renewed in the near future. This was a sign of the declining importance, in the government's view, of these payments to the West Bank. Tall's suggestion had been accepted because of the government's real economic difficulties, but the political significance of this measure could not be overlooked. It was also presumably intended to signal to the West Bankers the extent of their dependence on the government in Amman, a factor which they could not afford to ignore in any political calculation in future.

When the prestige of the PLO soared in the West Bank (at Jordan's expense) after the Yom Kippur War, the payment of salaries to Jordanian civil servants on the West Bank was resumed. Priorities had changed and the payments became more important.

## TALL AND THE FUTURE OF THE WEST BANK

Tall's determination to restabilize the country and to ensure government control was naturally detrimental to those of dubious loyalty to the regime. Many in this category were Palestinians. Since Tall was less inhibited and less hesitant than Husayn when it came to taking action against Palestinians, he acquired an infamous anti-Palestinian reputation. Tall was said to have belonged to a group in the upper echelons of the Jordanian political elite, which included Husayn's younger brother, Hasan, the Queen Mother Zayn, and Husayn's uncle, Nasir bin Jamil, who were reputed to favour Jordan's final disengagement from the West Bank and dissociation from the Palestinian question.[53] Such non-conformist attitudes were never publicly expressed and it is therefore difficult to assess the precise nature of the differences between the King and this group, but one may contend with some assurance that, as in other similar instances, the picture was considerably more complex than its portrayal in some of the sources.

Husayn, Tall and Hasan all strove to ensure the existence of Jordan in its traditional form under the leadership of the Hashimite dynasty, supported by the Trans-Jordanian political elite. One may safely assume that Tall and Hasan, like Husayn, believed that, in order to ensure its own survival, Jordan had to prevent the formation of a hostile Palestinian entity on the West Bank, especially if such an entity were to be under the control of the PLO. They had no intention of abandoning Jordan's links to the West Bank, or of passively standing by while an undesirable process (from their point of view), developed unhindered. At the same time, however, they tended to attach less importance to Jordan's relations with the Arab world in general, and with Palestinians in particular. After the civil war, Tall, Hasan and others in the political leadership showed greater readiness than Husayn to reconcile themselves to the situation that resulted from the Six Day War. As in his attitute to Jordan's entry into the Six Day War and in his treatment of the Fida'iyyun, so also in regard to the question of future relations with the West Bank Tall was inclined to prefer immediate considerations. Husayn, by contrast, thought most of all of the long-term legitimacy of the regime.

One may assume that Husayn was also well aware of the advantages of Israel (rather than himself) bearing the onus of preventing the rise of a Palestinian entity, hostile to the Hashimite regime, in the West Bank. Nor was he likely to overlook the advantage of the policing of the Palestinian population there having become an Israeli problem rather than a Jordanian one. However, because of his assessment that no one in the Arab world would accept Israeli rule over the whole of Palestine, Husayn found it preferable to co-operate with the Arab states in the

161

political effort to bring about an Israeli withdrawal to the 1967 borders. Tall and Hasan, at this juncture, opted for a more passive course which, at least temporarily, accepted the post-1967 status quo. Their position was primarily due to their fear that political or military co-operation with the other border states was likely to bring Arab pressure to bear on Jordan to join an 'Eastern Front'. This could possibly force Jordan into another undesirable war, or confront the Kingdom with demands to make unsavoury concessions to the Palestinians and the PLO in order to obtain the necessary inter-Arab backing for negotiations with Israel to retrieve the West Bank.

Tall must have realized that Jordan, with its massive Palestinian population on the East Bank, could not realistically detach itself from the Palestinian question and the future of the West Bank, but during his last term of office he was apparently of the opinion that as long as Israel controlled the West Bank, it was unnecessary to make any special effort to change the status quo. Certainly it was not worth making concessions to other Arab states and the PLO for that purpose. Tall could hold such opinions without actually rejecting the basic premise of Jordanian policy on the Palestinian question, according to which Jordan, in the final analysis, would have to maintain some form of control of the West Bank, if and when Israel withdrew. There were perhaps differences in emphasis, but there were no material or lasting differences of principle between Husayn and Tall on this issue.

Tall's design to demolish the fida'i power-base in Jordan was not intended to weaken Jordan's ties with the West Bank at the same time. In fact, special measures were taken to preserve and reaffirm these ties. The most noticeable of these was the formation of the Jordanian National Union in September 1971. The formation of the National Union was actually the realization of one of Wasfi al-Tall's own ideas. Since the early 1950s Tall had been of the opinion that the country needed a national charter which would serve as an essential instrument of national guidance.[54]

The National Union was established under the same slogan as that employed by the first Tall government in 1962 – 'freedom, unity and a better life'. A return to this slogan suggested a revival of the mood of those earlier days – the perception that Jordan was yet again at the beginning of an era of consolidation, construction and renewal, after the years of internal strife and war against the PLO. However, in contrast to the Tall government's attempt in 1962 to rally the population around the regime and to broaden the base of its popular support by holding relatively free elections, the government now adopted a different course. By establishing the Union as the only legal political mass organization, with branches throughout the Kingdom, the regime sought to buttress the loyalty of the populace, Jordanians and Palestinians alike.

The ideological framework for this quest was embodied in the charter of the National Union, drawn up by Tall, together with Trans-Jordanian Ibrahim Habashna and the Palestinians, 'Adnan Abu 'Awda and Mustafa Dudin.[55] The ideas and objectives of the charter were strikingly similar, and at times identical, to the White Paper issued by the Tall government in 1962, on Jordan's position on Palestine and inter-Arab relations. Like the White Paper, the charter stressed Jordan's devotion to Jordanian–Palestinian unity because the 'unity of the people (sha'b) on both Banks of the Jordan is a fateful, guiding unity, stemming from the unity of history, land, objective and fate, the tragedy of the present and the hopes of tomorrow'.[56]

The National Union was not particularly active in the four and a half years of its existence and was abolished in February 1976. The liquidation of the fida'i presence in Jordan precipitated the collapse of all other centres of opposition in the Kingdom and the National Union, as an instrument to consolidate the stability of the regime, soon proved superfluous.

### BETWEEN TALL AND HUSAYN

During Tall's last term of office as Prime Minister there was much rumour and conjecture about friction between him and Husayn, particularly in regard to Jordan's policy towards the Fida'iyyun. Tall, with his outspoken resolve, his occasionally cynical behaviour, his acid tongue and his utter disdain for his critics, contributed, perhaps intentionally, to the creation of an impression that he was not simply the orchestrator of that policy but also its architect and prime mover, thereby, as it were, overshadowing Husayn, who was more inclined towards moderation and compromise.

Against the background of the fighting in Jordan in January

1971, the Egyptians blamed those at the head of the Jordanian Army and government for having created an atmosphere of distrust between the regime and the Fida'iyyun.[57] Their impression was that Crown Prince Hasan and Tall had taken advantage of the absence of King Husayn (who was in London at the time) to launch an offensive against the Fida'iyyun. President Sadat therefore appealed to Husayn, suggesting that he restrain the Crown Prince and the Prime Minister. Operating on a similar premise, the chairman of the Arab Follow-up Committee, Bahi al-Adgham, went to London to consult with the King. Their attempts were of no avail. On the contrary, Husayn, in a letter to Hasan, fully endorsed the measures taken by the government.[58]

At the end of March, in the wake of the bout of fighting during which the Fida'iyyun were dislodged from Irbid, Tall announced in the Chamber of Deputies that he had ordered the army into the town himself and assumed full personal responsibility for the scale of the clashes between the army and the Fida'iyyun. In response, the Egyptian government published an official statement calling upon those 'who have a say in Jordan' to try to prevent a new massacre of Palestinians.[59] The Egyptians were indicating to Husayn that they expected him to restrain his Prime Minister. Husayn, however, did not accede to this request. Once again he gave full backing to Tall's forceful policy and, at the beginning of April, he himself exerted heavy pressure on the Fida'iyyun to evacuate all their forces from Amman.

At the beginning of June, the Fida'iyyun, unwilling to meet representatives of the Tall government, approached Husayn directly to sound out his attitude. They were apparently not sure whether the King really favoured the ongoing confrontation with the Fida'iyyun.[60] Husayn's reply was immediate and decisive. It was given in the form of a public condemnation of the Fida'iyyun coupled with instructions to Tall to take firm action against them (see above).

The fact that from time to time Husayn was required to give public support to Tall, and to express his full confidence in his policies, could have created the impression that it was Tall who dictated the turn of events and that Husayn was left with no choice but to concur and give his blessing *ex post facto*. This, however, was not the case. By virtue of his post as Prime Minister, his resolution, his independence and his strong personality, Tall was the man who directed the operation of ridding Jordan of the fida'i presence. In other instances in the past – when the *éminence grise* of Jordanian politics, Samir al-Rifa'i, was prime minister or during Tall's term of office in 1966–67 – a strong and independent prime minister often served as a 'lightning conductor', deflecting and absorbing criticism of policies which had really been formulated by the King. The contention that it was Tall and people close to him in the royal family, such as Crown Prince Hasan, who imposed their own hard line on an unwilling King[61] appears exaggerated. Husayn was no more willing to compromise than Tall, although it is true that Husayn was more cautious when it came to taking drastic measures, and there were a number of people at court, Tall among them, who relentlessly pressured him to take a tougher line (see Chapter 6). However, once Husayn had made up his mind to crush the Fida'iyyun in Jordan, his decision was final and his determination complete. His appointment of Tall to the premiership was as clear an indication as any of his own single-minded resolve.

Any differences between Tall and Husayn focused more on style and tactics than on fundamental ideals. Husayn did have reservations at times about some of Tall's actions and there was more than a grain of truth in the occasional reports of tension between the King and his Prime Minister. During 1971 there were frequent rumours that Husayn was about to dismiss Tall in order to improve Jordan's relations with the Arab world and reach some form of accommodation with the Fida'iyyun.

The Arab Follow-up Committee and its corps of military observers ceased functioning at the end of March 1971, a result of Egypt's decision to recall its representatives on the committee on the grounds that they were being prevented from carrying out their mission.[62] According to Bahi al-Adgham, Tall had made it quite clear to members of the committee and the observers that he had no need for their activities and would prefer to see them leave the country. Husayn's attitude was presumably no different. Husayn, however, was concerned about Tall's manner in his dealings with the committee members, being more sensitive than Tall to the inter-Arab repercussions of Jordan's struggle with the Fida'iyyun. Husayn did not believe that the campaign against the Fida'iyyun should be halted because of Arab censure, but he thought that it ought to have been handled in such a way as to reduce friction with other Arab states. He did not want to relinquish any principle of policy but, while pursuing it, would rather not irritate the Arab world by unnecessarily provocative behaviour.

Their respective styles in conducting the campaign against the Fida'iyyun were markedly different. Tall openly declared that he had initiated the intensification of the confrontation in Irbid. By contrast, the King succeeded a few days later in bringing about the evacuation of Amman without resorting to force, using only his powers of persuasion and intimidation. It is, of course, possible that it was the government's use of force in Irbid which enabled Husayn to dispense with force in Amman a week later but, even so, these incidents are an indication of the different modes of operation employed by the two men.

In an interview for Lebanese television in May 1971, Tall was asked to comment on the sensitivity of some Arab governments to his role as Prime Minister. He replied with his usual outspoken candour that 'we here in Jordan are not compelled to change our behaviour in order to reduce sensitivities' and that Jordanians said and did only what they believed in, and did so openly.[63] Husayn was not always as frank in matters related to Arab 'sensitivities'. Thus, for example, after the final eviction of the Fida'iyyun in July, and even before then, Tall expressed his opinion that the terms of the Amman agreement had been overtaken by events. In the new circumstances, he contended, they were no longer valid. Tall's statements were sharply criticized in the Arab world, where Jordan was accused of failing to abide by its commitments. Husayn responded with a note to Arab leaders in which he took pains to stress that Jordan had neither abandoned nor rejected any agreement. He refrained from going into details[64] but created the impression that he was willing to compromise and that he and Tall were at loggerheads over this issue.

In a speech on 23 July 1971, President Sadat of Eygpt complained that while Husayn maintained that he still accepted the agreements, Tall had rejected them.[65] Radio Amman accused Sadat of trying to drive a wedge between Husayn and Tall, and noted that Tall had not rejected the Cairo agreement.[66] The radio made no mention of the Amman agreement, which neither Husayn nor Tall intended to revive and actually implement. Husayn was not prepared under any circumstances to allow the Fida'iyyun to regroup in Jordan, as provided for by the Amman agreement but, unlike Tall, he did not openly say so. The Egyptian daily *al-Ahram* therefore blamed Tall for having been personally responsible for the failure of the conciliation talks with the Fida'iyyun in Jedda. The paper said that Tall's uncompromising directives to the Jordanian delegation had actually allowed him to conduct the Jedda talks 'from his office in Amman'.[67] It is hardly likely that the position taken by the Jordanian negotiators at the Jedda talks was not agreed upon beforehand, in consultation with the King as well as the Prime Minister. However, because of his inflexibility, Tall constantly created the impression that there were fundamental policy differences between him and Husayn.

The Egyptians and the Saudis, co-sponsors of the Jedda talks, presented the Jordanians with a joint working paper in August 1971, as a basis for the resolution of the crisis with the PLO. In terms of the working paper, Jordan was to declare that it was fully committed to the Cairo and Amman agreements, and that it would agree to a renewal of the operations of the Arab Follow-up Committee to supervise the implementation of the agreements. Husayn accepted the working paper 'in principle', but Tall would not hear of it and was not even prepared to discuss it with the Egyptian and Saudi mediators.[68] The mediators concluded that while Husayn was interested in an agreement with the Fida'iyyun, Tall was not and they therefore felt it advisable to bring about the replacement of the Tall government.[69] It is indeed possible that Husayn was more interested than Tall in an agreement of sorts with the Fida'iyyun, but one may safely assume that Husayn's acceptance 'in principle' of the working paper would, in practice, have rendered the Amman agreement void of any real content. Husayn's flexibility was purely a question of tactics and public relations, for which Tall had no patience.

Tall's contempt for them and for the recent mediation effort caused the Fida'iyyun to demand his removal. In September they claimed that Husayn had promised the Egyptian and Saudi mediators that he would make changes in his government. Once it became clear that he was not going to do so, they accused Husayn of being responsible for the failure of the first round of the Jedda talks as he must have known all along that Tall wanted the talks to fail. The appointment of the strongly anti-fida'i, Riyad al-Muflih, as head of the Jordanian delegation was, in their view, clear evidence of the government's ill-will.

It is difficult to believe that Husayn did undertake to replace Tall, but it is possible that the mediators sensed that he had certain reservations about his Prime Minister. This would not have been an unfounded impression; some evidence for it can be found in a report on a meeting which took place at the end of September, involving Bahjat al-Talhuni (Tall's long-standing rival and a former prime minister), Qasim al-Rimawi (a member of the Chamber of Deputies), Tall and King Husayn. At this meeting Talhuni assailed the Tall government, holding it responsible for Jordan's isolation in the Arab world, for the severing of relations with Jordan by a number of Arab states, and for the closure of Jordan's border with Syria and Iraq. Husayn did not defend Tall on this occasion. His silence was consequently understood as a tacit agreement with Tall's critics.[70] Husayn may have been considering Tall's replacement, although he could not afford to appear to be submitting to external pressure. Moreover, Tall had served the King extremely well, despite his faults.

## THE ASSASSINATION IN CAIRO

At the peak of his political career, and in the throes of an energetic rehabilitation of the Jordanian state, Wasfi al-Tall was assassinated in Cairo on 28 November 1971 by members of the Black September organization,[71] an arm of Fath. The gunmen lay in wait for Tall at the entrance of the Sheraton Hotel in Cairo and shot him at close range as he was about to enter. His wife Sa´diyya, who was in the hotel at the time, rushed into the lobby screaming: 'Are you happy now, Arabs – sons of dogs!' A Jordanian officer knelt down at Tall's side and kissed his forehead, just after one of the assassins had vented his hatred and lust for vengeance by licking Tall's blood as it poured from his wounds onto the marble floor.[72] Four suspects were apprehended by the Egyptian authorities very shortly thereafter.

Tall was buried the next day, with full military honours, in the Royal Cemetery adjoining Husayn's palace in Amman. King Husayn, who was said to have been 'desolated' by Tall's death,[73] could not hold back his tears as he headed the thousands of mourners who accompanied Tall on his last journey. The coffin was lowered into the grave by army officers, amidst cries for revenge from the crowd.

Tall, who had arrived in Cairo on 26 November to take part in the discussions of the Arab Defence Council, went to Egypt against King Husayn's advice. Because of his anti-Egyptian record Tall was considered *persona non grata* in Egypt. On the eve of his arrival in Cairo, he was specifically advised of this by Jordan's ambassador to Egypt. Since his appointment as Prime Minister in October 1970, the Egyptians made no effort to conceal their distaste for Tall. They criticized 'those around King Husayn', and in February 1971, the Egyptian daily *al-Ahram* disclosed that Husayn had cancelled a visit to Egypt after he had been notified by the Egyptians that they would not allow Wasfi al-Tall to accompany him.[74] Tall did not care about improving his image in the eyes of the Egyptians. On the contrary, he was deliberately provoking. He appointed Akram Zu'aytar Jordanian ambassador to Cairo despite the fact that Zu'aytar was known to be unsympathetic to Egypt since he had served as Tall's Foreign Minister in 1966. In the more distant past, as a journalist, Zu'aytar had consistently attacked 'Abd al-Nasir on the pages of the Lebanese daily *al-Hayat* and he had consequently been barred from entering Eygpt.[75] The Egyptians considered Zu'aytar's appointment as a provocation and refused to accept him.

Egypt's hostility to Tall had prompted Husayn to fear for Tall's safety on the grounds that he might not receive adequate protection during his visit to Cairo. After Tall's assassination, Jordan and Egypt exchanged mutual recriminations regarding the protection given to Tall, but there is no evidence to suggest that the Egyptian authorities were implicated in the murder. Husayn made no such accusations, but there were others in the royal palace who believed that the assassination had been financed by Libya and had been carried out with the tacit consent of the Egyptians.[76]

Immediately after the assassination, President Sadat expressed his sorrow over what had happened and promised Husayn that all those found guilty after proper investigation would be duly punished. Yet, only a few days later, the Egyptian press expressed its sympathy for Tall's assassins. In an article in *al-Ahram*, its editor, Muhammad Hasanayn Haykal, justified their action. According to Haykal, the assassination was an understandable and predictable reaction by young Palestinians after all they had gone through in Jordan. Tall's visit to Cairo, according to Haykal 'was an unjustifiable provocation' of Arab public opinion and the Palestinian movement. Haykal argued that by coming to Cairo Tall had tried to demonstrate that he could be accepted in any Arab state, as though nothing had happened, and that Jordan could do as it pleased.[77] Haykal's approach heralded a change in the attitude of the Egyptian judiciary. The prosecution began to examine 'the political aspects' of the assassination, especially the political motives of the accused, in light of the events which had taken place in Jordan from September 1970 until Tall's assassination. Jordan objected to this line of investigation. In Jordan's view, this was a politicization of the proceedings and had no place in a murder trial. The Fida'iyyun, on the other hand, welcomed the new departure. In their view, the four suspects were neither criminals nor murderers but fighters who had fulfilled their mission. According to Salah Khalaf, a senior member of the Fath Central Committee and the 'godfather' of Black September,[78] after the heavy casualties suffered by the Palestinians in the fighting in Jordan and the death in battle of their revered commander of the Jarash–ʿAjlun area, Abu ʿAli Iyad, the despair in the ranks of Fath soon gave way to a desire for revenge. In assassinating Tall 'justice had been done, one of the hangmen of the Palestinian people had been executed'.[79]

At their trial, the accused were defended by Ahmad al-Shuqayri, and in the end all four were released. The courtroom became a platform for a barrage of anti-Jordanian propaganda. Shuqayri contended that Tall was assassinated not only for his direct responsibility for the events of September 1970 and their consequence, but because he was 'a target' that symbolized the Hashimite regime which 'bore great responsibility . . . for all the tragedies' visited upon the Arab nation.[80] For the Fida'iyyun and for longstanding arch-Nasserists like Haykal, Tall was indeed a symbol of Hashimite staying power. Jordan's very survival as a Hashimite Kingdom was ample proof of their frustrating failure to remove it from the Arab scene.

The assassination of Wasfi al-Tall was a severe blow to Husayn but it did not lead to any changes in the regime's attitude and policy towards the Fida'iyyun. As a symbol of continuity and as an expression of appreciation for Tall, the government which he had formed, now headed by Ahmad al-Lawzi, continued to function after his death. ´Abdallah al-Tall, Wasfi's cousin, replaced him in the Senate, and Sa´diyya, his widow, was appointed a member of the Executive Committee of the newly formed National Union.

The Trans-Jordanian political elite has yet to produce a successor to Wasfi al-Tall. Another forceful, energetic and aggressive leader of his stature and calibre has yet to emerge in Jordan.

# Conclusion: Wasfi al-Tall and the East Bank Political Elite

Wasfi al-Tall was an exemplary representative of 'the Jordanian entity' and the Trans-Jordanian political elite. More than any other individual of his time, with the single exception of King Husayn, Tall personified Hashimite Jordan, with unequalled force and resolution. He was the embodiment of that Trans-Jordanian elite whose unflinching support for the Hashimite regime has been a crucial factor contributing to its vitality and longevity. His contempt for the opponents of the regime made him enemies everywhere. But forceful and uncompromising opposition was his instinctive response to those who sought to undermine or overthrow the monarchy.

All the fundamental characteristics of the Hashimite regime in Jordan became an integral part of Wasfi al-Tall's political make-up. From an early stage of his political career he linked his fate with that of the regime. Regardless of whether his initial choice was one of political identification or self-serving opportunism, Tall's devotion was unswerving. He was protective of the independence of the state and suspicious of 'liberated' pan-Arabism. He had little respect for Nasserist or Ba´thi style revolutionism and he loathed and distrusted ´Abd al-Nasir.[1] Above all, he attached great importance to the persistent and untiring pursuit of clearly defined immediate political objectives in which pragmatic considerations completely overrode ideology.

Tall was a man of action in every sense of the word. This was his great strength but also his major weakness. In his ability to take decisive action against enemies of the regime, whether resorting to force or cunning, intrigue or subversion, Tall was an invaluable asset to King Husayn. On the other hand, Tall was, at times, impulsive, abrasive and rash. His arrogance and shortsightedness occasionally aroused the ire of the King who was compelled to restrain Tall and cover up or make amends for his mistakes.

Tall was convinced that Jordan's survival depended on a pro-Western orientation in foreign policy; in domestic politics he did not hesitate to use the army when necessary to put down challengers of the existing political order. In this way he was no exception in the Jordanian establishment. On the contrary, these had been the basic tenets of Hashimite policy since the very foundation of the Emirate of Trans-Jordan and during the entire course of Husayn's reign.[2] However, Tall was unique in his zealous pursuit of this policy, which led him at times to extremism and to a blatant display of tenacity and contempt towards the enemies of the state within and without. Tall showed little respect for the feelings or opinions of his opponents. He despised them.

There were no substantive differences in the political attitudes and positions of Tall and King Husayn, but there were differences of style, temperament and tactics, resulting from the different relative weights that the two leaders attached to the constraints of diplomacy and legitimacy. For Husayn, these were of prime importance. For Tall they were secondary. Husayn had a broader perspective and a more farsighted vision than Tall. The King was shrewder and more sophisticated. He was a better manoeuvrer. He was less outspoken. These differences were clearly manifested on the eve of the Six Day War, when Tall strenuously opposed Jordan's entry into the war, in total disregard for the possible Palestinian and general Arab reaction. Both Husayn and Tall feared that Jordan might lose the West Bank in the war, but Husayn had other concerns as well, relating to the long-term durability of the regime if it failed to rally to the Arab cause. In retrospect, it would seem that Husayn was vindicated. The Six Day War cost Jordan the West Bank, but Jordan's participation paved the way for the steady enhancement of Hashimite Arab legitimacy, eventually allowing Husayn to achieve a position of prominence in the Arab world that would have been unthinkable in the 1960s.

Husayn and Tall also had their differences in the war against the Fida'iyyun. Tall took the initiative and attacked without respite until they were finally driven out of Jordan, showing utter disregard for the criticism levelled against him in the Arab world. His actions did not run counter to Husayn's basic policy objectives, but Tall did not inform the King of every move, and his provocative manner did, at times, meet with royal disapproval and cause a certain measure of friction between Tall and Husayn.

Tall had charisma. He was self-confident and impressed those about him as a straightforward and decisive man. He said what he really thought and if a subject arose that he preferred not to discuss he would simply say so.[3] When convinced of the merit of any matter, he would give his support; when not, he would say so on the spot. People always knew where they stood with him. However, this did not mean that it was not easy to be drawn into a serious quarrel with him.[4]

Tall was the most powerful personality in Jordan, apart from the King.[5] Both he and the King were attractive, dynamic characters who generally got on well with each other. Husayn liked Tall, even though Tall did not always handle the King with sufficient tact. At times, Tall was 'like a bull in a china shop'.[6] He was one of the very few in Jordan prepared to speak his mind to King Husayn and had no inhibitions about stating his opinions fully and forcefully so as to persuade and influence the King, even if this meant being disagreeable to the point of arousing the King's anger. Indeed, it was precisely because of his candour that he won Husayn's trust and became one of his closest confidants and advisers. Tall had a much better rapport with the King than his predecessor, Samir al-Rifa'i. Like Tall, Rifa'i was a forceful personality, but between Husayn and Rifa'i there was an uneasy relationship that stemmed from an unbridgeable generation gap that did not exist between Tall and Husayn. Tall's contemporary and rival for the premiership, Bahjat al-Talhuni, was far less dynamic than Tall. The two men disliked each other intensely. Talhuni handled Husayn well, but he lacked Tall's independent mind and forceful character. In Talhuni's dealings with the King, it was always Husayn who took the lead.[7] Consequently, Talhuni never achieved the stature of Tall in the upper echelons of the establishment. Tall's status in the leadership gave him considerable influence with Husayn, and he was therefore part of that small coterie close to the King who were intimately involved in policy-making and who shared the responsibilities of government. While Prime Minister, Tall was the only non-Hashimite to participate in the regular family councils held by the King.[8]

Husayn has always been the linchpin of Jordan's political system and his premiers, whatever their characters, political perceptions and predispositions, were expected to implement the policies the King found applicable at that particular juncture. When forceful characters like Wasfi al-Tall or Samir al-Rifa'i were in office, they attracted much of the criticism for unpopular policies because of their image as powerful and influential personalities who occasionally forced their opinions on the King. Thus, by serving concurrently as a 'bulldozer' and a 'lightning conductor', these leaders spared the King undesirable exposure to public criticism, whether at home or in the Arab world at large. As such, they were invaluable assets which the King never failed to appreciate.[9]

Wasfi al-Tall's 'philosophy of government' did not depart from the norm in the Arab Middle East. His political concepts were deeply rooted in the predominantly authoritarian political tradition of the region, in which there was little place for the ideas and institutions accepted in the political life of Western democracies. A genuine parliamentary system or 'loyal opposition' were alien concepts to Husayn and Tall. Their political lexicon included such elementary terms as 'respect for the authority of government', 'positive freedom', and 'constructive criticism', all of which reflected a deep-seated intolerance of any real opposition. If in that sense Tall was a true product of the predominant political culture of the Middle East, in another he was quite exceptional, though not unique. Tall, in his self-confident and candid style, tended to dismiss the widely accepted 'plot theories', customarily used to explain the failures of the Arabs. Thus, he frankly explained the Arab defeat in 1948 as a direct result of the failings of the Arabs themselves. His attitude to the Six Day War was the same. He did not believe ´Abd al-Nasir's story of Anglo-American intervention on Israel's side, even 'for a moment'.

Wasfi al-Tall's position towards Israel was complex and pragmatic. On the one hand, he fought for the Palestinian cause and described Zionism as 'an aggressive, racist, expansionist, fascist movement, a base for imperialism and a bridgehead for war against liberation'.[10] On the other hand, he respected Israel's power and even admired its prowess. He had little confidence in his Arab brethren, and tended to underrate the Palestinian national movement. When he sought to avoid war with Israel, he was prepared to act with an iron fist against those who strove to destabilize the situation on the border with Israel and drag Jordan into an untimely and unequal confrontation with the Israeli Army. As with others in the Jordanian leadership, there was no reason to assume that Tall's expression of hostility towards Israel and the

Zionist movement was less than genuine. His admiration for Israeli resolve and his consequent appeal to the Arabs to learn from the Israelis were the consequence of his basic hostility towards Israel and a desire to meet like with like in dealing effectively with the Israeli challenge. There was nothing particularly original about this. It was very much in line with longstanding Islamic teachings of confronting or resisting the enemy with his own devices (*al-muqabala bil-mithl* or *al-muqawama bil-mithl*).[11] Yet the main task of ensuring the survival of the Hashimite regime dictated co-existence with Israel and recognition of the interests that Jordan and Israel shared in regard to the Palestinian question. Thus an attitude of hostility in principle had to co-exist with an actual policy of restraint.

There has always been a paucity of prominent and decisive leaders in the Jordanian elite who could share the burden of government with the King under conditions of constant pressure and crisis. Of the few of this calibre, pride of place must go to Wasfi al-Tall, along with Tawfiq Abu al-Huda and Samir al-Rifa´i, who had preceded him, and Zayd al-Rifa´i (Samir's son) and Sharif ´Abd al-Hamid Sharaf, who followed him. Sharaf, a brilliant young man, had served as Tall's Minister of Information in the 1960s when still only in his twenties. Sharaf was more of an idealist than Tall, but the two men were on the best of terms and learnt from each other.[12] As Patrick Seale has aptly pointed out,

> Wasfi was an earthier more home-grown product, who could claim to know every hill-top, every chieftain, the name of every camel. He was a leader rooted in Jordanian soil. ´Abd al-Hamid did not know the country so intimately. He was not a man of the masses. He was happier with ideas than with instincts, but he shared with Wasfi a dream of what their country could become.[13]

Sharaf may have become Tall's true successor, but he did not possess the charisma and forceful character of Wasfi al-Tall. Unfortunately for Husayn and Jordan, Sharaf died from a heart attack when he was 41, during his first term of office as Prime Minister.

The life of Wasfi al-Tall is, in many respects, the story of the evolution of the Trans-Jordanian political elite – the East Bank politicians, soldiers and bureaucrats who, with the King, form the backbone of Hashimite Jordan. In weathering Jordan's troubles from the challenges of Nasserism, Palestinian nationalism or Islamic fundamentalism, more credit is due to this political elite than is generally given. The portrayal of Jordan's struggle for survival as that of a lonely but 'plucky little king' propped up by foreign aid is way off the mark, primarily because it ignores the role of the East Bank elite – the Talls, Rifa'is, Majalis, 'Ajlunis, Habashnas, Badrans, Tarawnas, Khasawnas and many more.

A combination of three main factors can explain Hashimite Jordan's longevity: the quality of leadership, political astuteness and acumen of the Hashimite kings, 'Abdallah and Husayn; the cohesion of the East Bank elite and its determination to protect and preserve its political patrimony; and the constant interest of world and regional powers in maintaining the political status quo in Jordan. Situated at the geopolitical heart of the Fertile Crescent, a buffer between Israel and Iraq and at the core of the Arab–Israeli conflict, the destabilization of Jordan could pave the way for regional havoc.

Jordan is an artificial creation, but not any more so than the other states of the Fertile Crescent. Just as a sense of Iraqi, Syrian or Palestinian identity has developed over the last 70 years, so has the Jordanian entity and identity. Generations of East Bankers have evolved a conviction that Jordan is their political birthright and patrimony. They have no other. Nor do they have any intention of resigning themselves to subordination to Damascus, Baghdad, the Palestinians or Israel.

Jordan was born partly from the British need for compromise over Palestine. Jordan's fate has consequently been linked to that of Palestine, and the emergence of a Jordanian sense of collective territorial identity is also, in some ways, a product of the Jordanian–Palestinian relationship and confrontation. The conflict with the Palestinians in the 1960s and early 1970s was not only a battle for political supremacy, but also a formative experience which accelerated the development of a distinctive group identity for Jordanians and Palestinians alike. It widened the divide between the communities and endowed both Palestinians and Jordanians with an added sense of national consciousness, embodied and nurtured by the likes of Wasfi al-Tall on the one hand and the PLO leadership on the other.

Tall's career reached its climax through the conduct of this struggle. His own political character was moulded in this ferocious contest. Yet, at the same time, he set the pace and shaped the contours of confrontation. He set an example for others to follow and to his peers, including the King, radiated an aura of confidence, reassurance and determination to preserve their own state.

Jordan as Uriel Dann has shown is not the King's one-man show.[14] Though Tall was perhaps the most impressive of the East Bank stalwarts of the Jordanian entity, he was neither the first nor the last. In the early 1950s, in the aftermath of King 'Abdallah's assassination, the future of Jordan as an independent entity was shrouded in uncertainty. Iraq sought to take advantage of the situation and bring Jordan under its influence. Even though Iraq was then still a Hashimite monarchy, its unionist endeavours were rebuffed by the Jordanian political elite. They wanted to preserve their political independence, even in the absence of an authoritative King.[15]

During the Second World War a new generation of educated and politically active young men had matured in the towns of the East Bank. They, according to Mary Wilson, had begun to challenge 'Abdallah's patriarchal ways and his continued reliance on Great Britain.[16] This is only partly true for many of this new generation – like Hazza' al-Majali and Wasfi al-Tall – became pillars of the existing order. Moreover, it is precisely because so many of that and subsequent generations have become ardent supporters of the Jordanian entity and the political status quo that expectations for the demise of the anachronistic Jordanian monarchy have not been fulfilled. In addition, Tall and his peers were acutely aware of the need to impart to future generations a distinctive sense of Jordanian pride and patriotism.[17]

The emergence of Jordanian and Palestinian territorial identity is not just a result of the struggle between the two, but is also due to major trends that have swept the Arab world in general. The most important of these, in this context, has been the eclipse of pan-Arabism.

The defeat inflicted by Israel on Egypt, Jordan and Syria in the Six Day War was not only a military débâcle but an ideological setback from which the messianic and revolutionary pan-Arabism of the Nasserite or Ba´thi strands never fully recovered. The 'end of pan-Arabism'[18] paved the way for a new era in the Arab world. The dichotomy between 'progressive' and 'reactionary' regimes became increasingly irrelevant. Ideology lost its importance as a factor in inter-Arab relations as well as in relations between Arab states and the superpowers, and even in Arab attitudes towards Israel.

In some respects, these developments bode well for Jordan. The fading of pan-Arab ideological fervour brought to an end the 'Arab Cold War'.[19] The end of pan-Arabism enhanced the legitimacy of the nascent states of the Arab Middle East, including Jordan, The Hashimite regime consequently enjoyed greater room for manoeuvre in the generally more flexible network of inter-Arab relations.

At the same time, however, Jordan's initiative in the Palestinian question was steadily curtailed. The decline of pan-Arabism and the entrenchment of the nation-state legitimized the idea of Palestinian particularism and the Palestinian demand for independent statehood. Coupled with the Palestinian national resurgence that came in the wake of the 1967 defeat, these developments continued to pose a potential challenge, in the long run, to Jordan's domestic stability and to the legitimacy of the Hashimite Kingdom. It is these contradictory processes that are at the heart of Husayn's Palestinian dilemma. In order to maintain the inter-Arab legitimacy of the Jordanian state, in the short term Husayn has little choice but to acquiesce in an Arab consensus on the Palestinian question that is potentially detrimental in the longer term to his own stability and legitimacy.

Jordan's rearguard battle against the Palestinian national revival suffered a severe setback in 1967. The process of 'Jordanization' was halted after Jordan's loss of control over the West Bank while the 're-Palestinization' of the West Bankers (and other Palestinian communities) was accelerated. Jordan's efforts to stem the tide continued unabated, but with steadily diminishing returns. The PLO gradually established itself in the occupied territories and in the Arab and international arenas as the 'sole legitimate representative of the Palestinian people'. The outbreak of the *intifadah* in December 1987 finally turned the tables on Husayn. It rapidly developed into the PLO's major political asset and the scales in the Jordanian–Palestinian equation were now tipped heavily against Jordan.

Husayn's decision in July 1988 to disengage from the West Bank was an admission of Jordan's weakness. Husayn conceded that Jordan could not assimilate or subdue the Palestinians. However, for historical, demographic, geographical and strategic reasons, Jordan could not simply disengage from the Palestinian question but now strove for a more equitable partnership with the Palestinians, while placing special emphasis on the fact that the East Bank was not part of the Palestinian patrimony, even if some Palestinians and Israelis thought so. The new slogan was 'Jordan is Jordan and Palestine is Palestine'. It was no longer 'Jordan is Palestine and Palestine is Jordan' of the 1960s. If Jordan could not assimilate Palestine, it had to prevent Palestine from absorbing Jordan. Jordan, therefore, had to disengage to ensure the preservation of the East Bank for the East Bankers.

Relations with the PLO improved after the disengagement. The Palestinian challenge, although never entirely absent, became more subtle and less immediate. A more salient and pressing domestic challenge now comes from elsewhere: severe economic crisis has provided a receptive environment for Islamic militancy.

Following the rise and fall of oil power numerous Arab societies, including Jordan, have gone through a period of prosperity followed since the mid-1980s by a period of economic recession. The imbalance between a rapid growth of population and a sluggish or even negative economic growth has thrust Jordan into its worst economic recession. With the decline of pan-Arabism and the collapse of Communism, the Arab left has precious little to offer by way of ideology and political guidance in a time of crisis. Islamic fundamentalism has superseded pan-Arabism as the major challenge to stability in the Middle East and it is Islamism which today claims to provide the panacea for all the social and political ills that Nasserism sought to eradicate a generation ago.

The Trans-Jordanian political elite, therefore, faces a novel challenge to its basically secular, pragmatic and non-ideological worldview. Islamic radicals propose an authentic alternative to the nature of the Jordanian state as an essentially Westernized entity. Against a background of severe unemployment, socio-economic dislocation and hardship, Islamic radicals have gained much public support. Indeed, the mantle of leading the opposition in the Kingdom has shifted from Palestinian nationalists to Islamic fundamentalists.

However, as always, as long as the determination of the King, the cohesion of the East Bank elite and external support all remain intact it will be difficult to overturn the status quo. Foreign states continue to bail out Jordan's faltering economy on a regular basis; Husayn is as astute as ever; but without the loyalty, solidarity and determination of the Talls, Majalis and ´Ajlunis of the East Bank – whether as politicians, soldiers or bureaucrats – foreign aid and a wise king will not sufffice.

# Notes

INTRODUCTION, pp. 1–8

1. Y. Nevo, ´Abdallah and the Palestinian Arabs (Tel Aviv: Shiloah Center, Tel Aviv University Students' Union Publishing House, 1975), p. 11 (Hebrew).
2. These characteristics are based on the analysis of Uriel Dann, 'Regime and Opposition in Jordan Since 1949', in M. Milson (ed.), Society and Political Structure in the Arab World (New York: Humanities Press, 1973), p. 146.
3. Reliable data on the Palestinian population in Jordan is hard to obtain. Estimates range from fewer than 40 per cent, to over 60 per cent. Jordanian spokesmen have at times suggested that the Palestinians are a majority, but on other occasions have chosen to refute such claims, made by both PLO and Israeli sources. For a discussion of this politically charged subject, see Valerie Yorke, 'Jordan is not Palestine: The Demographic Factor', Middle East International, 16 April 1988. Due to the influx of Palestinians from Kuwait in the aftermath of Iraq's invasion of that country, Palestinians are now probably a majority on the East Bank.
4. P.A. Jureidini and R.D. McLaurin, Jordan: The Impact of Social Change on the Role of the Tribes (New York: Praeger, The Washington Papers/108, 1984), p. 15.
5. P. Gubser, Jordan: Crossroads of Middle Eastern Events (Boulder: Westview, 1983), p. 25.
6. Dann, 'Regime and Opposition', p. 149.
7. Jureidini and McLaurin, pp. 36–58, 61–8.
8. A.R. Day, East Bank/West Bank: Jordan and the Prospects for Peace (New York: Council on Foreign Relations, 1986), p. 80.
9. In a major survey published in 1976 more than one-third of the responding heads of Bedouin households were in the military. Gubser, p. 29.
10. For an illuminating discussion of these changes see Linda L. Layne, 'Tribesmen as Citizens: "Primordial Ties" and Democracy in Rural Jordan', in Linda L. Layne (ed.), Elections in the Middle East: Implications of Recent Trends (Boulder: Westview, 1987), pp. 113–51.
11. Day, p. 81.
12. Dann, 'Regime and Opposition', pp. 150–51.
13. Kamel Abu Jaber, 'The Legislature of the Hashemite Kingdom of Jordan: A Study in Political Development', Muslim World, 59 (1969), p. 244.
14. This measure excluded the Muslim Brotherhood, which was officially designated as a social organization and not as a party and with whom the regime had an established modus vivendi, founded, to a large degree, on their shared antipathy for ´Abd al-Nasir and his ideology. For the 'Nabulsi interlude' and the crisis of April 1957 see Uriel Dann, King Hussein and the Challenge of Arab Radicalism: Jordan, 1955–1967 (New York: Oxford University Press, 1989), pp. 39–67.

CHAPTER 1, pp. 9–13

1. Sulayman Musa, 'Wasfi al-Tall: sura shakhsiyya', in Wasfi al-Tall, Kitabat fi al-qadaya al-´Arabiyya (Amman: Dar al-liwa lil-sahafa wal-nashr, 1980), p. 18.
2. Munib al-Madi and Sulayman Musa, Ta'rikh al-Urdunn fi al-qarn al-ishrin (Amman,

1959), p. 10.
3. Sulayman Musa, *A'lam min al-Urdunn: safahat min ta'rikh al-'Arab al-hadith* (Amman: Matabi' dar al-sha'b, 1986), pp. 97–8.
4. Ibid., p. 120.
5. Ibid., pp. 99–100; Mamduh Hawamida, *Wasfi al-Tall bayn al-madi wal-hadir* (Amman, 1971), pp. 24–5.
6. Sulayman Musa, *A'lam min al-Urdunn*, p. 99.
7. Y. Arnon-Ohanna, *The Internal Struggle within the Palestinian Movement, 1929–1939* (Tel Aviv: Yariv Hadar, Shiloah Center for Middle Eastern and African Studies, 1981), pp. 265–6 (Hebrew).
8. Sulayman Musa, *A'lam min al-Urdunn*, p. 99.
9. A. Hourani, *Arabic Thought in the Liberal Age, 1798–1939* (Cambridge: Cambridge University Press, 1984), p. 309.
10. Sulayman Musa, *A'lam min al-Urdunn*, p. 102.
11. Ibid., pp. 101, 161.
12. Ibid., pp. 163–5.
13. Ibid., p. 161.
14. Ibid., p. 102.
15. Ibid., p. 103.
16. James Lunt, *Hussein of Jordan: A Political Biography* (London: Macmillan, 1989), p. 71.
17. Sulayman Musa, 'Sura shakhsiyya', p. 25.
18. Sulayman Musa, *A'lam min al-Urdunn*, pp. 104–5; Lunt, op. cit.

## CHAPTER 2, pp. 14–22

1. In a document by the 'Arab Offices', probably drawn up at the end of 1945, a list of the staff of the offices in Jerusalem, London and Washington is provided. Tall is not mentioned ('The Arab Offices', *Israel State Archives*, Section 65, File 3916, Container P/413). However, his name does appear in a list of the staff of the Jerusalem office for 1 March 1946, when that office was directed by Ahmad al-Shuqayri, Tall's future enemy (Y. Shimoni, *The Arabs of Palestine* (Tel Aviv: Am Oved, 1947), p. 325 (Hebrew)).
2. G. Furlonge, *Palestine is My Country: The Story of Musa Alami* (London: John Murray, 1969), pp. 136–9; Shimoni, op. cit.; 'The Arab Offices' (note 1 above).
3. 'Taqrir 'an a'mal al-maktab al-'arabi fi London mundhu ta'sisihi fi ayyar sana 1945 lighaya nisan 1947', *Israel State Archives*, Section 65, File 3916, Container P/413.
4. Sulayman Musa, *A'lam min al-Urdunn*, pp. 106–7.
5. Furlonge, pp. 150–51.
6. Sulayman Musa, *A'lam min al-Urdunn*, p. 107.
7. Shimoni, p. 325; *Palestine Post*, 16 April 1947; *Palestine Press Review*, 31 Aug. 1947.
8. Public Record Office (London), FO 371, Eastern Dept., General 1947, E11764/11763/65.
9. Nevo, p. 77.
10. 'Arif al-'Arif, *Al-Nakba*, Part I (Beirut: Al-maktaba al-'asriyya, n.d.), p. 38.
11. 'Al-qissa al-kamila lijaysh al-inqadh al-mu'allaf litahrir Filastin', Part II, *Filastin*, 17 Sept. 1955.
12. Sulayman Musa, *A'lam min al-Urdunn*, p. 109.
13. Husni Za'im even had ideas for more than just an armistice agreement with Israel. See Itamar Rabinovich, *The Road Not Taken: Early Arab–Israeli Negotiations* (New York: Oxford University Press, 1991), pp. 65–110.
14. Sulayman Musa, *A'lam min al-Urdunn*, pp. 109–10 and 'Sura shakhsiyya', pp. 28–9.
15. L. Collins and D. Lapierre, *O Jerusalem!* (New York: Simon and Schuster, 1972), pp. 156, 294.
16. Ibid., p. 156; Walid Khalidi, 'The Arab Perspective', in Wm Roger Louis and Robert

W. Stookey (eds.), *The End of the Palestine Mandate* (London: I.B. Tauris, 1986), pp. 104–36.

17. Collins and Lapierre, pp. 294–5.
18. Sulayman Musa, *A'lam min al-Urdunn*, p. 108.
19. 'Arif al-'Arif, Part II, pp. 458–64; Muhammad Fa'iz al-Qasri, *Harb Filastin*, Part II (Damascus, 1962), pp. 239–61.
20. Sulayman Musa, *A'lam min al-Urdunn*, p. 111, quoting from a series of articles written by Wasfi al-Tall in the weekly *al-Hadaf*, from 17 Feb.–12 May 1950.
21. Tall, *Kitabat fi al-qadaya al-'Arabiyya*, p. 264; Tall's account conflicts with Qawuqji's, who maintains that *Jaysh al-Inqadh* had 'put up a magnificent show' at Tirat Zvi. See Fawzi al-Qawuqji, 'Memoirs 1948', Part I, *Journal of Palestine Studies* (Summer, 1972), p. 36.
22. 'Arif al-'Arif, Part II, pp. 459–60.
23. Y. Slutzky (ed.), *The History of the Haganah*, Vol. III, *From Struggle to War*, Part II (Tel Aviv: Am Oved, 1973), p. 1266 (Hebrew).
24. Sulayman Musa, *A'lam min al-Urdunn*, pp. 111–12.
25. Ibid.
26. 'Arif al-'Arif, Part II, p. 460, quoting from the above-mentioned series of articles by Tall in *al-Hadaf*.
27. Wasfi al-Tall, 'Asbab hazimat al-'Arab al-'askariyya fi Filastin', Parts II and III, *Filastin*, 27, 28 Sept. 1955.
28. Jordan's understandings with the British and the Jews in Palestine, before and during the 1948 war have been dealt with extensively in a number of recent works: Uri Bar-Joseph, *The Best of Enemies: Israel and Transjordan in the War of 1948* (London: Frank Cass, 1987); Avi Shlaim, *Collusion Across the Jordan: King Abdullah, the Zionist Movement and the Partition of Palestine* (Oxford: Clarendon, 1988); Mary Wilson, *King Abdullah, Britain and the Making of Jordan* (Cambridge: Cambridge University Press, 1987).
29. Tall, 'Asbab hazimat al-'Arab', Part III; Hawamida, pp. 63–7.
30. On the pervasiveness of such plot theories see, for example, Hisham Sharabi, *Nationalism and Revolution in the Arab World* (Princeton: Van Nostrand, 1966), p. 101.

## CHAPTER 3, pp. 23–35

1. Hawamida, pp. 61–2.
2. S. Mishal, *The Conflict between the West and East Banks during the Period of Jordanian Rule and its Impact on the Patterns of Government and Adminstration in the West Bank, 1949–1967* (unpublished Ph.D. thesis, submitted to the Senate of the Hebrew University, Jerusalem, 1974), p. 138 (Hebrew).
3. Furlonge, p. 87.
4. A. Cohen, 'Political Parties in the West Bank under the Hashimite Regime', in M. Ma'oz (ed.), *Palestinian Arab Politics* (Jerusalem: Jerusalem Academic Press, 1975), p. 45.
5. Sulayman Musa, *A'lam min al-Urdunn*, pp. 112, 115.
6. Wasfi al-Tall, *Kitabat fi al-qadaya al-'Arabiyya*, pp. 390–401.
7. Sulayman Musa, 'Sura shakhsiyya', pp. 34–5.
8. Dann, 'Regime and Opposition', pp. 159–60, and *King Hussein and the Challenge of Arab Radicalism*, pp. 21–30.
9. *Al-jarida al-rasmiyya lil-Mamlaka al-Urdunniyya al-Hashimiyya*, 1955, p. 1073.
10. *Al-Urdunn 1962, Ma'lumat rasmiyya 'an al-Mamlaka al-Urdunniyya al-Hashimiyya* (Amman: al-Mudiriyya al-'ama lil-matbu'at wal-nashr, April 1963), p. 58.
11. Dann, 'Regime and Opposition', p. 159.
12. Ibid., pp. 159–60.
13. Ibid., p. 160.

14. Sulayman Musa, *A 'lam min al-Urdunn*, pp. 116–17.
15. Ibid., p. 117.
16. Ibid., p. 115.
17. Tall, *Kitabat fi al-qadaya al-'Arabiyya*, pp. 410–11.
18. Ibid., pp. 404–5.
19. Sulayman Musa, 'Sura shakhsiyya', pp. 37–8.
20. Sulayman Musa, *A 'lam min al-Urdunn*, p. 119.
21. G. Harris, *Jordan, Its People, Its Society, Its Culture* (New Haven, CT: HRAF Press, 1958), pp. 99–100.
22. Radio Amman, 17 Aug. 1959, 1 Nov. 1960.
23. Y. Oron (ed.), *Middle East Record (MER) 1960* (London: Weidenfeld and Nicolson, n.d.), pp. 126–7.
24. Ibid., pp. 148, 150.
25. Ibid., pp. 129–30.
26. Ibid., p. 131.
27. Sulayman Musa, *A 'lam min al-Urdunn*, p. 121.
28. Radio Cairo, *Sawt al-'Arab*, 31 Aug., 3 Sept. 1960.
29. Radio Amman, 1, 3 Sept. 1960.
30. *MER 1960*, p. 158.
31. Radio Amman, 21, 23 Sept. 1959.
32. *MER 1960*, p. 159.
33. Radio Amman, 21 Dec. 1959.
34. *MER 1960*, pp. 159–60.
35. Radio Baghdad, 19 Dec. 1960.
36. Y. Oron (ed.), *Middle East Record (MER) 1961* (Jerusalem: Israel Program for Scientific Translations, n.d.), pp. 155–6.
37. *MER 1961*, p. 138; *al-Jarida*, 19 Jan. 1962.
38. *MER 1961*, pp. 398–9.
39. *Al-Hayat*, 10 Jan. 1962.
40. Radio Amman, 21 May 1962; *Filastin*, 22 May 1962.
41. *Al-Jarida*, 30 May 1962.
42. Among the enemies of Jordan and of Tall there were even some who alleged that he himself was a member of the party. See, for example, Ribhi Jum'a Halum, *Ha'ula'i a'da' al-taharrur fi al-Urdunn* (n.p., n.d.), p. 62. No confirmation of this can be found in more reliable sources. However, it is possible that Tall was a supporter of the party at one time or another. During the Baghdad Pact crisis Tall and this party shared similar views and people associated with the party were in contact with him. But he strongly denied that he himself was a member of the party. See Sulayman Musa, *A 'lam min al-Urdunn*, p. 117.
43. M. Suleiman, *Political Parties in Lebanon* (Ithaca: Cornell University Press, 1967), pp. 99, 116–19.

## CHAPTER 4, pp. 36–69

1. *Al-Difa'*, 28 Jan. 1962.
2. C. Bailey, 'Cabinet Formation in Jordan 1950–1970', *New Outlook* (Nov. 1970), p. 18.
3. Peter Snow, *Hussein* (London: Barrie and Jenkins, 1972), p. 140, 149–50, Lunt, p. 71.
4. *Al-Difa'*, 28 Jan. 1962.
5. Sulayman Musa, *A 'lam min al-Urdunn*, p. 122.
6. Radio Amman, 27 Jan. 1962; *Filastin*, 28 Jan. 1962.
7. Radio Amman, 28 Jan. 1962; *al-Difa'*, 29 Jan. 1962.
8. *Al-Difa'*, 23 Feb. 1962.
9. *Al-Difa'*, 28 Feb. 1962.
10. Wasfi al-Tall, 'Problems of the Arab World', *India Quarterly*, 3 (4) (1947), p. 432.
11. *Filastin*, 22 May 1962.

12. *Filastin*, 21 Oct. 1962.
13. Radio Amman, 6 Feb. 1962; *al-Manar*, 7 Feb. 1962.
14. Abu Jaber, p. 240.
15. Ibid., *MER 1961*, p. 358.
16. Radio Amman, 26 Sept. 1962.
17. *Filastin*, 21 Oct., 8 Nov. 1962.
18. Tall at news conference on 7 Nov. 1962 (*Filastin*, 8 Nov. 1962).
19. Radio Cairo, 26 Oct. 1962.
20. *Filastin*, 8 Nov. 1962.
21. *Filastin*, 22 Nov. 1962.
22. *Filastin*, 21 Oct. 1962.
23. *Al-Difa'*, 23 Nov. 1962.
24. Abu Jaber, op. cit.
25. Based on files of the Jordanian Security Services cited in Eliezer Be'eri, *The Palestinians Under Jordanian Rule* (Jerusalem: Truman Institute, Hebrew University, 1978), pp. 48, 61–2 (Hebrew); *The Economist*, 8 Dec. 1962.
26. *Mideast Mirror*, 1 Dec. 1962.
27. N. Aruri, *Jordan: A Study in Political Development, 1921–1965* (Ann Arbor: Xerox University Microfilms, 1974), p. 226.
28. *Al-Difa'*, 26 Nov. 1962.
29. *Filastin*, 30 Nov. 1962; *al-Urdunn 1962*, pp. 361–2.
30. *Al-Difa'*, 26, 27 Nov. 1962; *Filastin*, 27 Nov. 1962.
31. Radio Amman, 1 Dec. 1962.
32. Laurie Brand, 'Nasir's Egypt and the Reemergence of the Palestinian National Movement', *Journal of Palestine Studies*, 66 (Winter, 1988), pp. 29–45; Issa al-Shuaibi, 'The Development of Palestinian Entity-Consciousness', Part I, *Journal of Palestine Studies*, 33 (Autumn, 1979), pp. 67–84.
33. Y. Harkabi (ed.), *The Arabs and Israel (3–4), The Resolutions of the Palestine National Councils* (Tel Aviv: Am Oved), 1975, pp. 17–18 (Hebrew).
34. *Filastin*, 22 May 1962.
35. *Al-Jihad*, 26 April 1962.
36. Husayn to refugee delegations, *al-Manar*, 26 April 1962, and in speech commemorating Jordan's independence day, *Filastin*, 27 May 1962.
37. *Mideast Mirror*, 5 May 1962.
38. Ibid.
39. Be'eri, pp. 17, 47–8; *al-Sayyad*, 26 April 1962.
40. *Mideast Mirror*, 2 June 1962.
41. Al-Mamlaka al-Urdunniyya al-Hashimiyya, Wizarat al-Kharijiyya, *Al-Urdunn wal-qadiyya al-Filastiniyya wal-'alaqat al-'Arabiyya* (n.p., n.d.).
42. *Filastin*, 3 July 1962.
43. *Al-Urdunn wal-qadiyya al-Filastiniyya*, pp. 29–37; Tall, *Kitabat fi al-qadaya al-'Arabiyya*, pp. 114–20.
44. Harkabi, pp. 18–20; *Sawt al-'Uruba*, 4 Aug. 1962; *Akhbar al-Yawm*, 8 Sept. 1962.
45. *Al-Hawadith*, 1 June 1962.
46. Radio Amman, 31 Dec. 1962.
47. Radio Amman, 12 Feb. 1963.
48. Lunt, p. 72.
49. M. Kerr, *The Arab Cold War: Gamal Abd al-Nasir and his Rivals, 1958–1970* 3rd edn (New York: Oxford University Press, 1977), pp. 23, 27; *MER 1961*, pp. 145–7.
50. *Al-Urdunn wal-qadiyya al-Filastiniyya*, pp. 10–11, 24–5.
51. Radio Amman, 19 April 1962; *Filastin*, 3 July 1962.
52. Radio Amman, 18 Aug. 1962; *Filastin*, 19 Aug. 1962.
53. Radio Cairo, 19 Aug. 1962.
54. *Filastin*, 19 Aug. 1962.
55. *Filastin*, 30 Aug. 1962.

56. Radio Amman, 2 Sept. 1962.
57. Ibid.
58. Radio Amman, 3 Sept. 1962.
59. *Filastin*, 21 Oct. 1962.
60. Ibid.
61. Radio Amman, 3 Nov. 1962.
62. Radio Cairo, Radio Amman, 12 Nov. 1962; Middle East News Agency (MENA), 13 Nov. 1962.
63. Lunt, p. 72.
64. Radio Amman, 2 Dec. 1962.
65. *Filastin*, 28 Dec. 1962.
66. *Al-Difa'*, 28 Dec. 1962; *Filastin*, 29 Dec. 1962.
67. *Filastin*, 4 Jan. 1963.
68. S. Mishal, *West Bank/East Bank; The Palestinians in Jordan 1949–1967* (New Haven, CT: Yale University Press, 1978), pp. 34–5.
69. Sulayman Musa, *A 'lam min al-Urdunn*, p. 128.
70. Ibid.
71. Ibid.
72. *Filastin*, 4 Jan. 1963.
73. *Filastin*, 10 Jan. 1963.
74. Radio Cairo, 16 Jan. 1963.
75. BBC Radio, London, 11 Jan 1963; Voice of Israel, 11 Jan. 1963.
76. *Filastin*, 13 Jan. 1963.
77. Ibid.
78. C. Bailey, *The Participation of the Palestinians in the Politics of Jordan* (Ann Arbor: Xerox University Microfilms, 1974), pp. 213–14.
79. *Filastin*, 13 Jan. 1963.
80. *Al-Manar*, 14 Jan. 1963.
81. Editorial note in the BBC's *Summary of World Broadcasts*, 9 April 1963.
82. *Filastin*, 10 March 1963.
83. See, for example, a news conference he gave on 16 March and a speech he made during a tour of army units on 25 March (*Filastin*, 17, 26 March 1963).
84. *Akhbar al-Usbu'*, 15 March 1963; BBC Radio, London, 20 March 1963; *al-Difa'*, 21 March 1963.
85. Radio Amman, 27 March 1963.
86. For example, *al-Difa'*, 1 April 1963; *al-Manar*, 2 April 1963; Radio Cairo, 17 April 1963.
87. Kerr, *The Arab Cold War*, p. 77.
88. Snow, p. 154; *Mideast Mirror*, 27 April, 4 May 1963.
89. *Al-Nahar*, 24 April 1963; *Mideast Mirror*, 27 April 1963.
90. Aruri, p. 229.
91. Radio Amman, 21 April 1963; *Mideast Mirror*, 27 April 1963.
92. Abu Jaber, p. 242.

## CHAPTER 5, pp. 70–122

1. Kerr, *The Arab Cold War*, pp. 77–95.
2. Ibid., p. 114.
3. *Al-Jarida*, 25 Dec. 1964; *al-Hawadith*, 22 Jan. 1965; *al-Nahar*, 13 Feb. 1965.
4. *Filastin*, 14 Feb. 1965.
5. *Al-Nahar*, 13, 14 Feb. 1965.
6. Sulayman Musa, 'Sura shakhsiyya', p. 74.
7. *Filastin*, 14 Feb. 1965.
8. Ibid.
9. Radio Amman, 11 March 1965; *Filastin*, 12 March 1965.

10. *Filastin*, 2 May 1965.
11. Press conference, 1 May 1965 (*Filastin*, 2 May 1965).
12. Tall in policy statement to parliament, 11 March 1965 (*Filastin*, 12 March 1965).
13. Tall at news conference on 1 May 1965 (*Filastin*, 2 May 1965).
14. M. Kerr, *Islamic Reform: The Political and Legal Theories of Muhammad ´Abduh and Rashid Rida* (Berkeley, CA: University of California Press, 1966), p. 134.
15. *Filastin*, 16 March 1965; *Akhbar al-Usbu´*, 19 March 1965.
16. Radio Amman, 9, 10 March 1965.
17. Regional News Service (Beirut), 13, 16, 23 April 1965; MENA, 22 April 1965.
18. Radio Amman, 6 April 1965.
19. PLA regiments were established from Palestinian conscripts by Egypt, Syria and Iraq. The regiments were subordinated to the general staffs of each of the host countries. See Moshe Shemesh, *The Palestinian Entity, 1959–1974; Arab Politics and the PLO* (London: Frank Cass, 1988), p. 116. For summit details see D. Dishon (ed.), *MER 1967* (Jerusalem: Israel Universities Press, 1971), p. 107.
20. Kerr, *The Arab Cold War*, p. 115; *The Economist*, 9 April 1966.
21. *Filastin*, 28 May 1965.
22. *Al-Ahrar*, 2 June 1965.
23. Tall at news conference on 6 June 1965 (*al-Difa´*, 7 June 1965).
24. *´Amman al-Masa'*, 21 Sept. 1965.
25. *Filastin*, 19 Sept., 12 Oct. 1965.
26. Hussein of Jordan, *My 'War' with Israel*, as told to Vick Vance and Pierre Lauer (New York: William Morrow, 1969), p. 39.
27. Tall at news conference, 20 Feb. 1965 (*Filastin*, 21 Feb. 1965), and in policy statement to parliament, 11 March 1965 (*Filastin*, 12 March 1965).
28. Tall at news conference, 1 May 1965 (*Filastin*, 2 May 1965).
29. *Al-Hayat*, 24 Sept. 1965. Tall made additional statements in a similar vein, for example in a speech he made in the West Bank on 12 Dec. 1965 (*al-Difa´*, 13 Dec. 1965).
30. Harkabi, p. 24.
31. Ibid., pp. 24–5.
32. E. Ya´ari, *Fath* (Tel Aviv: Levin Epstein, 1970), p. 34 (Hebrew).
33. Harkabi, p. 25.
34. Ibid., p. 62.
35. Radio Amman, 13 Feb. 1965.
36. *Filastin*, 12 March 1965.
37. Radio Amman, 20 Feb. 1965; *Filastin*, 21 Feb. 1965.
38. Regional News Service (Beirut), 22 Feb. 1965.
39. *Al-Jumhuriyya* (Egypt), 24 Feb. 1965; *Filastin*, 25 Feb. 1965.
40. *Al-Jarida*, 4 March 1965.
41. Regional News Service (Beirut), 24 Feb. 1965.
42. Radio Cairo, Voice of Palestine, 6 May 1965.
43. *Al-Difa´*, 10 May 1965.
44. Regional News Service (Beirut), 9 May 1965.
45. *Al-Jihad*, 11 May 1965.
46. Radio Amman, 13 May 1965.
47. Radio Cairo, Voice of Palestine, 15 May 1965.
48. Ibid., 31 May 1965.
49. P.J. Vatikiotis, *Politics and the Military in Jordan* (London: Frank Cass, 1967), pp. 79–81.
50. *Filastin*, 16 March 1965.
51. Radio Amman, 13 May 1965.
52. *Al-Difa´*, 22 June 1965.
53. Ibid.
54. Harkabi, pp. 58–9; *al-Usbu´ al-´Arabi*, 19 July 1965; *al-Hurriyya*, 30 Aug. 1965.
55. MENA, 15, 16 Sept. 1965; *al-Nahar*, 17 Sept. 1965.
56. *MER 1967*, p. 107.

57. Radio Cairo, 17 Sept. 1965.
58. Radio Cairo, Voice of Palestine, 30 Sept. 1965.
59. Radio Amman, 4 Oct. 1965.
60. *Mideast Mirror*, 16 Oct. 1965.
61. *'Amman al-Masa'*, 9 Nov. 1965.
62. Al-Jumhuriyya (Egypt), 27 Oct. 1965.
63. MENA, 4 Nov. 1965; *al-Manar*, 9 Nov. 1965.
64. Ahmad al-Shuqayri, *'Ala tariq al-hazima, ma' al-muluk wal-ru'asa* (Beirut: Dar al-'awda, 1972), p. 114.
65. Ibid., p. 115.
66. Ibid., pp. 115–17.
67. Radio Amman, 6 Dec. 1965.
68. Ya'ari pp. 46–7, 60–2; there were reports that Shuqayri had already contacted Fath in mid-1965, in the hope of incorporating it into the PLO (Radio Baghdad, 15 July 1965).
69. Radio Amman, 6 Dec. 1965.
70. Ibid.
71. Radio Cairo, Voice of Palestine, 8 Dec. 1965.
72. Hazim Nusayba in his meeting with Arab diplomats on 6 Dec. 1965 (Radio Amman, 6 Dec. 1965).
73. Radio Cairo, Voice of Palestine, 8 Dec. 1965.
74. Ibid.
75. Ibid.
76. Radio Cairo, Voice of Palestine, 22 Dec. 1965.
77. Radio Cairo, Voice of Palestine, 21 Feb.; Radio Amman, 1 March 1966.
78. Radio Cairo, Voice of Palestine, 2 March 1966.
79. Radio Cairo, Voice of Palestine, 8 Dec. 1965.
80. *Al-Hurriyya*, 28 March 1966.
81. Tall at news conference on 4 July 1966 (*Filastin*, 5 July 1966).
82. *Filastin* (Lebanon), 29 Dec. 1966.
83. *Al-Muharrir*, 13 April 1966.
84. *Al-Hayat*, 14, 15 April 1966.
85. *Al-Hayat*, 15 April 1966.
86. *Al-Hayat*, 14 April 1966.
87. Ibid.
88. *Al-Hawadith*, 1 July 1966; *Ruz al-Yusuf*, 4 July 1966.
89. Radio Amman, 1 March 1966.
90. Tall at news conference on 4 July 1966 (*Filastin*, 5 July 1966).
91. *Filastin*, 8 May 1966.
92. *Al-Muharrir*, 4 May 1966.
93. Radio Cairo, Voice of Palestine, 9 May 1966.
94. Harkabi, pp. 69–70.
95. Tall at news conference on 4 July 1966 (*Filastin*, 5 July 1966).
96. Tall in speech to Chamber of Deputies, 16 July 1966 (*Filastin*, 17 July 1966).
97. Radio Amman, 30 June 1966.
98. Tall at news conference on 4 July 1966 (*Filastin*, 5 July 1966).
99. Radio Cairo, Voice of Palestine, 9 June 1966.
100. Lunt, p. 79.
101. *Filastin*, 15 June 1966.
102. BBC Radio, London, 18 June 1966; Radio Amman, Voice of Palestine, 20, 21 June 1966.
103. *Al-Anwar*, 21 June 1966.
104. Radio Cairo, Voice of Palestine, 17 June 1966. The rhetorical effect of these slogans was enhanced by the rhyme between the imperative 'revolt', *thuri*, and Nuri.
105. BBC Radio, London, 19 June 1966; Shuqayri in interview with *Ruz al-Yusuf*, 4 July 1966.
106. Radio Cairo, Voice of Palestine, 25 Oct. 1966.

107. Shuqayri's father, As'ad al-Shuqayri the former Mufti of Acre, had indeed sold land to Jews in Palestine. Tall, of course, did not mention the fact that the Amir 'Abdallah had not been averse to land deals of his own with the Jews. See Y. Porath, 'The Land Problem in Mandatory Palestine', *The Jerusalem Quarterly*, 1 (Fall 1976), p. 23 and K. Stein, *The Land Question in Palestine, 1917–1939* (Chapel Hill: University of North Carolina Press, 1984), pp. 194–9, 237.
108. *Filastin*, 5 July 1966.
109. Radio Cairo, Voice of Palestine, 5 July 1966.
110. *Filastin*, 17 July 1966.
111. Radio Amman, 16 July 1966.
112. Kerr, *The Arab Cold War*, p. 114.
113. Ibid., p. 110; *MER 1967*, p. 108.
114. Radio Riyadh, 2 Feb. 1966; *Mideast Mirror*, 5 Feb. 1966.
115. *Filastin*, 1 Feb. 1966.
116. Kerr, *The Arab Cold War*, p. 121.
117. *Al-Jihad*, 15 May 1966.
118. Kerr, *The Arab Cold War*, p. 122; *MER 1967*, p. 109.
119. Regional News Service (Beirut), 30 May 1966.
120. *Filastin*, 5 July 1966.
121. Kerr, *The Arab Cold War*, p. 120. On 23 February 1966, a military coup took place in Syria, the ninth in 17 years. It was carried out by an extreme faction of the Ba'th and was aimed against the veteran leadership of the party. During the coup, the house of President Amin al-Hafiz was destroyed by artillery fire, and Michel Aflaq and Salah al-Din al-Bitar, the founders of the Ba'th, were arrested.
122. Regional News Service (Beirut), 5 May 1966.
123. Radio Cairo, 2 Sept. 1966.
124. *Filastin*, 16 Sept. 1966; *Mideast Mirror*, 24 Sept. 1966.
125. Radio Cairo, 1 Oct. 1966.
126. See, for example, Tall's news conference on 6 Aug. 1966 (*Filastin*, 7 Aug. 1966).
127. Radio Cairo, 6 Oct. 1966.
128. *Akhbar al-Usbu'*, 29 July, 27 Oct. 1966.
129. Ya'ari, pp. 25–6, 37–52; Helena Cobban, *The Palestinian Liberation Organisation: People, Power and Politics* (Cambridge: Cambridge University Press, 1984), p. 32.
130. Harkabi, p. 63.
131. Ya'ari, p. 66.
132. Ibid., p. 67.
133. Ze'ev Schiff and Eytan Haber (eds.), *Israel Security Lexicon* (Jerusalem: Zamora, Bitan, Modan, 1976), pp. 384–5 (Hebrew); Samir Mutawi, *Jordan in the 1967 War* (Cambridge: Cambridge University Press, 1987), pp. 77, 198.
134. Snow, p. 168; *The Economist*, 26 Nov. 1966; *Mideast Mirror*, 26 Nov., 3 Dec. 1966.
135. Radio Cairo, Voice of Palestine, 13 Nov. 1966.
136. Radio Damascus, 14 Nov. 1966.
137. Radio Amman, 19 Nov. 1966.
138. Tall at news conference on 21 Nov. 1966 (Radio Amman, 21 Nov. 1966).
139. *MER 1967*, p. 401.
140. Mutawi, p. 58.
141. Radio Amman, 21 Nov. 1966; *Filastin*, 22 Nov. 1966.
142. Radio Cairo, 21 Nov. 1966.
143. Radio Damascus, 7 Dec. 1966.
144. Kerr, *The Arab Cold War*, p. 117; Radio Cairo, 23 Dec. 1966.
145. Radio Cairo, Voice of Palestine, 23 Nov. 1966.
146. Radio Cairo, Voice of Palestine, Regional News Service (Beirut), 3 Dec. 1966; *The Economist*, 10 Dec. 1966.
147. Britain's ambassador to Jordan in the late 1950s, Charles Johnston, wrote of this phenomenon in reference to Samir al-Rifa'i; Charles Johnston, *The Brink of Jordan* (London: Hamish Hamilton, 1972), pp. 69–70.

148. When Tall was appointed Prime Minister in 1962 and again in 1965, he displaced Bahjat al-Talhuni. The two were known for their mutual rivalry.
149. ´Akif al-Fa'iz, the paramount Chief of the Banu Sakhr tribe, became one of the supporters of the National Gathering (al-Tajammu´ al-Watani), the opposition body led by Sulayman al-Nabulsi which was active in Jordan between 1968 and 1970 in support of the fida'i presence in the country.
150. Al-Nahar, 16 Dec. 1966.
151. Radio Amman, Filastin, 23 Dec. 1966.
152. MER 1967, p. 316.
153. Radio Amman, 7 Jan. 1967.
154. Radio Amman, 25 Jan. 1967.
155. MER 1967, pp. 65, 122–6, 128.
156. Ibid., p. 395.
157. Ibid., p. 396; see also interview with Mahmud Ya´ish, one of the owners of al-Jihad, quoted in Dahir ´Abd al-Karim, The Press and the Regime in Jordan, 1949–1967 (unpublished paper for seminar 'Trans-Jordan and Jordan', supervised by Dr U. Dann, Tel Aviv University, 1970), pp. 74–5.
158. Filastin, 26 Feb. 1967.
159. Sulayman Musa, A ´lam min al-Urdunn, pp. 176–7.
160. MER 1967, pp. 396, 406.
161. Al-Majalla, 23–29 April 1986; al-Bayan, 18 May 1986.

## CHAPTER 6, pp. 123–40

1. Author's interview with Anwar Nusayba, Jerusalem, 13 Feb. 1980; Lunt, p. 89.
2. Hussein, p. 125.
3. Sulayman Musa, A ´lam min al-Urdunn, p. 138.
4. Ibid., pp. 138–9.
5. Mutawi, p. 145.
6. Hussein, pp. 125–6.
7. E. Kamm (ed.), Husayn Goes to War, The Six Day War in the Eyes of the Jordanians (Tel Aviv: Ma´arakhot, 1974), pp. 11–13 (Hebrew).
8. Hussein, p. 126.
9. Mutawi, p. 173.
10. Kamm, p. 14.
11. Hussein, pp. 126–7.
12. Kamm, p. 27n.
13. Ibid., pp. 14–15; author's interview with former US ambassador to Jordan, Findley Burns, Jr, Washington DC, 23 Sept. 1987.
14. Mutawi, pp. 100–4, 183.
15. Findley Burns interview.
16. Ahmad al-Shuqayri, Al-nizam al-Urdunni fi qafas al-ittiham (Cairo, 1972), pp. 151–3.
17. Kamm, pp. 12–13.
18. Hussein, p. 107.
19. Snow, p. 195.
20. Hussein, pp. 127–9.
21. Mutawi, pp. 91, 129, 161.
22. MER 1967, p. 496; MER 1968, pp. 735–6; Radio Damascus, 7 Sept. 1968.
23. MER 1967, p. 404.
24. Sulayman Musa, A ´lam min al-Urdunn, pp. 139, 146.
25. Wasfi al-Tall, 'Dawr al-khulq wal-´aql fi ma´rakat al-tahrir', Durus min al-hazima (Amman, 1969); Sulayman Musa, A ´lam min al-Urdunn, pp. 142–9.
26. Sulayman Musa, A ´lam min al-Urdunn, pp. 142–4.
27. Ibid., p. 143.

28. See Aaron D. Miller, *The Arab States and the Palestine Question: Between Ideology and Self-Interest* (New York: Praeger, Washington Papers/120, 1986).
29. Harkabi, pp. 84–5.
30. Ibid., pp. 122–3.
31. Sulayman Musa, *A'lam min al-Urdunn*, pp. 143, 146, 151–2.
32. Ibid.
33. Ibid., p. 146.
34. *MER 1968*, p. 592.
35. Ibid., p. 601.
36. Snow, p. 204; *MER 1969–70*, pp. 789–91.
37. *MER 1969–70*, p. 816.
38. *Al-Hawadith*, 5 Dec. 1969.
39. *MER 1969–70*, p. 822.
40. Ibid., p. 795.
41. Ibid., p. 818.
42. Ibid., p. 793.
43. Ibid., p. 799.
44. Ibid., pp. 805–6.
45. Snow, pp. 203, 213–14; *MER 1969–70*, p. 843.
46. *The Economist*, 12 Sept. 1970; *MER 1969–70*, pp. 790, 833.
47. Snow, pp. 219–21.
48. *MER 1969–70*, p. 1150.
49. Patrick Seale, *Asad of Syria: The Struggle for the Middle East* (London: I.B. Tauris, 1988), pp. 158–60.
50. *MER 1969-70*, p. 383.
51. Lunt, p. 147.

## CHAPTER 7, pp. 141–71

1. *MER 1969–70*, p. 867.
2. Ibid., p. 881.
3. Ibid., pp. 628–9.
4. *Al-Dustur*, 8 Nov. 1970.
5. *Al-Difa'*, 3 Jan. 1971.
6. *Al-Dustur*, 5 Jan. 1971.
7. *An-Nahar Arab Report*, 11 Jan. 1971.
8. *MER 1969–70*, p. 869.
9. *Al-Dustur*, 6 April 1971.
10. *Al-Difa'*, 3 Jan. 1971.
11. *Al-Ahram*, 31 Jan. 1971.
12. *Al-Difa'*, 3 Jan. 1971.
13. Tall at news conference on 7 Nov. 1970 (*Al-Dustur*, 8 Nov. 1970).
14. Tall in a speech before the Chamber of Deputies on 2 Jan. 1971 (*Al-Difa'*, 3 Jan. 1971).
15. *Al-Hayat*, 12 Jan. 1971.
16. *Al-Ahram*, 31 Jan. 1971; *al-Nahar*, 14 April 1971.
17. *Al-Dustur*, 15 Jan. 1971.
18. *Al-Dustur* and *al-Ahram*, 29 March 1971.
19. Radio Amman, 6 April 1971; *al-Difa'*, 7 April 1971.
20. Tall in interview on Lebanese TV, quoted by Radio Amman, 6 May 1971.
21. *Al-Dustur*, 12 May 1971.
22. *The Times*, 12 April 1971.
23. Radio Amman, 2 May 1971.
24. Radio Cairo, Voice of Fath (clandestine station), Voice of Palestine, 17 May 1971; *al-Dustur*, 1 June 1971.

25. *Al-Nahar*, 6 June 1971.
26. Radio Amman, 2 June 1971.
27. *Al-Nahar*, 6 June 1971.
28. Radio Amman, 23 June 1971.
29. Radio Amman, 27, 28 June 1971.
30. Radio Cairo, Voice of Fath, 3 July 1971.
31. Harkabi, pp. 171–4.
32. *Al-Dustur*, 16 July 1971.
33. Radio Amman, 17 July 1971; *International Herald Tribune*, 19 July 1971.
34. *Al-Dustur*, 20 July 1971.
35. Radio Amman, 19 July 1971.
36. *Al-Dustur*, 20 July 1971.
37. Radio Amman, 21, 22 July 1971; *al-Ahram*, *al-Hayat*, 22 July 1971.
38. *Al-Dustur*, 20 July 1971.
39. MENA and *al-Hayat*, 19 July 1971.
40. Radio Cairo, Voice of Palestine, 9 Nov. 1971; *al-Ahram*, 10, 15 Nov. 1971.
41. *Al-Dustur*, 8 Nov. 1970.
42. Radio Algiers, Voice of al-'Asifa [Fath], 24 Jan. 1971; *al-Ahad*, 31 Jan. 1971; *al-Hawadith*, 12 Feb. 1971.
43. *Al-Anba*, 6 Jan. 1971.
44. Radio Amman, 1 Dec. 1971.
45. *Al-Hayat*, 1 Jan. 1971.
46. *MER 1969–70*, p. 814.
47. Radio Baghdad, Voice of the [PLO] Central Committee, 13 Jan 1971; *al-Ahram*, 14 Jan. 1971.
48. Syrian Arab News Agency (SANA), 27 Sept. 1971; Radio Cairo, Voice of Palestine, 17 Oct. 1971; MENA, 19 Oct. 1971.
49. *MER 1969–70*, pp. 383, 883; *al-Quds*, 3, 11 March 1971; *al-Anba*, 18 April 1971.
50. *Al-Anba*, 17 May 1971.
51. *Ma'ariv*, 2 June 1971; *Ha'aretz*, 3 June 1971.
52. *Al-Dustur* and *al-Quds*, 20 June 1971.
53. *Al-Ahram*, 28 Jan. 1972.
54. *Al-Nahar*, 1 Sept. 1971; *al-Ahram*, 8 Sept. 1971; Hawamida, pp. 74–7.
55. Sulayman Musa, 'Sura shakhsiyya', p. 65.
56. *The Jordanian National Union – The Charter* (n.p., n.d.).
57. Radio Cairo and *al-Ahram*, 10 Jan. 1971.
58. Radio Amman, 11 Jan. 1971; MENA and *al-Ahram*, 12 Jan. 1971.
59. *Al-Ahram*, 30 March 1971.
60. *Al-Nahar*, 2 June 1971.
61. A. Susser, *The Trans-Jordanian Elite, Wasfi al-Tall and the War Against the Fida'iyyun* (Shiloah Center Occasional Papers, Aug. 1974), p. 7 (Hebrew).
62. Radio Cairo, 24, 30 March 1971.
63. Radio Amman, 6 May 1971.
64. Radio Amman, 22 July 1971.
65. Radio Cairo, 23 July 1971.
66. Radio Amman, 24 July 1971.
67. *Al-Ahram*, 20 Nov. 1971.
68. *Al-Ahram*, 14 Aug. 1971.
69. *Al-Hayat*, 15 Aug. 1971.
70. *An-Nahar Arab Report*, 11 Oct. 1971.
71. *The Times*, 29 Nov. 1971.
72. *Jerusalem Post*, 29 Nov. 1971; *The Times*, 29, 30 Nov. 1971. In a book by the British journalist Alan Hart, the author contends, on the basis of conversations with Khalid al-Hasan (a member of the Fath Central Committee), that Black September's claim to have assassinated Wasfi al-Tall 'was incorrect'. Wasfi al-Tall, according to this version, was indeed hit by bullets fired by one of the Black September gunmen,

but he was actually killed by bullets fired a few seconds earlier by a Jordanian secret service agent. According to Khalid al-Hasan's 'new evidence' and 'revelations', which Hart accepts without question, Tall's assassination was 'part of a plot involving President Sadat and, probably, one or some of [Henry] Kissinger's back-door associates to prevent ´Arafat and his Fath colleagues from advancing their cause by political means after their military defeat in Jordan'. The motive for the killing according to this Hart/Hasan version was the desire of its instigators to prevent the signing of an agreement that Tall and Hasan had concluded on the day before the assassination (27 Nov. 1971). By this agreement, which Tall had negotiated without consulting Husayn since 'he knew [it] would be opposed by many around the King', Jordan would accept a renewed political presence of the PLO in Jordan. The 'essence of the bargain that was struck' between Tall and Hasan was that 'in return for a PLO commitment to pursue the liberation struggle by political means alone, Jordan would recognize the PLO as the only legitimate representative of the Palestinian people'. Moreover, according to Khalid al-Hasan, in their talks Tall had implied that he would be 'prepared to oblige King Husayn to go into exile if he opposed the agreement with the PLO' (Alan Hart, *Arafat: Terrorist or Peacemaker?* (London: Sidgwick and Jackson, 1984), pp. 339–46).

The notion that two uncoordinated conspiracies, hatched in different corners of the globe, could be carried out at precisely the same time and at precisely the same place, has the makings of an 'imaginary detective story', as Sulayman Musa puts it, but nothing more. According to Wasfi al-Tall's wife, Sa´diyya, and senior Jordanian officials who had accompanied Tall on his visit to Cairo, he had not even met with Khalid al-Hasan on 27 November (Sulayman Musa, *A 'lam min al-Urdunn*, p. 203). Even if he had, the idea that Wasfi al-Tall, of all people, would have concluded such an agreement with the PLO is unbelievable. Were such an agreement to have been considered, Tall would have been the first of those 'around the King' to have opposed it. It ran counter to everything he had stood for since his rise to prominence in the Jordanian establishment in the early days of his political career. If anything, he was more and not less intransigent than the King on matters relating to the PLO. The suggestion that he, with the support of the army, would have deposed the King for the sake of an agreement with the PLO is rather far-fetched.

73. Lunt, p. 154.
74. *Al-Ahram*, 22 Feb. 1971.
75. *Jewish Observer and Middle East Review*, 3 March 1967.
76. *New York Times*, 12 Dec. 1971.
77. *Al-Ahram*, 3 Dec. 1971.
78. Lunt, p. 153.
79. *Al-Ra'y*, 6 Dec. 1971; Voice of Fath (clandestine station), 10 Dec. 1971; Abu Iyad (Salah Khalaf), *Palestinien sans patrie: entretiens avec Eric Rouleau*, Hebrew translation by Nurit Peled (Jerusalem: Mifras, 1979), pp. 145–6.
80. Ahmad al-Shuqayri, *Al-nizam al-Urdunni fi qafas al-ittiham*, pp. 67, 90–1, 166.

CONCLUSION, pp. 172–81

1. Findley Burns interview.
2. Dann, 'Regime and Opposition', p. 146.
3. Findley Burns interview.
4. Anwar Nusayba interview.
5. Findley Burns interview.
6. Author's interview with former US ambassador to Jordan, William B. Macomber, Washington DC, 24 Sept. 1987.
7. Ibid.
8. Findley Burns interview.
9. Johnston, pp. 69–70.

10. Wasfi al-Tall, 'Haqa'iq al-ma´araka', lecture at the University of Jordan on 1 June 1970 (text in *al-Ra'y*, 2 Dec. 1971).
11. On these concepts see Bernard Lewis, *The Muslim Discovery of Europe* (New York: W.W. Norton, 1982), p. 224; David Farhi, 'Nizam-i Jedid – The Military Reforms in Egypt at the Time of Muhammad ´Ali', *Hamizrah Hehadash*, 20 (4) (1970), pp. 325–6 (Hebrew).
12. Patrick Seale, 'Abd al-Hamid Sharaf', in Patrick Seale (ed.), *The Shaping of an Arab Statesman* (London: Quartet, 1983), p. 18.
13. Ibid.
14. Dann, 'Regime and Opposition', pp. 145–81.
15. Bruce Maddy-Weitzman, 'Jordan and Iraq: Efforts at Intra-Hashimite Unity', *Middle Eastern Studies*, 26 (1) Jan. 1990), pp. 65–75.
16. Wilson, p. 165.
17. See, for example, Tall's foreword to Sulayman Musa, *Ta 'sis al-Imara al-Urduniyya, 1921–1925*, 2nd edn (Amman, 1972), pp. 9–10. This was written by Tall in May 1971, shortly before his death.
18. Fouad Ajami, 'The End of Pan-Arabism', *Foreign Affairs*, Winter, 1978–79.
19. The term was coined by Malcolm Kerr in *The Arab Cold War*.

# Bibliography

## OFFICIAL PUBLICATIONS AND ARCHIVES

Al-Ittihad al-watani al-Urdunni, *Al-Mithaq*, n.p., n.d.

*Al-Jarida al-rasmiyya lil-Mamlaka al-Urdunniyya al-Hashimiyya*, 1955, 1956, 1957, 1958, 1959.

Al-Mamlaka al-Urdunniyya al-Hashimiyya, wizarat al-kharijiyya, *Al-Urdunn wal-qadiyya al-Filastiniyya wal-´alaqat al-´Arabiyya*, n.p., n.d.

*Al-Urdunn 1962, ma´lumat rasmiyya ´an al-Mamlaka al-Urdunniyya al-Hashimiyya*, Amman: al-mudiriyya al-´ama lil-matbu´at wal-nashr, April 1963.

*Al-Urdunn, al-kitab al-sanawi 1964*, Amman: wizarat al-i´lam, al-mudiriyya al-´ama lil-matbu´at wal-nashr, October 1964.

Israel State Archives, Section 65, File 3916.

The Public Record Office (London), FO 371, Eastern Department, General, 1947.

## PRESS

Daily Newspapers (Arabic)

Dubai
*Al-Bayan*

Egypt
*Al-Ahram*
*Al-Akhbar*
*Akhbar al-Yawm*
*Al-Jumhuriyya*

Israel
*Al-Anba*
*Al-Ittihad*
*Al-Quds* (after June 1967)

Jordan
*Al-Difa´*
*Al-Dustur*
*Filastin*
*Al-Jihad*
*Al-Manar*
*Al-Quds* (before June 1967)
*Al-Ra'y*
*Sawt al-Sha´b*

Kuwait
*Al-Siyasa*
*Al-Watan*

Daily Newspapers (Arabic) (cont)
Lebanon
*Al-Ahad*
*Al-Ahrar*
*Filastin*
*Al-Hayat*
*Al-Jarida*
*Al-Muharrir*
*Al-Nahar*
*Al-Safir*
*Al-Yawm*

Syria
*Al-Ba'th*

Weeklies (Arabic)
Egypt
*Akhir Sa'a*
*Ruz al-Yusuf*

Jordan
*Akhbar al-Usbu'*
*'Amman al-Masa'*
*Al-Liwa*

Weeklies (English)
*The Economist* (London)
*Jewish Observer and Middle
East Review* (London)

Daily Newspapers (Hebrew)
*Ha'aretz*
*Ma'ariv*

Daily Newspapers (English)
*International Herald Tribune*
(Paris)
*Jerusalem Post*
*New York Times*
*Palestine Post*
*Palestine Press Review*
*The Times* (London)

Lebanon
*Al-Hawadith*
*Al-Hurriyya*
*Kull Shay*
*Al-Usbu' al-'Arabi*

Syria
*Al-Hadaf*

*Mideast Mirror* (Beirut)
*An-Nahar Arab Report*
(Beirut)

## RADIO AND TELEVISION

Material from radio and television broadcasts has been collected
from the following monitoring services:

British Broadcasting Corporation, *Summary of World Broadcasts,
The Middle East and Africa.*
Itim Mizrah Agency (Hebrew).
US Foreign Broadcast Information Service, *Daily Report, The
Middle East and North Africa.*

BIBLIOGRAPHY

INTERVIEWS

Burns Jr, Findley, Washington DC, 23 September 1987.
Macomber, William B., Washington DC, 24 September 1987.
Nusayba, Anwar, Jerusalem, 13 February 1980.


UNPUBLISHED WORKS

´Abd al-Karim, Dahir, *The Press and the Regime in Jordan, 1949–1967* (unpublished paper for seminar 'Trans-Jordan and Jordan', supervised by Dr U. Dann, Tel Aviv University, 1970 (Hebrew)).
Mishal, Shaul, *The Conflict between the West and East Banks during the Period of Jordanian Rule and its Impact on the Patterns of Government and Administration in the West Bank, 1949–1967* (unpublished Ph.D. thesis, submitted to the Senate of the Hebrew University, Jerusalem, 1974 (Hebrew)).


BOOKS

Abu Iyad (Salah Khalaf), *Palestinien sans patrie: entretiens avec Eric Rouleau*, Hebrew translation by Nurit Peled (Jerusalem: Mifras, 1979).
Al-´Arif, ´Arif, *Al-Nakba* (Beirut: Al-Maktaba al-´asriyya, n.d.).
Arnon-Ohanna, Yuval, *The Internal Struggle within the Palestinian Movement 1929–1939* (Tel Aviv: Yariv Hadar, Shiloah Center for Middle Eastern and African Studies, 1981 (Hebrew)).
Aruri, Naseer, *Jordan: A Study in Political Development, 1921–1965* (Ann Arbor: Xerox University Microfilms, 1974).
Bailey, Clinton, *(The Participation of the Palestinians in the Politics of Jordan* (Ann Arbor: Xerox University Microfilms, 1974).
—, *Jordan's Palestinian Challenge, 1948–1983: A Political History* (Boulder: Westview, 1984).
Bar-Joseph, Uri, *The Best of Enemies: Israel and Transjordan in the War of 1948* (London: Frank Cass, 1987).
Be'eri, Eliezer, *The Palestinians under Jordanian Rule* (Jerusalem: Truman Institute, Hebrew University, 1978 (Hebrew)).
Cobban, Helena, *The Palestinian Liberation Organisation: People, Power and Politics* (Cambridge: Cambridge University Press, 1984).

198

Collins, L. and D. Lapierre, *O Jerusalem!* (New York: Simon and Schuster, 1972).

Dann, Uriel, *King Hussein and the Challenge of Arab Radicalism: Jordan, 1955–1967* (New York: Oxford University Press, 1989).

Day, Arthur, *East Bank/West Bank: Jordan and the Prospects for Peace* (New York: Council on Foreign Relations, 1986).

Furlonge, Geoffrey, *Palestine is my Country: The Story of Musa Alami* (London: John Murray, 1969).

Gubser, Peter, *Jordan: Crossroads of Middle Eastern Events* (Boulder: Westview, 1983).

Halum, Ribhi Jum´a, *Ha'ula'i a´da al-taharrur fi al-Urdunn* (n.p., n.d.).

Harkabi, Yehoshafat (ed.), *The Arabs and Israel*, No. 3–4, *The Resolutions of the Palestine National Councils* (Tel Aviv: Am Oved, 1975 (Hebrew)).

Harris, George, *Jordan, Its People, Its Society, Its Culture* (New Haven CT: HRAF Press, 1958).

Hart, Alan, *Arafat, Terrorist or Peacemaker?* (London: Sidgwick and Jackson, 1984).

Hawamida, Mamduh, *Wasfi al-Tall bayn al-madi wal-hadir* (Amman, 1971).

Hourani, Albert, *Arabic Thought in the Liberal Age, 1798–1939* (Cambridge: Cambridge University Press, 1984).

Hudson, Michael, *Arab Politics: The Search for Legitimacy* (London: Yale University Press, 1977).

Hussein of Jordan, *My 'War' with Israel*, as told to Vick Vance and Pierre Lauer (New York: William Morrow, 1969).

Johnston, Charles, *The Brink of Jordan* (London: Hamish Hamilton, 1972).

Jureidini, Paul and R.D. McLaurin, *Jordan: The Impact of Social Change on the Role of the Tribes* (New York: Praeger, Washington Papers/108, 1984).

Kamm, Ephraim (ed.), *Husayn Goes to War: The Six Day War in the Eyes of the Jordanians* (Tel Aviv: Ma´arakhot, 1974 (Hebrew)).

Kanovsky, Eliahu, *The Economy of Jordan* (Tel Aviv: University Publishing Projects, 1976).

Kerr, Malcolm, *Islamic Reform: The Political and Legal Theories of Muhammad ´Abduh and Rashid Rida* (Berkeley, CA:

University of California Press, 1966).

—, *The Arab Cold War: Gamal Abd al-Nasir and His Rivals, 1958–1970*, 3rd edn (New York: Oxford University Press, 1977).

Khalil Muhammad (ed.), *The Arab States and the Arab League*, Vol. I (Beirut: Khayats, 1962).

Lewis, Bernard, *The Muslim Discovery of Europe* (New York: W.W. Norton, 1982).

Lunt, James, *Hussein of Jordan: A Political Biography* (London: Macmillan, 1989).

Al-Madi, Munib and Sulayman Musa, *Ta'rikh al-Urdunn fi al-qarn al-ishrin* (Amman, 1959).

Miller, Aaron, *The Arab States and the Palestine Question: Between Ideology and Self-Interest* (New York: Praeger, Washington Papers/120, 1986).

Mishal, Shaul, *West Bank/East Bank: The Palestinians in Jordan, 1949–1967* (New Haven, CT: Yale University Press, 1978).

Musa, Sulayman, *Ta'sis al-Imara al-Urdunniyya* (Amman, 1972).

—, *A'lam min al-Urdunn; safahat min ta'rikh al-'Arab al-hadith* (Amman: Matabi' dar al-sha'b, 1986).

Mutawi, Samir, *Jordan in the 1967 War* (Cambridge: Cambridge University Press, 1987).

Nevo, Yosef, *'Abdallah and the Palestinian Arabs* (Tel Aviv: Shiloah Center, Tel Aviv University Students' Union Publishing House, 1975 (Hebrew)).

Nusseibeh, Hazem Zaki, *The Ideas of Arab Nationalism* (Ithaca: Cornell University Press, 1956).

Plascov, Avi, *The Palestinian Refugees in Jordan, 1948–1957* (London: Frank Cass, 1981).

Al-Qasri, Muhammad Fa'iz, *Harb Filastin* (Damascus, 1962).

Rabinovich, Itamar, *The Road Not Taken: Early Arab–Israeli Negotiations* (New York: Oxford University Press, 1991).

Schiff, Ze'ev and Eytan Haber (eds.), *Israel Security Lexicon* (Jerusalem: Zamora, Bitan, Modan, 1976 (Hebrew)).

Seale, Patrick, *Asad of Syria: The Struggle for the Middle East* (London: I.B. Tauris, 1988).

Sharabi, Hisham, *Nationalism and Revolution in the Arab World* (Princeton: Van Nostrand, 1966).

Shemesh, Moshe, *The Palestinian Entity, 1959–1974: Arab Politics and the PLO* (London: Frank Cass, 1988).

Shimoni, Y., *The Arabs of Palestine* (Tel Aviv: Am Oved, 1947 (Hebrew)).

Shlaim, Avi, *Collusion Across the Jordan: King Abdullah, the Zionist Movement and the Partition of Palestine* (Oxford: Clarendon, 1988).

Al-Shuqayri, Ahmad, *'Ala tariq al-hazima, ma' al-muluk walru'asa* (Beirut: Dar al-'awda, 1972).

—, *Al-Nizam al-Urdunni fi qafas al-ittiham* (Cairo, 1972).

Slutzky, Y. (ed.), *The History of the Haganah*, Vol. III, *From Struggle to War*, Part II (Tel Aviv: Am Oved, 1973 (Hebrew)).

Snow, Peter, *Hussein* (London: Barrie and Jenkins, 1972).

Stein, Kenneth, *The Land Question in Palestine, 1917–1939* (Chapel Hill: University of North Carolina Press, 1984).

Suleiman, Michael, *Political Parties in Lebanon* (Ithaca: Cornell University Press, 1967).

Al-Tall, Wasfi, *Kitabat fi al-qadaya al-'Arabiyya* (Amman: Dar al-liwa lil-sahafa wal-nashr, 1980).

Vatikiotis, P.J., *Politics and the Military in Jordan* (London: Frank Cass, 1967).

Wilson, Mary, *King Abdullah, Britain and the Making of Jordan* (Cambridge: Cambridge University Press, 1987).

Ya'ari, Ehud, *Fath* (Tel Aviv: Levin Epstein, 1970 (Hebrew)).

ARTICLES

Abu Jaber, Kamel, 'The Legislature of the Hashemite Kingdom of Jordan: A Study in Political Development', *Muslim World*, 59 (1969).

Ajami, Fouad, 'The End of Pan-Arabism', *Foreign Affairs* (Winter, 1978–79).

Bailey, Clinton, 'Cabinet Formation in Jordan, 1950–1970', *New Outlook* (November, 1970).

Brand, Laurie, 'Nasir's Egypt and the Reemergence of the Palestinian National Movement', *Journal of Palestine Studies*, 66 (Winter, 1988).

Cohen, Amnon, 'Political Parties in the West Bank under the Hashimite Regime', in Moshe Ma'oz (ed.), *Palestinian Arab Politics* (Jerusalem: Jerusalem Academic Press, 1975).

Dann, Uriel, 'Regime and Opposition in Jordan since 1949', in

M. Milson (ed.), *Society and Political Structure in the Arab World* (New York: Humanities Press, 1973).

Farhi, David, 'Nizam-i Jedid – The Military Reforms in Egypt at the Time of Muhammad ´Ali', *Hamizrah Hehadash* 20 (3) (1970).

Khalidi, Walid, 'The Arab Perspective', in Wm Roger Louis and Robert W. Stookey (eds.), *The End of the Palestine Mandate* (London: I.B. Tauris, 1986).

Layne, Linda L., 'Tribesmen as Citizens: "Primordial Ties" and Democracy in Rural Jordan', in Linda L. Layne (ed.), *Elections in the Middle East: Implications of Recent Trends* (Boulder: Westview, 1987).

Maddy-Weitzman, Bruce, 'Jordan and Iraq: Efforts at Intra-Hashimite Unity', *Middle Eastern Studies*, 26 (1) (January, 1990).

Musa, Sulayman, 'Wasfi al-Tall; sura shakhsiyya', in Wasfi al-Tall, *Kitabat fi al-qadaya al-´Arabiyya* (Amman: Dar al-liwa lil-sahafa wal-nashr, 1980).

Porath, Yehoshua, 'The Land Problem in Mandatory Palestine', *Jerusalem Quarterly*, 1 (Fall, 1976).

Al-Qawuqji, Fauzi, 'Memoirs 1948', Part I, *Journal of Palestine Studies*, 4 (Summer, 1972).

'Al-qissa al-kamila lijaysh al-inqadh al-mu'allaf litahrir Filastin', Part II, *Filastin*, 17 September 1955.

Seale Patrick, 'Abd al-Hamid Sharaf', in Patrick Seale (ed.), *The Shaping of an Arab Statesman* (London: Quartet, 1983).

Al-Shuaibi, Issa, 'The Development of Palestinian Entity-Consciousness', Part I, *Journal of Palestine Studies*, 33 (Autumn, 1979).

Susser, Asher, *The Trans-Jordanian Elite, Wasfi al-Tall and the War Against the Fida'iyyun* (Shiloah Center Occasional Papers, August 1974 (Hebrew)).

Al-Tall (Tell), Wasfi, 'Problems of the Arab World', *India Quarterly*, 3 (4) (1947).

—, 'Asbab hazimat al-´Arab al-´askariyya fi Filastin', Parts II and III, *Filastin*, 27, 28 September 1955.

—, 'Dawr al-khulq wal-´aql fi ma´rakat al-tahrir,' *Durus min al-hazima* (Amman, 1969).

—, 'Haqa'iq al-ma´raka', lecture at the University of Jordan on

1 June 1970 (text in *al-Ra'y*, 2 December 1971).
Yorke, Valerie, 'Jordan is not Palestine: The Demographic Factor', *Middle East International*, 16 April 1988.

YEARBOOKS

Dishon, Daniel (ed.), *Middle East Record, 1967* (Jerusalem: Israel Universities Press, 1971).
—, *Middle East Record, 1968* (Jerusalem: Israel Universities Press, 1973).
—, *Middle East Record, 1969–70* (Jerusalem: Israel Universities Press, 1977).
Oron, Yitzhak (ed.), *Middle East Record, 1960* (London: Weidenfeld and Nicolson, n.d.).
—, *Middle East Record, 1961* (Jerusalem: Israel Program for Scientific Translations, n.d.).

# Index

ʿAbbasid Caliphate, 32
ʿAbd al-Hadi, Naʿim, 75, 76
ʿAbd al-Karim, Dahir, 191
ʿAbdallah, Amir and King, 1, 3, 9, 15, 23,
   67, 116, 125, 177, 178, 190
ʿAbdallah bin Husayn, 41, 75
al-ʿAbdallah, Radi, 118, 129
ʿAbd al-Nasir, Gamal, 25, 27, 29, 31, 32, 48,
   53–7, 59, 61, 63, 64, 66–8, 70, 71, 73, 88,
   98, 104–7, 109, 115, 120, 124–6, 141, 169,
   172, 175, 182
ʿAbduh, Yusuf, 62
Abu al-Huda, Tawfiq, 12, 176
Abu ʿAsali, Talal, 108
Abu ʿAwda, ʿAdnan, 155, 157, 163
Abu Dis, 138
Abu Ghazala, Da'ud, 38
Abu Nuwar, ʿAli, 42
Abu Zayd, Salah, 56, 117
al-Adgham, Bahi, 147, 148, 164, 165
Aflaq, Michel, 190
*Al-Ahram*, 108, 142, 167, 169
ʿAjlun, 100, 117, 151–4, 170
al-ʿAjluni, Mazin, 138
*Akhbar al-Usbu'*, 158
al-ʿAlami, Musa, 14, 15, 23–5
Aleppo, 24
Alexandria, 14, 76, 78, 80
Algeria, 28, 106, 109
American University in Beirut (AUB),
   10–12, 38, 131
American University in Cairo, 38
ʿAmir, ʿAli, 77
Amman, 24, 26, 27, 30, 31, 33, 34, 40, 56,
   59, 75, 79, 82, 84, 85, 88, 94, 96, 101, 103,
   108, 119, 124, 126, 127, 129, 133, 134,
   136–9, 142, 144–52, 155, 156, 160, 164,
   166–8
Amman agreement, 144, 146–8, 152, 155,
   156, 166–7
*ʿAmman al-Masa*, 158
Amman protocol, 144, 152, 155
Aqaba, 33, 38, 57
Arab Club, 27
Arab Ceasefire Observer Corps, 147, 148,
   165
Arab Defence Council, 169
Arabia, 9
ʿArabkir, 9

Arab League, 14, 15, 30, 51–3, 56, 78, 80,
   88, 93, 119
Arab Legion, 3, 12, 17
Arab Liberation Front, 147
Arab Nationalism, 11, 32, 35, 38, 55, 73,
   115, 172, 178–80
Arab Nationalist Movement (*Harakat
   al-Qawmiyyin al-ʿArab*), 8, 11, 24, 25,
   27, 37, 38, 43, 46, 47, 79, 95, 96, 158
Arab Offices, 14, 15, 20, 88, 183
Arab Rebellion (Palestine), 10
Arab Summit Conferences, 70, 71, 72, 76–8,
   80, 81, 83, 87, 102–6, 120, 140
Arad, 110
ʿArafat, Yasir, 109, 134, 154, 157, 194
al-Asad, Hafiz, 139
al-Atasi, Nur-al-Din, 115
ʿAylabun, 16

Bab al-Wad, 18
al-Badr, Muhammad, 57
Baghdad, 11, 25–7, 29, 32–6, 106, 177, 185
Baghdad Pact, 25–7, 29, 106, 185
Bakr, Ibrahim, 147, 148
Bani Zaydan, 9
Baʿth Party, 2, 8, 23, 37, 42, 46, 47, 65–7,
   76, 79, 95, 96, 105–7, 109, 128, 129, 172,
   179, 190
Bedouin, 3–5, 10, 113
Beirut, 10–12, 25, 38, 56, 95, 96, 138
Ben Gurion, David, 120
al-Bina, Antun, 62
Bin Jamil, Nasir, 118, 123, 135, 136, 161
Bin Nasir, Husayn, 69, 70, 122
Bin Shakir, Zayd, 136, 138
al-Bitar, Salah al-Din, 129, 190
'Black Hand', 10
'Black September', 168, 170, 193
Bonn, 28
Bourguiba, Habib, 104
Britain, 2, 25, 28, 38, 41, 64, 178
British Army, 12–14, 25, 103
British Mandate, 1, 3, 21, 49

Cairo, 9, 15, 23, 26, 32, 38, 56, 76–8, 88, 93,
   101, 103, 107, 115, 120, 128, 133, 140,
   142–4, 146, 152, 153, 155, 166–70
Cairo agreement, 140, 143, 144, 146, 152,
   155, 166–7

Casablanca, 77, 87, 88, 104
Chamber of Deputies, 6–8, 39, 43, 45, 46,
    47, 59–63, 65, 66, 68, 69, 72, 74, 79, 81,
    83, 84, 90, 103, 117–21, 143, 144, 150,
    164, 168
Communists and Communism, 2, 8 , 33, 37,
    41, 42, 46, 47, 95, 180
'Constructive Enterprise', 23, 24

Da'ud Muhammad, 138, 141
Dajani, Kamal, 38
Dajani, Raja'i, 39
al-Dalqamuni, Fadl, 62
Damascus, 16, 108, 113–15, 129, 138, 158,
    159, 177
Damiya bridge, 16
Dann, Uriel, 178
Dead Sea, 79
Al-Difa´, 46, 121, 158
al-Dizdar, Ishaq, 62
Dudin, Mustafa, 157, 163
al-Durra, Sa´id, 10
Durrell, Lawrence, 12
Al-Dustur, 121

East Bank, 1–4, 7, 45, 62, 63, 67, 79, 82,
    84, 87, 153, 156, 160, 162, 172, 176–8,
    180, 181
Egypt, 17, 25, 26, 30, 31, 34, 42, 44, 47, 48,
    51, 54–8, 61, 62, 64, 66–8, 70, 71, 75, 76,
    90, 104–8, 110, 111, 114, 115, 117–20,
    122–8, 130, 132, 136, 137, 142, 147, 155,
    164–70, 178, 188

al-Fa´iz, Akif, 117, 191
Far´un, ´Abd al-Rahman, 42
al-Faruqi, Hamdi Taji, 42
Fath, 47, 86, 90, 100, 109, 110, 133, 134,
    143, 147, 151–3, 155, 156, 168, 170, 194
Fath, 158
Faysal, King of Iraq, 32
Faysal, King of Saudi Arabia, 104–6
Fertile Crescent, 34, 35, 177
Fida'iyyun, 90, 110, 111, 115, 116, 118, 127,
    132–67, 168, 170, 171, 173
Filastin, 47, 121
France, 51
Furlonge, Geoffrey, 24

Galilee, 16–19
Gardiner, Toni (Princess Muna), 37
Gaza, 33, 48, 57, 83, 99, 100, 115
General Intelligence, 5, 75, 94, 96, 97, 107
    108, 118, 129, 159

General Security (police), 5, 118, 129, 159
Ghuri, Emil, 49
Glubb, Sir John Bagot (Glubb Pasha),
    12, 27
Great Arab Revolt, 73, 144
'Greater Syria', 34
Guinea, 104

Habash, George, 24, 144, 146
Habashna, Ibrahim, 163
Al-Hadaf, 23, 158, 184
al-Hadidi, Sulayman, 76
al-Hafiz, Amin, 107, 108, 190
Haganah, 17
Haifa, 17, 108
Hammarskjold, Dag, 120
Hammash, ´Amir, 118
Hamuda, Yahya, 23, 133
Hart, Alan, 193, 194
Hasan, Crown Prince, 6, 73, 75, 161, 162,
    164, 165
al-Hasan, Khalid, 193, 194
Hashim, Ibrahim, 26
Hashimites, 1, 4, 7, 9, 15, 20, 21, 24, 25, 28,
    32, 33, 36, 42, 43, 50, 53, 54, 57, 73, 79,
    100–3, 119, 126, 132, 136, 139, 144, 153,
    161, 170, 172–4, 176–9
Hassuna, ´Abd al-Khaliq, 30
Hatum, Salim, 108, 129
Hawatima, Na'if, 144, 146
Al-Hayat, 25, 169
Haykal, Muhammad Hasanayn, 108, 170
Hebron, 110–12
Hijazi, ´Arafat, 23, 158
Hilmi, Ahmad ´Abd al-Hamid, 147
Hindawi, Dhuqan, 72
al-Hiyari, ´Ali, 75, 86, 87
Holy war (jihad), 131
Hourani, Albert, 11
Hulagu, 32
Husayn, King, 1–2, 6, 8, 25–8, 30–9, 41–4,
    46, 47, 49, 50, 53–9, 62–7, 69–73, 75,
    77–81, 83–5, 87, 88, 93–5, 100, 101,
    103–6, 112, 113, 115–27, 129, 130, 132,
    135–42, 149–52, 154, 157, 159–70,
    172–7, 179–81, 194
Husayn, Sharif (Amir), of Mecca, 73
Husayni camp (in Palestine), 3, 15
al-Husayni, Da'ud, 62
al-Husayni, Hajj Amin, 3, 15, 19, 49
al-Husayni, Munif, 49
al-Husayni, Musa, 23
al-Husayni, Rafiq, 35
al-Hut, Shafiq, 80

*Intifadah*, 179
Iran, 28, 29, 104
Iraq, 11, 14, 15, 17, 25, 28, 31–4, 48, 51, 56,
    65–8, 70, 76, 77, 90, 101, 102, 126, 127,
    130, 147, 168, 177, 178, 182, 188
Irbid, 3, 9, 10, 42, 62, 86, 137–9, 146, 149,
    150, 164, 166
Irshidat, Najib, 86, 87
Irshidat, Shafiq, 75, 98
Islam, 2, 11, 73, 74, 104–6, 121, 176, 177,
    180, 181
Islamic Liberation Party, 8
Israel, 3, 16–24, 28, 31, 48, 51–3, 55, 63,
    75–8, 82, 85–8, 90, 102, 109–15, 120,
    123–6, 128–35, 137, 139, 142, 145, 151,
    154–6, 160–2, 175–80
Istanbul, 9
Iyad, Abu ʿAli, 170

Jabri, Ihsan, 24
Jadid, Salah, 106
Jaffa, 17, 108
Jalazun, 112
Jarash, 147, 151–4, 170
*Al-Jarida*, 35
Jarring, Gunnar, 137
Jawad, Hashim, 34
*Jaysh al-Inqadh*, 14–19, 184
Jedda, 155, 156, 167
Jenin, 112
Jericho, 23
Jerusalem, 9, 14, 18, 23, 30, 38, 45, 47, 62,
    63, 65, 68, 79, 83, 88, 91, 92, 108, 111,
    112, 116, 119, 120, 123, 124, 138, 159
*Al-Jihad*, 121, 191
Johnson, Joseph, 50, 51, 56
Johnston, Charles, 190
Jordan River, 1, 82, 92, 159
Jordan Valley, 133, 150
Jordanian Army, 2–5, 9, 17, 27, 41, 50, 68,
    80, 83, 84, 89, 90, 95–7, 110, 113, 114,
    124, 127, 135–9, 147, 149, 151, 152, 157,
    164, 169, 172
Jordanian Bar Association, 65, 86, 98
Jordanian Communist Party, 41, 42, 46,
    47, 95
Jordanian National Security Council, 94
Jordanian National Union, 162, 163, 171
Jordanian Press Establishment, 158, 159

Kafr Manda, 16
Karak, 12, 41, 44
Karama, 133
al-Kayid, Hasan, 157

al-Kaylani, Muhammad Rasul, 108, 118,
    129, 136
al-Kaylani, Rashid ʿAli, 11
Khalaf, Hanna, 38
Khalaf, Salah, 170
Khalifa, ʿAbd al-Rahman, 74
al-Khatib, Anwar, 23
al-Khatib, Ruhi, 79
Kissinger, Henry, 194
Kuwait, 33, 34, 53, 90, 109, 140, 160, 182

Latrun, 41
al-Lawzi, Ahmad, 117, 171
Lebanon, 10, 16–18, 31, 34, 35, 56, 64, 96,
    106, 107, 121, 129, 166, 169
Libya, 140, 160, 169
London, 14, 15, 164

Madaba, 46
Maghar, 16
al-Majali, ʿAbd al-Wahhab, 38, 93, 95,
    107
al-Majali, ʿAtif, 128
al-Majali, Habis, 41, 152
al-Majali, Hazzaʿ, 26, 29–32, 41, 178
Mali, 104
*Al-Manar*, 121
Marxists, 30, 73, 102, 144, 152, 153
Mirza, Wasfi, 122
Mishmar Haemek, 18
Morocco, 104
al-Muflih, Riyad, 155, 168
al-Mufti, ʿIzz al-Din, 38
al-Mufti, Saʿid, 25, 26, 46
Muhammad, the Prophet, 73
Muhammad, ʿAbd al-Hafiz, 158
*Al-Muharrir*, 107
Mukhayba Dam, 76, 77
Musa, Sulayman, 194
Muslim Brotherhood, 74, 107, 182
al-Muʿayita, Qasim, 138

Nablus, 16, 59, 111, 112, 119, 159
al-Nabulsi, Sulayman, 8, 28, 42, 64, 76, 130,
    158, 182, 191
Najd, 9
al-Naji, Fathi, 159
Nakhla, ʿIsa, 49
Nashashibi camp (in Palestine), 3
Nasir, Musa, 31
Nasserism and Nasserists, 2, 26, 27, 32,
    34–7, 43, 45, 54–7, 63, 67, 70, 170, 177,
    179, 180
National Gathering, 158, 191

National Guard, 84
National Socialist Party, 8, 42
National Socialist Party (formerly PPS), 34, 35
National Water Carrier (Israeli), 76, 109
Na´was, ´Abdallah, 23
Nawfal, Sayyid, 88
Nazareth, 16, 17, 19
Nietzsche, 11, 12, 131
al-Nimr, ´Abd al-Halim, 28
Nusayba, Anwar, 62
Nusayba, Hazim, 23, 38, 49, 53, 62, 89–91

Operation Tariq, 124

Pakistan, 104
Palestinian Higher Arab Committee, 15, 49
Palestine Liberation Army (PLA), 70, 76, 80, 83, 87, 90, 96, 97, 111, 112, 127
Palestine Liberation Organization (PLO), 8, 70–2, 75, 76, 83–104, 109–12, 115–20, 125, 133–7, 143, 145, 147, 152, 153, 155, 156, 158, 160–2, 167, 177, 179, 180, 194
Palestine National Council, 52, 80, 84, 91, 92, 98, 99, 101, 133, 153
Palestinian National Union, 48
Palestinian Red Crescent, 156
Palestinian Refugees, 24, 49, 51, 88, 92, 112, 134, 135, 138
Parti Populaire Syrienne (PPS), 34
Popular Democratic Front for the Liberation of Palestine, 137, 144, 147
Popular Front for the Liberation of Palestine, 24, 133, 137, 144, 147
Port Sa´id, 115
Professional Gathering, 158

Qalqilya, 86
Qalya, 79
Qasim, ´Abd al-Karim, 32, 33, 48, 101
al-Qassam, ´Izz al-Din, 10
al-Qawuqji, Fawzi, 17, 184
Al-Quds, 121
Qunaytra, 16
al-Quwatli, Shukri, 16

Ra´d, In´am, 35
al-Rafi´i, Nizar, 159
Ramallah, 112
Ramtha, 128, 138
Al-Ra'y, 24, 158, 159
al-Rifa´i, Samir, 26, 27, 67–9, 165, 174, 176, 190

al-Rifa´i, Zayd, 39, 121, 123, 137, 176
al-Rimawi, Qasim, 38, 168
Riyad, ´Abd al-Mun´im, 124, 127
Rogers, William, 145
al-Rusan, Mahmud, 42

Al-Sabah, 158
Sadat, Anwar, 142, 164, 166, 169, 194
Safed, 17
Safwat, Isma´il, 15, 17
Sa´id, Ahmad, 64
al-Sa´id, Nuri, 101, 116
Al-Sa´iqa, 147
Sakhnin, 19
Salah, ´Abdallah, 151
al-Salih, ´Abd al-Qadir, 59
al-Salim, Khalil, 40
Salt, 3, 10, 12, 86, 135, 138
Samu´, 109–14, 116–18, 125, 126
Sarafand, 13
Sa´ud, King, 56
Saudi Arabia, 49, 56–8, 64, 71, 76, 77, 102, 104–6, 108, 118, 120, 155, 167
Sawt al-´Arab, 27, 32, 64
Sawt al-Sha´b, 121
Seale, Patrick, 139, 176
Senate, 6, 7, 46, 65, 79, 90, 130, 136, 171
Shakir, ´Abd al-Karim, 34
al-Shanti, Ibrahim, 158
Sharaf, ´Abd al-Hamid, 96, 121, 176
Shtura, 31, 56
al-Shuqayri, Ahmad, 23, 49, 50, 78–80, 82–96, 98–103, 109, 110, 112, 115, 126, 127, 133, 170, 183, 189, 190
al-Shuqayri, As´ad, 190
Shura, 73, 74
al-Silwani, Khalil, 62
Sinai, 57, 110, 113, 114, 120, 125
Six Day War, 23, 77, 123–8, 132, 133, 158, 161, 173, 175, 178
Soviet Union, 25, 26, 28, 54, 58, 106, 139
Straits of Tiran, 31, 125
Sudan, 104
Supreme Arab Follow-up Committee, 147, 148, 164, 165
Suwaylih, 138
Syria, 9, 15–17, 23, 24, 28, 30–2, 34, 36, 42, 54, 56, 64–8, 70, 90, 96, 100, 102, 104–11, 114, 115, 117–19, 125, 126, 128–30, 138, 139, 147, 151, 154, 168, 177, 178, 188, 190

Ta'if, 56, 105, 106
al-Talhuni, Bahjat, 36, 71, 84, 117, 136, 168, 174, 191

al-Tall, ´Abdallah, 9, 75, 171
al-Tall, Hajim, 122
al-Tall, Muraywid, 121
al-Tall, Mustafa Wahbi, 9, 10, 12
al-Tall, Sa´diyya, 24, 28, 168, 171, 194
Tanus, ´Izzat, 49
Tehran, 28
Tel Aviv, 17
Templer, General, 26
Tirat Zvi, 18, 184
Tubas, 16
Tulkarm, 112
Tunisia, 104, 147
Tuqan, Ahmad, 141
Turkey, 25, 51, 104

United Arab Command, 70, 76–8, 100, 114, 115, 119, 124, 127
United Arab Republic (UAR), 29–33, 36, 54, 66, 67, 109, 128, 142
United Nations, 14, 15, 23, 24, 31, 49–51, 53, 55, 57, 102, 114, 120, 124, 125, 137, 145
United States, 2, 38, 58, 64, 137, 139, 145
Al-Urdunn, 121

Voice of Palestine, 88, 96, 101, 103

Washington, 14
West Bank, 1, 5–7, 16, 21, 23, 26, 33, 37, 45, 46, 52, 59, 61–3, 79, 80, 82–5, 90, 101, 111, 112, 116, 118, 123–6, 128, 139, 143, 145, 153, 157, 159–63, 173, 179, 180
West Germany, 28, 120
'White Paper' (1962), 48, 51–3, 163
Wilson, Mary, 178

Ya´ish, Mahmud, 191
Yarmuk Battalion, 16
Yarmuk Forces, 16
Yarmuk River, 76
Yemen, 45, 57–9, 61, 62, 64, 66, 71, 104, 114, 120
Yom Kippur War, 160

Zabdani, 9
al-Za´im, Husni, 16, 183
Zarqa, 137, 138
Zayn, Queen Mother, 6, 161
Zionism and Zionists, 12, 27, 33, 52, 78, 98, 105, 131, 175, 176
Zu´aytar, Akram, 51, 169
Zurayq, Qustantin, 11